THE
FRIGATE
CONSTITUTION
AND OTHER
HISTORIC SHIPS

UNITED STATES FRIGATE "CONSTITUTION"

From a photograph made by Baldwin Coolidge about 1910

THE
FRIGATE
CONSTITUTION

AND OTHER

HISTORIC SHIPS

By

F. ALEXANDER **M**AGOUN

DEPARTMENT OF NAVAL ARCHITECTURE
MASSACHUSETTS INSTITUTE OF TECHNOLOGY

DOVER PUBLICATIONS, INC.

NEW YORK

Published in Canada by General Publishing Company, Ltd.,
30 Lesmill Road, Don Mills, Toronto, Ontario.
Published in the United Kingdom by Constable and Company, Ltd.

This Dover edition, first published in 1987,
is an unabridged republication of the work originally published
by the Marine Research Society, Salem, Massachusetts, in 1928.
Several of the illustration pages have been relocated
from considerations of space.

Manufactured in the United States of America
Dover Publications, Inc.
31 East 2nd Street
Mineola, N.Y. 11501

Library of Congress Cataloging-in-Publication Data

Magoun, F. Alexander, 1896–
The frigate Constitution and other historic ships.

Reprint. Originally published: Salem, Mass. :
Marine Research Society, 1928.
Includes index.
1. Constitution (Frigate)   2. Historic ships.
I. Title.
VM15.M3   1987   387.2′25   87-24577
ISBN 0-486-25524-7 (pbk.)

TO THE
WOMEN WHO HAVE WAITED
WHILE THE SEAS
RAN HIGH

INTRODUCTION

NOTHING with spars and sails can ever fail of beauty, whether it floats upon the briny deep or rests in miniature upon some mantelpiece. There is an irresistible lure about the sailing ship which holds men to it, once they have felt its power. Many a model is but the expression of a sailor's love; many a toy boat but the manifestation of that inalienable right of every boy,—the desire to experience the sharp tang of damp salt air, the noise of the rattle and slap of lignum-vitae blocks, and the magnificent awfulness of heavy weather out to sea.

Some men are wise enough never to grow old; far-seeing enough to preserve the spirit of the boy lest it be lost in the apathy of the man. To them, life is something more than raiment for their bodies, food for their sustenance, and new sensations for their jaded nerves. At evening they sit in their workshops, tying clove-hitches in tiny ratlines which help to recreate for them the ships of yesterday. With all the enthusiasm of youth they set the sails of their minds for one of those high voyages of the imagination which gives to history its clearest meaning and brings back the heroes of the past as living men in the very glow of great adventure.

It is for such happy men that this book has been written: those who fashion their ship models and let fancy play around their handiwork. They who so lose themselves in their creations that for a time they are Vikings, they are Pilgrim Fathers, they are fishermen: strong, resourceful, resolute. That which to others is only a model of the *Constitution*, to them is a vessel of sublime audacity, sailing against the Barbary corsairs to teach them grim lessons at the cannon's mouth. What though the *Mauretania* can steam across the Atlantic in four days, ten hours, and forty-one minutes? Did not their *Flying Cloud* establish a world's record for the voyage around the Horn? Beauty, wonderment and longing; these are the things which such men find. For them, to build a model is almost akin to the experience of knowing the ship herself. There is no pleasanter way to understand the sea and its conquest, from the wonderful workmanship of the Vikings, to the complexity of the clipper ships, and to understand it without danger of that "terrible misgiving in the front of the back" which is the landsman's malady.

Some of my colleagues have criticized the inclusion of the *Bluenose*, instead of a Gloucester fisherman, as being unpatriotic; a charge which to me is less odious than that of being unable to see beyond the shipyards of Massachusetts. Are not the *Constitution* and the *Flying Cloud* sufficient? Let those who say "no," console themselves with the realization that fishing schooners are as alike as two belaying pins in the port rail.

There is here no new material except the plans pertaining to "Old Ironsides," for in a field so carefully gleaned one could hardly hope to be both accurate and original. But perhaps the happy combination of the structure and the "biography" of ships, undertaken with the conscious intention of conjuring up the romance of by-gone days for those who previously have seen nothing but a "model," is here presented for the first time.

It is our misfortune that so much has been irretrievably lost in the dim traditions of seamanship; those who could have told us having been much handier with the marlin spike than with the pen. Yet, by recreating their ships, we find ourselves in a mood which appreciates and values the things that they did.

The plans have been a gradual development, growing out of insistent demands for accurate information. No previous attempt has been made to commercialize them, but the desire to publish may be comprehended from the fact that blueprints of the *Flying Cloud* have gone out to such divergent places as the workbench of a six-year old boy, the novelty shop of a state penitentiary, and the advertising agents of an automobile company.

That errors have crept in, in spite of the conscientious struggle for truth which should be no less than a passion with every man of science, is a foregone conclusion. Such is the unhappy fate of any human document. But every effort has been made to discover and to correct the inaccuracies in both text and drawings; a task made doubly difficult in the latter case because no vessel remains the same throughout the various repairs and alterations which inevitably intersperse her career; nor for that matter the same under the command of any two successive captains. Thus one may confidently anticipate much kindly criticism similar to that of the old sailor who insists that the water casks of the *Flying Cloud* should be beneath the ladders leading to the quarter-deck. His location appears to be correct for a number of her more latterly cruises but not, I think, for her maiden voyage.

One other element remains. No work of this sort could possibly be accomplished without the generous coöperation of others. To them belongs much of the credit and none of the censure. The book was undertaken at the suggestion of my talented friend, Eric F. Hodgins, managing editor of "The Youth's Companion." Vice Admiral Don Honorio Cornejo, of the Royal Spanish Navy, furnished information for the *Santa Maria*. The gracious personality of Henry Royal, curator of Pilgrim Hall, Plymouth, Mass., made an examination of the Anderson model of the *Mayflower*, and various historic documents, a positive joy equalled in every way by the pleasure of obtaining additional information under the guidance of George Ernest Bowman of the Massachusetts Society of Mayflower Descendents. The consent of Rear Admiral Philip Andrews, U. S. N., to use the official plans for the 1927 restoration of the *Constitution*, was but the auspicious beginning of invaluable aid rendered by Captain C. M. Simmers, Industrial Manager of the Boston Navy Yard, Lieut. John Lord, Reconstruction Officer, and Warren D. Liebman, delineator of plans whose excellencies put mine to shame. The kindly criticism and encouragement of such men as Forrest VanLoon Ryder and St. Clair Smith, both of whom have built models of the *Flying Cloud* from Plans XI, XII, and XIII, has been most helpful. W. J. Roué, naval architect of Halifax, N. S., permitted the use of plans of his famous fishing schooner.

Nor are these all. Greater than any of them in patient effort is the typist who in the small hours of the morning has transcribed from an almost undecipherable handwriting a manuscript filled with unfamiliar and possibly to her meaningless words.

A series of acknowledgments of this kind is considered to be no proper place for a recognition of that so-often-mistakenly-taken-for-granted coöperation without which a husband, if he writes at all, does so only by sheer force of will. A woman who calmly accepts continued tardiness at meals, persistent demands for quiet, and complete if temporary loss of companionship, has often actually contributed more to the making of a book than any of those recognized in the acknowledgments. In this particular case she also deserves credit for many helpful criticisms dealing with the presentation of material, as well as for her careful work on the proof.

The urge to write has come from many sources, none more prolific than the 1919, the 1922, and the 1923 "models," who have continuously clamored at my study door for pencils and paper that they too might be busy about their own mighty affairs of belles-lettres. Some day, when maturity has given them a more discriminating judgment, may they read these pages and scan these drawings with the same enthusiasm which they now show.

And last of all, one word of thanksgiving for the pine woods, laden with the spicy suggestion of tar and oakum, the glint of sunshine over dancing water, and the inimitable song of the wood thrush which make a heaven of the spot where these chapters were put into words. What could be a finer benediction to the day's work than the calmness of impending twilight and the cool caress of evening?

F. ALEXANDER MAGOUN

Mashapaug, Connecticut
August, 1927

NAVY YARD. BOSTON

23 November 1927.

Mr. F. Alexander Magoun,
Department of Naval Architecture,
Massachusetts Institute of Technology,
Cambridge, Massachusetts.

Dear Sir:-

The Commandant has received and examined a set of
the plans of the U. S. Frigate CONSTITUTION which you have
prepared, with the consent of the Navy, from the official
plans for the 1927 restoration. These official plans are
complete and exact, so far as research can show, and are the
only plans which the Navy Department endorses.

Your work will prove of value to model enthusiasts,
since prior to this time there has been no accurate and complete information, even in the files of the Navy Department,
concerning the construction of this historic ship.

You doubtless recognize the unique value of the information which has been placed at your disposal and the
amount of conscientious research which it represents on the
part of those engaged in the 1927 restoration. We appreciate your desire to make available to the public in this
particular form the results of our efforts to restore the
CONSTITUTION, in so far as is humanly possible, to the condition in which she was originally built.

Sincerely yours,

Philip Andrews,
Rear Admiral, U.S.N.,
Commandant.

CONTENTS

PLATES AND PLANS

PLATES AND PLANS

PLATES AND PLANS

THE
FRIGATE
CONSTITUTION
AND OTHER
HISTORIC SHIPS

I

THE VIKING SHIPS

ISTORY records no more picturesque conquerors of the rolling, restive, all-surrounding ocean than the Norsemen. Without instruments for measuring speed, with neither chart nor compass, knowing no system of dead reckoning, they were the first to deliberately sail out upon the open, trackless sea.* Other men might cling timidly to the coastline by day and prudently cast anchor in some protecting inlet by night, but the Vikings were awed neither by the appalling immensity nor by the fantastic terrors of the stormy North Atlantic.

The sun, the moon, and the stars were theirs to sail by. They realized that the water of the Gulf Stream is a purer blue than the greenish brown of the current along the coast. The artifice of letting captive birds loose and following their flight back to land was not unknown to them. But none of these navigational aids were effective in a fog. Under such adverse circumstances the pilot steered his vessel by a marvelous instinct developed to an uncanny degree.

It is probable that the Norsemen took some soundings, not from the fear of running aground, since their vessels drew scarcely more than five feet, but because the depth of water gave them a rough indication of their position off shore.

From the time King Solomon's ships traded with Ophir, the sailors of southern Europe were stimulated by the commercial instinct. Not so the Vikings. Their sails were driven by the necessity of plundering from more favored neighboring countries what their own could not supply, and by a desire to establish colonies in a milder climate. Thus the Norsemen spurned the secure toil of agriculture and devoted themselves to a precarious but romantic life of piracy and exploration.

Were it not for the burial customs of the Vikings, knowledge of their ships would be almost entirely limited to the saga accounts.

At the beginning of the Iron Age the ship itself served as a pyre on which to cremate the departed hero together with various personal possessions thought necessary to him in the next world. Such was the law of Odin: that all dead men should be burned upon their pyre. "In Samlingen of Norske Oldsager i Bergens Museum" (pages 153-161) gives an account of the ceremony of cremation. The author, Mr. Lorange, explored the ship-grave of *Mokklebyst*, Eids Parish, Norway, and has based his description on actual observation of what remains of this crematory.

The ship was hauled ashore on great rollers. Shields decorated her bulwarks. Arms and instruments of war were placed upon the deck beside the now lifeless body of her bold commander. Silently the crew stood by while the torch was applied. Flames consumed all save a few charred bones and the metal fastenings of the vessel. Then the remains were carefully collected and placed within a great bronze kettle. An iron

* Nansen: *In Northern Mists*, II, page 233.

arrow-head, dice, bone chessmen, and other trinkets were thrown in, and the kettle covered with the bosses of twelve shields. At the time of excavation, these bosses were so firmly stuck to the kettle by a process of gradual incrustation that it was necessary to remove the bottom in order to examine the contents without destroying the cover.

The caldron was then placed in an excavation at the bottom of what was to be the mound. Above it were piled spears, shields, swords, and the bit of a horse's bridle. Wrapped in an untanned goatskin were more arrow-heads, iron utensils, and some unburned animal bones which may have been intended to sustain the deceased on his long journey from the funeral pyre. The unburned metal fastenings of the ship's hull were then strewn about the kettle, and a huge mound of sand thrown over it.

A modified form of this procedure was to place the ashes of the dead in a suitable container and to deposit this, with appropriate accompanying articles, inside the ship, over which a mound was then raised. The *Borre Ship*,* excavated in Norway during 1852, offers an illustration of this method.

The vessel was drawn ashore to the desired location after the upper layer of soil and gravel had been removed. Sand was then thrown around the outside of the hull, and the interior filled with very fine sand, particularly in the vicinity of whatever articles or animals were deposited in it.† The approved arrangement called for three or four horses on the starboard side, smaller animals such as dogs and domestic fowl on the port side, and a bull in the stern. Thus equipped, the departed hero might either sail or ride to his Valhalla.

Amidships was left a hole in the sand sufficiently large to receive the kettle in which the ashes were collected after a litter with the body of the dead Viking had been placed upon the pile and burned. The hole was then filled with sand, and the mound erected.

From various passages in the old sagas one infers that after the Roman invasion the general custom was to inter the dead without cremation. In a large grave-chamber of wood, especially constructed abaft the mast, the body was laid to rest. This chamber was formed of round logs reaching from the sides of the vessel to the ridge pole, like a pitched roof. The ends consisted of planks. When the unburned remains of the dead and those of his effects which were considered necessary had been deposited in this chamber, a mound was thrown over the vessel as usual.

Some twenty such ship-tombs have been excavated, most of them in Norway, but in practically all instances, the material of the mound has been such as to offer little protection from moisture and air. Most frequently, therefore, the vessel has been so decayed that no information could be obtained concerning its construction, form, or dimensions. In two notable instances the ships have been sufficiently preserved to permit restoration: the *Tune Ship* found at Hangen, Norway, in 1867, and the *Gokstad Ship* unearthed near the entrance to the Christiania Fjord, Norway, in 1880. Both vessels were covered by a mound of blue clay which is an excellent preserver of wood.

Of these, the larger and more complete is the *Gokstad Ship*. Mr. Nicolaysen, then President of the Society for the Preservation of Norwegian Antiquities, under

* N. Nicolaysen: *Om Borrefundet.*
† Boehmer: *Prehistoric Naval Architecture,* page 606.

whose direction the excavation was undertaken, says in his description of the relic:*

"That there may yet be found in many parts of our country, near the coast, tumuli containing ships in tolerable preservation is by no means uncertain . . . Certain, nevertheless, it is that we shall not disinter any craft which, in respect to model and workmanship, will outrival that of Gokstad. For, in the opinion of experts, this must be termed the masterpiece of its kind, not to be surpassed by aught which the shipbuilding craft of the present age could produce. Doubtless, measured by our present ideas, this is rather a boat than a ship; nevertheless, in its symmetrical proportions and the eminent beauty of its lines is exhibited a perfection never since attained until, after a much later but long and dreary period of clumsy unshapeliness, it was once more revived in the clipper-built craft of our own country."

Upon completion of the excavation the vessel was taken to Christiania, where it is now one of the most valuable exhibits in the Archaelogical Museum of the Royal Frederiks University.

Very wisely the authorities decided to restore the ship only in so far as it was possible to do so without adding anything new to replace damaged or lost pieces.

There is reason to believe that this ship, although comparatively small, does not differ materially in shape or manner of construction from the more powerful warships of the period, or from those used for long voyages such as to Iceland and even to the shores of North America itself where a colony was established nearly five hundred years before the birth of Columbus.

Unfortunately the *Gokstad Ship* was — probably not long after the interment — visited by grave-robbers. There was unmistakable evidence that they had dug into the mound on the port side, making entrance by cutting through the ship's side and the timbers of the grave-chamber, of which large pieces are missing. This accounts for the fact that many of the bones of the Viking's body had disappeared; that all weapons of war had been removed; and that there were disappointingly few articles of antiquarian value compared with what had been reasonably anticipated. The miscellaneous character of those which were found would seem to indicate the completeness with which the deceased had been originally equipped. Quoting from a translation of Professor Rygh's article printed in "Ny Illusteret Tidende":

"Of articles of antiquarian value only a few trifles were found, but some of these are of considerable interest. A great quantity of mountings for belts and straps — partly gilt bronze, partly lead — deserve special mention. The bronze mountings are excellent samples of the best style of ornamentation of the Viking period. A small, delicately executed round mounting, of which two specimens were found, is remarkable for the rareness of the subject represented: a warrior, with lance in rest, on a galloping horse. Several fish-hooks were found among other things, and a turned draughtsman of bone or horn.

"Two of the favourite animals of the deceased had been deposited with him in the chamber; there were the skeleton of a very small dog, and the bones and feathers of a pea-fowl, which he had probably brought home with him from one of those expeditions to the West which were so common at that time. A great number of other animals must have been sacrificed on the occasion of the burial; the bones of eight or nine horses and some dogs were found near the ship.

"When interred, the ship had been decorated with shields hung along the rail, as was customary at a far later period when a ship was dressed on festive occasions.

* N. Nicolaysen: *Langskibet Fra Gokstad Ved Sandefjord*, page 17.

Large round shields were attached to the rail on both sides nearly right fore and aft, so close together that they sometimes overlapped each other. Traces of paint, yellow and black, are found on the shields. The thin boards forming the shields have unfortunately suffered much from the pressure of the superincumbent soil; but a few of them have been successfully restored and placed in position, so as to give an idea of the appearance of the whole.

"Outside of the grave-chamber a number of articles of various kinds were found collected in the ship. All these must have formed part of the inventory, or been intended for the use of the crew. We can here mention only a few of the most remarkable of these articles.

"There are fragments of three oak boats. They had been broken up before they were deposited, and cannot now be put together. The length of keel may, however, be determined with accuracy. (The lengths are 7.2, 5.6, and 4.2 metres.) The boats are as sharp at the ends as the ship. They are provided with rudders of the same pattern as that of the ship, and with mast and thwarts. Instead of holes for oars, they have rowlocks fastened to the gunwale of the same shape as those now used in the west and north of Norway.

"There were several carved pieces of wood; the carved parts had been painted in various colours. These have special interest as specimens of the style of ornamentation in wood of the Viking period, of which so very little has been preserved. Two of these carved pieces evidently were the side-pieces of a chair or a high seat. Four long boards, of which the carved portion is shown (Fig. 1), were the supports for the tent. They had been placed so as to form two crutches, one at each end of the tent, pivoted on a long pole, which passed through the hole below the carved part and connected the crutches with each other. The tent thus formed a gable-ended roof, extending from the pole to the rail at the sides of the ship, the carved ends of the supports projecting above the tent at each end.

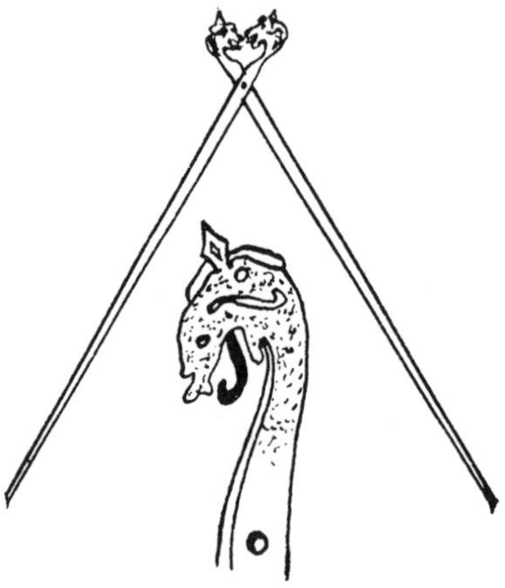

FIG. 1. TENT SUPPORTS OF GOKSTAD SHIP

Copied from N. Nicolaysen: "Langskibet fra Gokstad"

"Of kitchen utensils, there were found, among other things, a very large and solid copper kettle, bits of an iron kettle, an iron chain for suspending the pot over the fire, several buckets of different sizes, and some small wooden drinking-cups. The cooking utensils can scarcely have been used at sea; it does not seem to have been possible to cook on board such a vessel. They have, therefore, only been of service while coasting, and when a harbour could be gained at night; and this mode of travelling was, no doubt, usually practised whenever possible.

"The fragments of sleeping berths found show that a part, at least, of the crew have been provided with sleeping accommodations. A couple of these berths have been restored. They are bedsteads of the same shape as we use now — low and very wide. They are put together with fids, so as to be readily taken to pieces and stowed away under the bottom boards."

PRINCIPAL DIMENSIONS

In spite of the fact that the hull of the vessel is still extant, there is not complete agreement as to the dimensions of the *Gokstad Ship*.

PLATE II

Photograph by O. Varing

STERN VIEW OF THE "GOKSTAD SHIP." BUILT ABOUT 900 A.D.

PLATE III

Photograph by A. J. Olmstead

MODEL OF THE "GOKSTAD SHIP" IN THE SMITHSONIAN INSTITUTION, SHOW-
ING MAST AND YARD STOWED, BUT WITH A STUMP OF THE MAST HELD
ERECT IN THE FISH PIECE

Photograph by A. J. Olmstead

MODEL OF THE "GOKSTAD SHIP" IN THE SMITHSONIAN INSTITUTION
UNDER FULL SAIL

According to Professor William Hovgaard,* himself a Dane, and one of the foremost of living naval architects:

Length over all	101' - 0"
Load water-line	85' - 0"
Beam	16' - 7"
Draft	3' - 8"
Freeboard amidships	3' - 0"
Distance between frames	3' - 3"
Displacement	30 tons
Complement	40 men
Weight of hull	18 tons
Crew and effects	7 tons
Length of oars	20' - 0"

Mr. George H. Boehmer,† in a report from the Smithsonian Institution, gives the following:

Length between stems	79' - 4"
Load water-line	67' - 0"
Beam	16' - 2"
Draft	3' - 7"
Freeboard amidships	2' - 11"
Displacement	30.2 tons
Oars on each side	16
Distance between oars	3' - 0"
Length of middle oar	18' - 6"
Complement	70 men
Crew and effects	10 tons

Mr. Colin Archer,‡ an English naval architect, obtained his information with the help of Professor Rygh, Chief of the Archæological Section of the Christiana University. Mr. Archer himself took off her lines "with as much accuracy as circumstances would permit" and gives the data as:

Length between rabbets at gunwale	77' - 11"
Load water-line	73' - 3"
Beam	16' - 7"
Draft	3' - 8"
Depth from top of keel to gunwale amidships	5' - 9"
Distance between frames	3' - 3"
Displacement	28.4 tons
Complement	100 men
Crew and effects	10 tons

It is generally agreed that the *Gokstad Ship* is an example of the smaller seagoing vessels of her period. This is evident from the knowledge that the smallest ships which the various districts were required by law to furnish the king in time of war had twenty oars on a side. The Gokstad relic has only sixteen. Each oar required two men, who served by turns, from which it may be concluded that fully manned, her crew numbered seventy or eighty.

HULL

The vessel is clinker built and the material all of oak, like boats still constructed in parts of Norway. The sixteen strakes of outside planking are connected by hand-

* W. Hovgaard: *Voyages of the Norsemen to America*, page 51 *et sequentes.*
† Boehmer: *Prehistoric Naval Architecture*, page 627.
‡ Archer: *Transactions of the Institution of Naval Architects*, 1881, page 298.

wrought iron nails which are still in excellent condition. These nails have the diameter of an ordinary three-inch spike and were made with large flat heads about an inch across. Spaced at from six to eight inches and riveted over on the inside (except at the ends where the sharpness of the vessel made it necessary to reverse the process) they offer a fastening not unlike the copper rivets used in the clinker-built row boats of today.

The garboard strake is fastened to the keel with precisely the same sort of iron rivet as those used for joining the strakes to each other. There is nothing in the entire structure which faintly resembles a bolt, the strongest iron fastening being the rivets in the scarfs of the keel which are no larger than ordinary four-inch spikes.

Water-tightness was secured by oakum, made from cow's hair spun into three-stranded cord. This was probably laid between the seams when the vessel was built; not caulked in afterward with hammer and caulking iron as is our custom.

FIG. 2. METHOD OF FASTENING PLANKS

Copied from Nicolaysen: "Langskibet fra Gokstad"

Varying in length from eight to twenty-four feet, the outside planking has an average thickness of one inch, and a width of from seven to nine inches. Exceptions to this are found in the tenth strake, which is an inch and three-quarters thick in order to form a "shelf," for the beam ends, and the fourteenth strake, which is an inch and one-quarter thick. This plank, which should be referred to as the "main wale," is perforated with holes about four inches in diameter for the oars. A slit at the after and upper edges of each hole was cut to allow the blades of the oars to be passed through from inboard. The two upper strakes are the thinnest of all, being scarcely more than three-quarters of an inch in thickness. Inside the top strake and secured in the usual manner is the gunwale, three inches by four and one-half inches.

The connection of the planking to the frames is as ingenious as it is peculiar. The planks were apparently worked down from two-inch stock in such a way as to leave a ridge one-inch high running along the middle of the plank on the inner surface.

The ridge was then removed, except in way of the frames, so that the completed plank was provided with a series of cleat-like projections. Through one-quarter inch holes in these cleats and corresponding fore and aft holes in the frames, ties of birch roots were passed, thus securing the planking to the strength members of the hull by a strong yet flexible connection. With the triple exceptions of the nails driven through the "shelf" and riveted over on the extreme ends of the floors; the iron rivets which fasten the bottom planks to the keel; and the wooden trenails used to fasten the two top planks to the frames, these ties constitute the only attachment between the outside planking and the frames.

The craftsmanship of the Viking shipbuilders will be better appreciated when one realizes that in these complicated parts no trace can be found of a saw mark. All was accomplished with an axe.

Unfortunately the extreme tips of the vessel were not covered by the clay and have consequently suffered complete decay. The damage is sufficiently restricted so that the sharp and exceptionally beautiful lines of the bow and stern may still be seen.

This sharpness made it necessary to taper off the planks at the ends, and causes them to rise rapidly, producing the great sheer which, in combination with the broad beam, made the Viking ships so seaworthy.

It is impossible to determine whether the stem and stern posts were once surmounted by some fantastically carved ornamentation, but in the opinion of Professor Rygh such adornments were confined to vessels of larger size than the *Gokstad Ship*.

So gentle is the sweep with which the stem and stern posts run into the keel that no one could tell by looking at the plan where one ended and the other began. However, the timber which a shipwright would term the keel is fifty-seven feet long; fourteen inches deep, eleven inches of which are below the rabbet; four and one-half inches thick at the bottom; and only three inches thick where the rabbet has been cut out. The top of the keel measures seven inches across, offering a large surface of contact for the garboard strake.

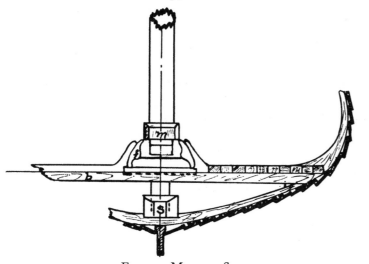

FIG. 3. MIDSHIP SECTION

Copied from Archer: *Institution of Naval Architects*, 1881

The floor timbers, as the lower portion of the frames are called, are nineteen in number, spaced thirty-nine inches apart. Instead of connecting to the keel they lie free above it (Fig. 3) and terminate at the height of the tenth strake or "shelf" already referred to. The beams (*b*) are supported on top of the floors and shelf, thus producing a stout structure upon which rests the comparatively light upper hull. These beams not only serve to support the deck planking, but are essential to resist the tendency of the water pressure to crush the sides of the vessel together: a function which the frames are quite unable to perform.

From the beams the upper frame timbers, more correctly called the knees, extend to the height of the fourteenth strake. Further strength is secured by short timbers fitted between alternate frames and extending downward from the gunwale. Similar supports are mortised into the beams with their lower ends cut so as to straddle the bottom timbers.

Being seven inches wide by four inches thick, the beams are wider than the knees, which are fastened to them by oak trenails. This leaves a ledge on each side into which the deck planking fits from beam to beam. Those instances in which the knees are not sufficiently long to meet in the center, are dealt with by nailing a strip of wood on top of the beam as a continuation of the knee.

Support is given to the middle of the beams by pillars which rest on the throats of the floors.*

The fifteen and sixteenth strakes, consisting of the thin planks previously mentioned, are fastened to the rest of the hull by independent timbers fitted between the knees and extending from the bottom of the gunwales almost to the deck.

Thus the upper and the lower portions of the vessel are not connected by continu-

* Afloat the term "floor" refers to that part of the "frames" between the keel and the turn of the bilge. It is never properly used to mean "deck."

ous framing. Consequently, any weights carried were necessarily stowed on the deck instead of on the bottom of the ship. Otherwise there would have been a dangerous tendency for the two sides of the ship to come apart.

The dual function of the lower portion was to supply the necessary buoyancy and to offer the least possible resistance to propulsion. A study of the midships section will show that the load from the super-structure is taken entirely by the beams, the floor timbers, and pil-lars which trans-mit the stresses along the center line to the keel. Therefore, practi-cally no strain is placed on the birch-root ties because there are no localized internal forces, and the water pressue from without holds the planking to the frames.

FIG. 4. CARVED TILLER OF THE GOKSTAD SHIP
Copied from Nicolaysen: "Langskibet fra Gokstad"

The upper portion contained the crew and their effects together with such cargo as was put aboard. It should be borne in mind that the load was always small as compared to the possible carrying capacity, and consisted principally of "live weight" which subjects a vessel to much smaller stresses in a seaway than would be the case with a similar "dead weight."

Mr. Archer* calls attention to the extraordinary resemblance in shape between the hull of the *Gokstad Ship* and that of an ordinary canoe. His table of dimensions for a fourteen-foot model of the Viking craft emphasizes this.

Length	14' - 0"
Beam	3' - 0"
Draft	0' - 8"
Depth	1' - 0½"
Displacement	5.77 cu. ft.

The bottom of the hull may have been payed with tar, although Professor Hovgaard considers it unlikely. The hull was unquestionably very pliable, the members working on one another in a manner which would alarm a modern sailor. Yet this very elasticity made it possible for the ship to survive storms which would have quickly destroyed an unduly rigid vessel of such construction.

HULL FITTINGS
Steering Gear

The sagas mention only one form of rudder, invariably fitted over the right-hand side of the stern. It consisted of one piece of wood beveled off on both edges, the forward one being particu-larly sharp. The rudder-head itself is six inches in diameter with a square hole to receive the tiller. This cut toward the upper end was beautifully carved as befitted an implement usu-ally taken in charge by the commander of the ship. The blade of the rudder is seven inches thick at the pivot and decreasing in thickness toward the foot. The breadth is fifteen inch-es at the pivot, increasing to a maximum of twenty-two.

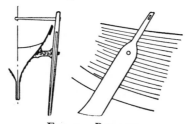

FIG. 5. RUDDER
Copied from Nicolaysen:
"Langskibet fra Gokstad"

The pivot about which the rudder swings is as simple as it is effective. A conical piece of wood, sufficiently long to keep the rudder clear of the ship's side, is fitted with its base to the outside planking. Through a hole in

* Archer: *Transactions Institution of Naval Architects*, 1881, page 304.

the cone and a corresponding one in the rudder, a stout rope is passed, the outer end of which is knotted and the inner end made fast aboard. This rope acts as a pivot which at once both supports and allows the rudder to turn.

To an iron staple near the lower end of the rudder is attached a line by which the blade could be raised when in shallow water or when the vessel was hauled ashore on rollers as was frequently done.

A wooden pillow or rubbing strip in way of the rudder-head takes the wear which would otherwise have been on the gunwale.

SPARS AND RIGGING

Until late in the Middle Ages the vessels of the Norsemen had but one mast, which carried only a single square sail. The jib was unknown to them. It is impossible, from what remains, to give accurately all the dimensions of the mast and yard of the *Gokstad Ship*, but the diameter was twelve and one-half inches, a ten-foot

piece of the butt having
entire length was probably
er estimates the yard to have
eight and one-half inches
three and one-half inches
Because the mast was
against a head-wind or
battle, some quick and con-
plishing this operation was
The mast step (*s*) is a
feet long, nineteen inches
deep at the middle.
by mortising it over
floors to which it is
knees not shown in
The fish (*f*),† a
oak, lies along the cen-
above the step. It is
feet two inches wide,
thick at the center. In
posed to represent the
ing on a flat slab or
is four inches thick.
tised over the beams
them by knees.

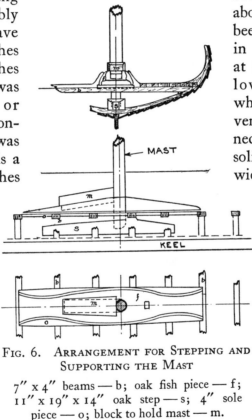

FIG. 6. ARRANGEMENT FOR STEPPING AND SUPPORTING THE MAST

7″ x 4″ beams — b; oak fish piece — f;
11″ x 19″ x 14″ oak step — s; 4″ sole
piece — o; block to hold mast — m.

been found in the ship. Its
about forty feet. Mr. Arch-
been thirty-five feet long,
in diameter at the sling,
at the arms.*
lowered when rowing
when clearing the ship for
venient means of accom-
necessary.
solid block of oak, eleven
wide, and fourteen inches
Rigidity was assured
the throats of the
fastened by small
Fig. 6.
tremendous piece of
ter line of the ship
sixteen feet long, three
and fourteen inches
shape it may be sup-
tails of two fish rest-
sole piece (*o*), which
This slab is also mor-
and strongly secured to

From a point slightly forward of its center and toward the stern, a slot is cut in the fish equal in width to the diameter of the mast. The length of this slot is five feet nine inches. By stepping the mast through the forward end of this slot it can be secured in position by a heavy block (*m*) which just fits into the remainder of the slot. In order to lower the mast it is then only necessary to remove the block and slack off on the forestay. Lest the beam just abaft the mast should interfere with this manoeuver, it is cut out to allow the mast to fall back the entire length of the slot.

The three stanchions seen in the photograph of the Smithsonian model (Plate

---

* *Transactions Institution of Naval Architects,* 1881, page 302.
† Even today the Norwegian technical term applied to what we call the mast partners is *Fisken* — the fish.

III), which are fitted at the top with cross-pieces having semi-circular depressions, are intended for stowing the mast and yard when not in use. The height of these stanchions is about eight feet.

Besides the arrangement for stepping and supporting the mast it is further secured by a forestay and two backstays. The forestay attaches to the stem with a surprisingly good imitation of the hearts and lanyard of later years for taking up the slack. The backstays are secured through holes in the floor timbers, as shown in Fig. 7.

FIG. 7. METHOD OF SECURING BACKSTAYS

Courtesy of the Smithsonian Institution

For fastening the yard to the mast, in such a way that it can be either raised or lowered, the Norsemen adopted the simple artifice of nailing a cleat to the yard. A semi-circular hole in this cleat fitted the mast and could be closed by tying a thong across the mouth.

With nothing even faintly resembling pulley blocks by which to raise and lower the yard, the only means of accomplishing this was to pass the halliard through a hole in the mast which had been rounded off, forward and aft, to allow the line to be handled through it without excessive chafing.

Braces from each end of the yard were fastened abaft the mast or held by the helmsman. Presumably it was necessary to lower the yard whenever it was desired to shorten sail.

The rope found in the ship was of various materials; cattle hair, leather, and twisted bark. The only hemp was in the cords used for fastening the tent. Most of the ship's rope, of which many pieces were recovered, was made of bast.

EQUIPMENT

Sails

The materials employed for sails were frieze and canvas; a great advance from the time of Cæsar's naval campaign against the Veneti, in 54 B.C., when skins and thin dressed leather were in use.*

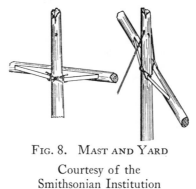

FIG. 8. MAST AND YARD

Courtesy of the Smithsonian Institution

The courses were sewed together with thread and reinforced at the edges by a leech to which were fastened the rings for securing the sheets. There is evidence to show that the Vikings were already familiar with the use of reef points.

Great pride was taken in making the sail a thing of beauty. White sails striped with blue and gold, historic designs, dragons painted or embroidered on, and even velvet linings are recorded in the sagas as the embellishments of a well-appointed vessel.

Ship's Tent

Some remains of the ship's tent are left. It was made of a fine, white woolen material with red stripes sewed on. Four supports for the ridge-pole were found, each eleven feet eight inches long. The upper extremities are beautifully carved and painted to represent the head of some mythical animal as shown in Fig. 1.

Although much of the gunwale is decayed, enough remains to indicate that a strip with rectangular openings was fitted to it, supposedly for tying the cords by which the ship's tent was stretched when it was necessary for the crew to seek shelter

* Cæsar: *De Bello Gallico*, iii, cap. xiii.

against the weather. To these the shields may also have been attached when stowed along the side.

Oars

In addition to sail power the ship was equipped with thirty-two oars; sixteen on each side. Instead of being plied between thole-pins on the gunwale or in oar-locks of any kind, the oars were passed through holes cut in the side of the ship about eighteen inches below the rail.

In order to prevent the sea from coming in through these holes when the oars were unshipped, a shutter swung on a spike driven above them. When the oar was removed, the shutter dropped into place covering both the hole and the slit for the blade. As is the case with even insignificant articles, the oars were found to have elaborately carved ornamentations.

The oars were spaced midway between each pair of knees and diminished slightly in length from amidships toward the ends, the longest ones measuring between nineteen and twenty feet.

No benches for the rowers were found. It may be that the oars were plied in a standing position, although the word *sess*, meaning seat, as applied to the number of oars by which the vessel was classified, would indicate otherwise. In further substantiation of this it is known that small portable seats were fitted on each side of the beams in the larger ships.

Anchor

The remains of an iron anchor, probably of the Admiralty type, were found forward on the starboard side. The iron being practically entirely corroded, there is left only the wooden stock.

Windlass

Between the seventh and eighth frame from the bow, a large wooden block is secured, possibly intended to support a windlass of some rude sort. A more logical conclusion would be that it is indicative of a single wooden bitt.

Implements of War

As previously stated, this interesting part of the record is denied us due to the antecedent action of grave-robbers — quite a different type both in motive and in method from the archæologist.

Whatever we may have been denied in the way of arrows, javelins, and swords, examples of the shields have been left to us. Of the original thirty-two, some disappeared during earlier attempts to open the mound, and some have been bent out of shape. At least four remain nearly intact.

Three feet in diameter, constructed of thin boards with a plate of iron in the center to protect the hand, and painted alternately with black and yellow, they form one of the most ornamental parts of the ship's equipment. Apparently the shields were once provided with a metallic rim, which, however, has disappeared. By being hung over the side from somewhat forward of the first oar to slightly abaft the last, they serve the dual purpose of raising the side of the ship and being out of the way when not needed. These shields are peculiar to vessels of war, and were not found on merchantmen.

Miscellaneous

A number of other items deserve mention in the equipment of the ship. A two and three-quarter inch oak gangplank, twenty-four feet long and ten inches wide, provides further evidence of artistic tastes of the Vikings, its face being beautifully carved in a manner which provides both ornamentation and a more secure footing.

Fragments of four sleeping berths have been pieced together with a result not dissimilar from the bedsteads still used by the Norwegian peasantry: low, and secured by fids so as to be readily taken to pieces and stowed.

Bits of a wooden chair, possibly the high seat of the ranking chieftain, are still in an excellent state of preservation. At the top of the side-pieces are carvings precisely similar to those adorning the upper extremities of the tent poles.

Cooking utensils were found in great variety. A large copper kettle with its iron chain, wooden dishes, and drinking cups, numerous tubs, buckets, and plates of varying sizes form the major portion of these. There being no trace of any provision by which to build a fire on board, the natural assumption is that cooking utensils were of service only when coasting. The crew, like the dove sent out by Noah, could then go ashore for food.

As mentioned in at least six of the sagas* great rollers were an essential part of the equipment, not only for launching the ship, but for hauling it ashore, as was generally done at night whenever proximity to and the character of the beach permitted. The sail was then lowered, serving double duty by forming a tent under which the crew slept.

The vessel was evidently bailed out with buckets or with scoops, as there were no bilge pumps of any description.

Flags

"The pennant, spun by women, played at the masthead."† In shape it was probably narrow and long like the homeward-bound pennants of later days. A standard-bearer, who stood beside the leader in battle, often took station at the prow of the ship. The standards were elaborately worked, some being embroidered in gold.

Small Boats

According to the saga accounts all large ships were provided with boats, often two or more. These were taken aboard when going to sea. Like the vessels themselves, these boats were clinker built, and sometimes also fitted with mast and sail. Propulsion could always be accomplished by means of oars which were worked through crude oar-locks fastened to the gunwale. Each man handled two oars, the total number of pairs ranging from one to six.

As already stated, fragments of three such boats were unearthed with the *Gokstad Ship*. Although too completely broken up to permit restoration, the rudders, mast-steps, thwart, bottom-boards, etc., which could be identified, clearly indicated a general similarity to the mother ship.

These small boats were of oak, were unpainted, and were sharp at the ends. The three keels are approximately twenty-five, eighteen, and thirteen and one-half feet in length. Apparently the boats had no beams — simply detached thwarts. The provision for stepping the mast resembled that of the ship itself, no mast partners having been found.

Like everything taken from the mound, these boats are specimens of skillful workmanship in every respect. Since they constitute the only examples of this type

* St. Olaf, Egils, Fagrskinna, Ragnar Lodobroks, Harold Hardradi, Olaf Trygvason.
† Egils' *Saga:* c. XXXVII.

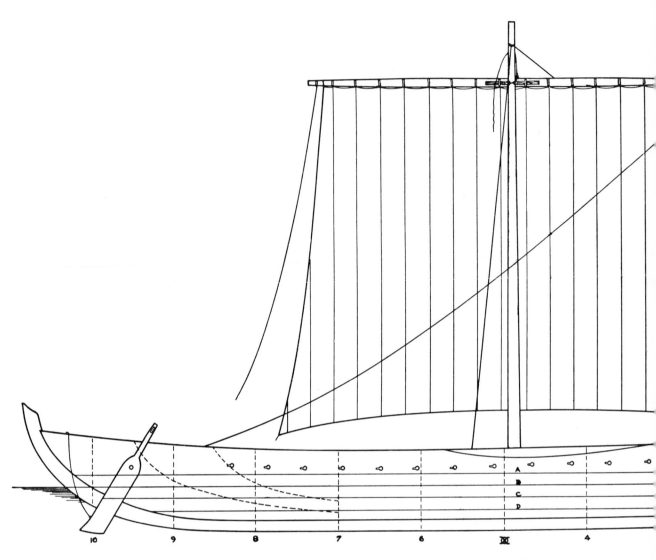

SHEER PLAN

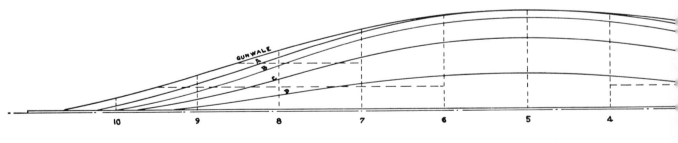

LINES

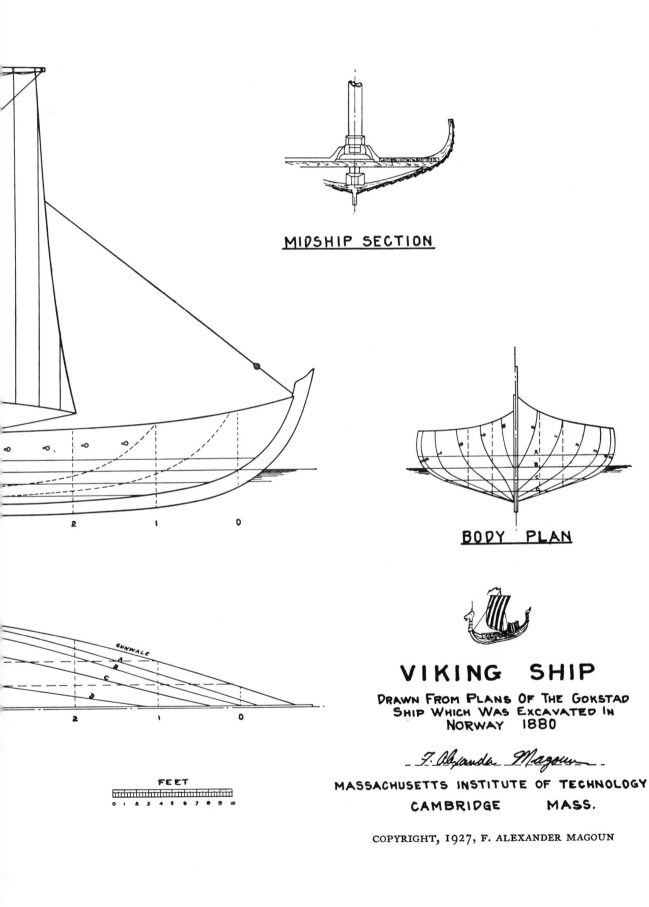

MIDSHIP SECTION

BODY PLAN

GUNWALE

FEET

VIKING SHIP

Drawn From Plans Of The Gokstad Ship Which Was Excavated In Norway 1880

F. Alexander Magoun

MASSACHUSETTS INSTITUTE OF TECHNOLOGY
CAMBRIDGE   MASS.

of craft known to exist from the period, their antiquarian value is possibly even greater than that of the ship itself.

Food

The Vikings probably enjoyed the classic if monotonous diet of the sailor: salt meat and salt fish. Nansen asserts that the larger ships may have had cattle aboard. The known aversion of the Norsemen to farming on dry land makes any such attempt to anticipate the marvels of condensed milk all the more heroic. Professor Hovgaard substantiates the conclusions of Nansen:*

"The vessels used in the Vineland voyages during the early prosperous times of the Greenland Colony were probably somewhat larger in general than the *Gokstad Ship*, and may, in several cases, have been of about fifty tons displacement. This would give a cargo carrying capacity of some fifteen tons, or about thirty-three thousand pounds.† On this weight there could be carried a crew of some forty to fifty men with provisions for about four weeks, besides live cattle with feed, tools, weapons, etc., as was necessary for expeditions like those to Vineland."

OPERATION

Substantial evidence of the seaworthiness of the *Gokstad Ship* was furnished in 1893 when a replica sailed from Bergen, Norway, to Newport, Rhode Island, with a crew of eleven men. To the original square-sail rig was added a jib, since the square rig will not permit beating into the wind. The maximum speed of eleven knots compares very favorably with that attained by such later ships as the *Santa Maria* and the *Mayflower*. By maintaining an average of nine knots, the replica, which started on May first, arrived June thirteenth.

Her great beam and flat bottom allowed the ship to follow the wave slope without the unpleasant and dangerous accumulation of rolling. Broad beam and shallow draft always give tremendous initial stability.

Being provided with both sails and oars, the Norsemen enjoyed all the advantages of wind propulsion and were at the same time independent of it. This gave them a flexibility never realized in the larger, later ships until steam was introduced during the nineteenth century. At will, they could sail the high seas or row safely into the restricted waters of some fjord.

Knowing the character and the capacity of the vessels in which the Norsemen sailed; that without compass, quadrant, personal experience, or previous discovery, they were guided by the stars, supported by their own meager resources, and impelled by a spirit of adventure which no unexpected dangers could repress, one cannot but be amazed at the success of the Norsemen who are believed to have been the first Europeans to discover America. However discouraged at the outset, Columbus eventually obtained the generous support of a wealthy monarch. He had workable scientific aids to navigation. His course lay far south of the Arctic circle. He has been acclaimed a world hero, the Admiral of the ocean, the discoverer of a new continent. Yet, in an open boat, the Norsemen endured and outlived the terrors of the North Atlantic, making their voyages to America nearly five hundred years before the keel of the *Santa Maria* was laid.

* Hovgaard: *The Voyages of the Norsemen in America,* page 58.
† The shipbuilder's ton is always 2240 pounds.

II

THE "SANTA MARIA"

ERY early on the morning of Friday, August 3, 1492, three small vessels weighed anchor in the port of Palos, Spain. When Christopher Columbus, standing on the quarter deck of the flagship *Santa Maria*, had given the order to spread the sails in the name of Jesus Christ, his fleet was at last embarked upon a venture for the realization of which the great admiral had labored over seventeen years. No discovery in the entire history of geographical exploration is comparable to the far reaching results which came from the persistence with which the son of a Genoese wool-weaver held to the idea that great discoveries would reward the navigator who had the courage to sail directly west.

It was the surmounting of the moral difficulties which gives to "Christofero Colombo" his position as a man of superlative genius. His opinions were contrary to the established ideas of the preceding ages. His proposed voyage to westward conjured up all the old superstitions that a vessel would sail off the edge of the world. His poverty made it impossible for him to accomplish anything until he had succeeded in sufficiently overcoming the prejudices of influential men to secure the necessary funds for outfitting and operating his fleet.

Of the early life of Columbus we have practically no accurate information. The year of his birth is variously given as 1435 by the French biographer, Roselly de Lorgues, whose work was published under the auspices of the Pope; as 1446 by John Lord, the American historian; and as 1451 by another Frenchman, Henry Vignaud, who presents so much evidence in support of his contention that his date is at present the most generally accepted one.

There were neither nobles nor sailors in the explorer's ancestry, the belief that one or both of the admirals named Colombo were his kin being due to the mistaken efforts of early biographers who endeavored to bolster up his lowly origin to the level of the distinction which later came to him. The story of his having been a student at the University of Pavia when a boy of but ten or twelve is now also discredited, the probability being that his early education was not in any way dissimilar from the schooling of the sons of other weavers.

One of his letters contains the statement that at fourteen he "went to sea," the expression probably referring to some sort of coastwise trip. Certain it is that, although still practicing the trade of a wool-weaver as late as 1472, at an early age Columbus acquired a love for and a confidence in the rolling ocean.

The series of events which led directly to the discovery of America began when he shipped on a Genoese vessel which was one of a convoy bound for England. This convoy was attacked off Cape St. Vincent by corsairs on August 13, 1476. Two of the vessels, one of which carried young Christopher, were able to reach Lisbon.

Early biographers assert that Bartholomew Columbus, a brother, was already established there in the business of making plans, charts, and maps for the use of navigators. In this new environment Christopher learned much which was to be of later value besides the widening of his horizon from the limiting shores of the Ligurian Sea to the unknown expanse of the Atlantic.

The period was one in which the Mediterranean peoples were tense with excitement and expectancy in regard to maritime discovery, not only on account of contemporary achievement, but because the belief that the world might be spherical was being more and more widely accepted as a possibility. This gave rise to the idea that the Atlantic might be the common boundary of both Europe and Asia. The opinion that new continents, or at least verdant islands, could be reached by following the setting sun laid hold upon Columbus with all the tenacity of a strong conviction. The reasons for his belief multiplied. He became a monomaniac.

While still considering Portugal as his home, the voyage to England became a reality. If he sailed still further north to Iceland, as some believe, he must certainly have heard of the Viking voyages to "Vineland"; information which he may indeed have acquired in England. The preponderance of evidence seems to indicate that the visit to Iceland is only a myth. To quote Doctor Stevenson: "To such an event no reference is made by himself in his journal, or in his frank statement to his sovereigns that he was fully competent to pass upon the unusual excellence of the harbors in the new islands, for he had explored 'the coasts from Guinea on the south, to England on the north.' It would have been in keeping with his disposition then to have referred to such an expedition to the farther North, for he was ever ready to talk of his adventures."*

Even his marriage to Philippa Moniz Perestrello shortly after his arrival in Portugal conspired to prepare Columbus for giving the order on August 3, 1492, which spread the sails of three small ships in the Port of Palos. While Philippa's alleged noble relationship is not definitely established, she was instrumental in their going, about the year 1479, to live on the island of Porto Santo, one of the Madeiras. The island itself was of no importance, but being a western outpost in the Atlantic it brought to Columbus an experience which was sufficient to invite a bold, adventurous man to investigate the secrets of the western Atlantic.

Of all the incidents which may have influenced him, none is more interesting or more convincing than the story of the shipwrecked sailor who sought shelter in the home of Columbus. Far from being improbable, there is much which entitles the essential features of this narrative to full credence.

It seems that Pero Vazquez de la Frontera, a pilot of Huelva, set out from a Spanish port for England, but encountering contrary storms was driven westward until at length he sighted islands lying far beyond any shown on the charts. The attempt to determine the bearings of these islands was made by means of such navigational instruments as were then available, notably the astrolabe which afforded a crude measure of latitude. The wind, shifting to the west, allowed the pilot to alter his course toward home, but not until so much time had elapsed that practically all the crew died of exposure and starvation before the ship cast anchor in Madeira harbor. Here de la Frontera fell in with Columbus at whose house he presently passed away, not, however, until he had confided to his benefactor the discovery of new is-

* Stevenson: *Christopher Columbus and his Enterprise.*

lands, and had given him a chart on which these new lands were roughly located.

The determination to organize an expedition now possessed Columbus with growing enthusiasm. The two necessary characteristics for pursuing the project to a successful conclusion were his: enterprising will power, and goading ambition. Obviously the discovery of land beyond the Azores, which then marked the western extremity of the known world, would bring glory, honor, and everlasting fame to him who could show the way thither.

It was more the lack of adequate instruments for determining positions at sea than the so-called perils of the deep which had so long limited voyages to the coastline. With the coming of Martin Behaim's improved astrolabe and a more reliable compass these difficulties were largely removed. But of the many seamen who day-dreamed of western exploration, none felt so certain of success, nor had such a definite goal, nor thought of such possible wealth and honor as did Christopher Columbus.

Modern research makes it seem that no years of study, no scientific theories, no emancipation from the prevailing geographical ideas preceded the sailing of the *Santa Maria*. It is doubtful if the great Italian thinker, Toscanelli, ever entered into correspondence with Columbus, or suggested to the King of Portugal that a shorter and better route to India than the southern one around Africa could be found by sailing west. Columbus had something more than a good "hunch," and his almost arrogant ambition made him the most persistent man of history with the exception of Noah, who while engaged in the apparently foolhardy task of building his famous *Ark*, withstood for well over one hundred years the ridicule and the disparagement of his iniquitous neighbors.

Sufficient funds could be raised only through the support of a thriving nation or wealthy prince; yet, what man of exalted station would furnish them to thread-bare maker of charts who demanded such unheard of honors and rewards as to be nothing short of offensive?

Nevertheless, in 1484 he gained an audience with King John II of Portugal — a newly ascended monarch — who was deeply interested in the progress of navigation. Various accounts of the interview may be found. One relates that His Majesty was much impressed by the boldness of the Italian's plans; indeed, so much so that he was willing to furnish ships for the undertaking, but that he could not agree to the immense recompenses which were demanded. Another story is that the subject was referred to a maritime junto and to a high council, both of which rejected it as absurd. A third account suggests that King John, jealous for his own glory, invited Columbus to submit a written report to the government containing maps, charts, and a description of his proposals, which was then literally used to examine the practicability of the venture by dispatching a caravel to trace the route indicated. The ship set out, but soon returned, her crew appalled at the boundless horizon.

Discouraged at his failure to find a patron in King John, and perhaps due to the additional calamity of his wife's death, Columbus emigrated to Spain in 1485. From Lisbon he travelled to Palos, and thence probably to Huelva where a sister of his deceased wife resided. En route with his little son, Diego, he knocked one night at the door of the monastery of Santa Maria de la Rabida, dedicated to the Virgin Mary and inhabited by Franciscan friars. With the opening of this door came the beginnings of success.

The Superior, Juan Perez de Marchena, was a man of no mean parts, for he seems to have combined something of the astronomer, the devotee, and the poet. To him the would-be discoverer confided his plans, which met with encouragement not only because the priest was a man of imaginative vision, but also because he was undoubtedly familiar with recent explorations to the south and west and may even have known the story of the Huelva pilot.

Additional and very important influence was soon gained from a Spanish nobleman, the Duke of Medina-Coli, through whose happy offices the attention of the Court was finally gained. After a long period of suspense Columbus was summoned to appear at Cordova to explain his proposals. Further delays were here encountered because of royal preoccupation in the war against the Moors, which had now reached a critical stage. On his arrival Columbus found the city so absorbed in military preparations that months intervened before the King and Queen granted him an audience.

This enforced delay was not an entire loss, however, as his host, Alonzo de Quintanilla, treasurer of Castile, became an enthusiastic supporter who introduced him to other men of influence including the Grand Cardinal of Spain. With the aid of such encouraging adherents arrangements were at last perfected for laying the plan before Ferdinand and Isabella.

No detailed account of what took place at this audience exists, but it appears that Ferdinand was at least sufficiently impressed to appoint a commission to consider the matter. In November, 1486, the royal commission met at Salamanca for conference, but with the characteristic circumlocution of political bodies, its time was wasted in useless discussion which led to no definite conclusions. When a decision was finally rendered, the junto hid its conservatism behind the pretext that there were insufficient funds in the treasury.

Once more, when the court was again at Cordova during the following April, Columbus urged his scheme, this time receiving the assurance that his proposals would not be forgotten, and in support of this the Queen gave him the passive encouragement of attaching him to her retinue.

Led by inactivity to seek sympathy and inspiration somewhere, his affair with Beatriz Enriquez, who was neither rich nor noble, provided the necessary stimulus. She bore him a son, Fernando, who afterward became his father's biographer.*

From time to time the Court gave hope that Columbus' project might be reconsidered. There were equally discouraging periods when Columbus thought of again seeking aid from Portugal. At last, disgusted by the time he had wasted awaiting the condescension of the wealthy, he returned to the abby of his friend Marchena, bearing the unmistakable marks of "poverty, fatigue and exhausted patience."

Marchena at once wrote an eloquent letter to Queen Isabella, who, although engaged in war and harassed by financial trouble, had the foresight not only to send for her protégé, but to appropriate twenty thousand maradevis (about seventy dollars) with which he might purchase a horse and suitable clothing.

Columbus arrived at Santa Fé just before the surrender of Grenada which closed the struggle between the Crescent and the Cross. Preceded by the happy rejoicing of this victory, his appearance before the Queen took place under very favorable circumstances.

Convinced of the practicability of the venture, Isabella discussed it from two points of view: the equipment necessary, and the recompense to be awarded to Columbus in case of success. Whatever extravagant and preposterous demands he may

* Only the Italian translation published in Venice, 1571, remains, copies of the original having all disappeared. Fernando's authorship is both warmly defended and denied by various authorities.

have made of King John there is no reason to believe that any discouragement influenced him to reduce them. The conditions which he fixed were that:

"He should receive the title of Grand Admiral of the Ocean.

"He should be Viceroy and Governor-General of all islands and mainlands he might discover.

"He should levy eight to ten per cent tax for his own benefit upon all productions — whether spices, fruits, perfumes, gold, silver, or precious stones — discovered in, or exported from, the lands under his authority.

"His titles should be transmissible in his family forever, by the laws of primogeniture."

A committee appointed to consider these claims regarded them as insolent and impossible. Such awards would possibly raise the son of a wool-weaver above the rank of the noblest dukes and grandees in all of Spain. Columbus, however, would not reduce his demands one jot nor one tittle in spite of the fact that after years of fruitless effort he now saw his hopes again being dashed to earth. Mounting his mule, he left the city resolved to seek the aid of Charles VIII of France.

Moved by the persuasions of friends, the Queen dispatched a messenger for Columbus who was overtaken a few miles from Grenada. She authorized the enterprise on April 17, 1492, not as the wife of the King of Spain, but independently as Queen of Castile. Ferdinand remained indifferent, although he signed the formal papers.

Documents granting the privileges and titles demanded were given to Columbus on April 30th. These papers contain no mention of a new route to India; nor is there any mention of it in any of the negotiations which refer only to the attempt to "discover and take possession of certain islands in the sea of whose existence Columbus knew." In the Las Casas résumé of the *Santa Maria's* log two references to India appear, the great probability being that it was an expedient by which the Admiral sought to reassure his crew. The royal letter acknowledging the receipt of dispatches sent by courier when the expedition returned, is the first official document to refer to India. No mention of it is made in the Papal bulls sanctioning the rights of their Catholic Monarchs, Ferdinand and Isabella, to the newly discovered territory.

The harbor of Palos, to which the Admiral went on the twelfth of May, was selected as the port of departure; and its citizens, whose taxes consisted in furnishing two caravels annually to the government, were instructed to place these at the disposal of Columbus within ten days. In order to raise a crew, criminals awaiting trial were offered the opportunity of escaping verdict and punishment by embarking on this mysterious and perhaps fatal voyage.

These tidings were received with dismay by the merchants of Palos. Owners of vessels secreted them in distant harbors. The authorities did nothing toward securing the required vessels. Finally stringent measures had to be adopted by the government, which seized and laid up for repairs a caravel named the *Pinta*. With all the sagacity of a modern labor movement, every carpenter became ill, and every ship chandler possessed neither rope, canvas, nor fittings.

Marchena, the zealous Franciscan, did his utmost to secure the coöperation of his people but without success. A change of attitude was effected only when the news became current that the three Pinzon brothers were to accompany Columbus. All sea-faring men whose influence in Palos was great, their decision to sail and to offer the *Nina*, a caravel belonging to the youngest brother, sufficiently overcame opposition for the city to furnish its second vessel, the *Gallega*, making three in all.

This last addition, properly classed as a carack, though old and heavy was still seaworthy and was much larger than the other two. She was, therefore, selected as the flagship and rechristened the *Santa Maria* after the La Rabida monastery from which Columbus had received so much encouragement.

Towards the end of July, when all was nearly in readiness, he retired to the monastery for a few days of prayer and meditation which, however, did not prevent him from returning at unexpected intervals to the shipyard, where on one occasion he surprised the sailors who had been condemned to accompany him, engaged in tampering with the rudder of the *Pinta* so that it would be carried away by the first storm.

On August 3, 1492, equipped with stores to last a year, the voyage began. Three days later there was trouble with the *Pinta's* steering gear—a mishap having been more successfully brought about the second time by her terrified crew. But the damage was successfully repaired at the Canary Islands, from which the little fleet set sail on September 6th.

The shrewdness with which the Admiral sought to allay the fears of his comrades began to function immediately. He kept two logs; an accurate one for himself, a second recording less than the distance actually sailed, for the benefit of the crew.

Familiar constellations disappeared. Others took their places. The water became more limpid. The climate changed. On September 13th, Columbus observed that the compass needle, which until then had pointed toward the North Star, was diverging to the west. So far as is known, he was the first to note this westerly declination, a discovery which he kept discreetly to himself until the voyage was over.

On several occasions the sailors became seriously alarmed and threatened mutiny. The floating vegetation on what is now known as the Sargasso Sea was the first taken as an indication of land. None appeared, even though the weeds so retarded the ships as to make extrication seem impossible. The continuing east wind supported the apprehension that it would be impossible to sail back to Europe. At the crucial moment a contrary wind sprang up which, as Columbus wrote in his journal, "came very opportunely, for my crew was in great agitation, imagining that no wind ever blew in these regions by which they could return to Spain."

At sundown on September 25th the captain of the *Pinta* shouted "Land! Land! My lord, I was the first to see it!" Sailors climbed excitedly into the tops and Columbus fell upon his knees in prayer. But in the morning there was nothing but limitless ocean, nothing but sky and waves.

On the first of October the crew became newly alarmed by the thought that they were seventeen hundred miles from the Canaries, the distance being actually twenty-one hundred miles according to Columbus' private reckoning. Disappointed so many times by signs which seemed to indicate the vicinity of land, the crew was now openly mutinous. A plan was laid to throw the Admiral into the sea and to report on their return to Spain that he had "fallen into the waves while gazing at the stars."

Dissatisfaction and fear came to a head on October 10th when the *Pinta* and *Nina* came alongside the *Santa Maria*. The Pinzon brothers, followed by their men, leaped to the deck of the flagship and commanded Columbus to put his ship about for the return voyage.

How this indomitable man by sheer force of personality overcame the superstition, the terror, and the rebellion of over one hundred others is not recorded. In the light of the next day's developments it was a dramatic thing.

Pigeons flew over the ships. A bush covered with red berries was taken from the water by the *Nina*. A piece of wood, apparently hacked with some sort of iron implement was picked up by the *Pinta*. The fleet continued to sail westward in spite of the fact that no land could be seen.

At evening the ships came together and Columbus announced that their suspense was at an end. He felt sure land was near, and ordered the pilots to shorten sail after midnight. Two hours after midnight a gun from the *Pinta*, which was the most rapid sailer and therefore somewhat in advance, announced that land had been sighted. The first to see is was Redrigo de Triana who thus won the velvet pourpoint which Columbus had promised.

At the sound of the *Pinta's* gun the man who had worked so persistently for this moment sank to his knees singing the *Te Deum Laudamus*. Sails were furled and the fleet lay to. In the morning the great mystery would be solved.

At dawn, accompanied by officers in full regalia, Columbus landed on one of the Bahamas now known as Watling's Island, carrying a drawn sword in one hand and the standard of Spain in the other. Naming the land San Salvador in memory of the Savior, he took possession of it for the Crown of Castile. The crews recognized him as Grand Admiral of the Ocean; Viceroy and Governor-General; one who already had in his gift great wealth and powerful positions.

The object of his enterprise was now attained. The land was not, to be sure, where he had thought it to be, but so much further westward that he wondered if what we know as Cuba were not a projection of Asia. This error was the cause of the North American savages being called "Indians" — an error which can never be corrected.

For several weeks he explored the region, sailing along the Cuban coast and discovering Haiti on December 6th. To this island he gave the name of "Hispaniola" because it reminded him of the fairest tracts of Spain. Here the captain of the *Pinta* deserted, hoping to make discoveries and gain glory on his own account.

Christmas Eve, being a calm night, the Admiral went below at 11 P.M. whereupon the steersman, drowsy in the tropical air, fell asleep. Thus the *Santa Maria* was carried ashore by the tide before anyone realized the danger. The pounding on the beach roused Columbus, who immediately ordered a boat over the side and a kedge anchor laid astern by which to pull his flagship off. The men who manned the boat disregarded the order and fled, panic stricken, to the *Nina*. An attempt to lighten the *Santa Maria* by throwing a great quantity of stores overboard was unavailing. She had to be abandoned.

The problem of caring for the crew, now that the largest of the ships was lost, presented difficulties of no mean order. It was eventually solved by building a fort from the timbers of the wreck in which forty-two men were left to be rescued on a later voyage.

Transferring his flag to the *Nina*, Columbus weighed anchor on January 11, 1493. Shortly afterward he fell in with the *Pinta* by chance, accepting the fictions which Pinzon invented as his reasons for abandoning the fleet. The two vessels now set sail for Spain.

The tranquil weather of their autumnal voyage had now given way to winter tempests. On February 12th a storm of such violence struck them that to survive it seemed impossible. To invoke Divine aid, "a quantity of dried peas, equal in number to the number of men on board the *Nina*, were placed in a sailor's woolen cap, one of them being marked with a cross. He who should draw this pea, was to go on a pilgrimage to the Church of St. Mary at Guadeloupe, bearing a candle weighing five pounds in case the ship were saved. Columbus was the first to draw, and he drew the marked pea."*

During the most terrific part of the storm the Admiral withdrew to his cabin where he wrote out two separate narratives of his discoveries. These he enclosed in wax, placing each in a separate barrel one of which was immediately thrown into the sea, and the other attached to the poop of the *Nina* from which it was to be cut loose in the event of the ship going down.

Happily the storm subsided so that on February 17th the *Pinta* and the *Nina* arrived at one of the southernmost islands of the Azores. Here half the crew were taken prisoners by the Portuguese. With only three able seamen aboard, the *Nina* put to sea again, this time to narrowly escape shipwreck in a storm which carried her to the coast of Portugal.

At mid-day on March 15, 1493, over seven months after his departure, Columbus arrived at Palos. Alonzo Pinzon had already arrived in the *Pinta*, and supposing the *Nina* to have gone down in the storm, had sent a courier to the Court with news of the discovery together with a claim that the honors and rewards should be awarded to him. For this deception Queen Isabella is said to have administered so stinging a rebuke that Pinzon died of shame.

On his way to Barcelona, whither the Court had gone, Columbus discharged the holy pilgrimage which had fallen to him by lot to perform. He visited his friend Marchena at the monastery of La Rabida. He received a more enthusiastic and colorful reception from the people who gazed at him than had ever been previously accorded to an explorer. His discovery had stirred all Spain. He was welcomed by the thunder of cannon and the ringing of bells.

The Spanish Sovereigns received him with princely honors, rising at his approach, and seating him beside themselves on their gilded and canopied throne. Pope Alexander VI confirmed the claims of Spain and Portugal to all discoveries made, or to be made, of "lands which lay to west or east of the meridian henceforth to be known as the Line of Demarcation."

A new expedition was soon fitted out which sailed from Cadiz on September 25, 1493. This time Columbus commanded a fleet of seventeen vessels carrying five hundred sailors, soldiers, and servants, and one thousand colonists of whom three hundred had "stowed away" on board.

Returning to Hispaniola where he had left the forty-two men, he found the fort destroyed and the garrison massacred. Undismayed, he founded the city of Isabella on another part of the island. Here new hostilities broke out for the Spaniards did many things to outrage and alienate the natives. They rapidly dwindled away from disease and poor food; jealousies arose and starvation threatened in spite of the fertility of the soil. All this created bitter disappointment for which the leader of the expedition was naturally blamed. On March 10, 1496, he put back toward Spain with only two ships, one the staunch *Nina*. The discovery of Jamaica, which had been named in honor of Saint James, represented the only progress achieved by this unhappy effort at securing a foothold in the New World.

Upon his return Isabella forgot the calumnies of which he had been the object and the accusations which his disillusioned followers had heaped upon him. But it was not until May 30, 1498, that another fleet, numbering six caravels, set out. Three of these ships were loaded with supplies and reinforcements for the colony

* Goodrich: *Man Upon the Sea*, page 150.

at Isabella, the other three were intended to furnish Columbus with means of further exploration.

It was on the 31st of July that strange land was sighted to westward — three mountain peaks ascending from the same base. With characteristic religious fervor the great discoverer called the region Trinidad, signifying the Trinity.

But his colonists did not prosper. Influence was exerted to prejudice the mind of Ferdinand and in July, 1500, the King dispatched a representative who placed Columbus in chains. In the same small vessel which had brought him home a world hero only seven years before, the Admiral was carried back to Spain a prisoner. How seriously this affront offended him may be guessed by the story that he kept the fetters with which he was bound until his dying day, and ordered that they be enclosed in his coffin.

However, public opinion was, even in those monarchial days, a factor to be reckoned with. So strong was the protest against this treatment of Columbus that his sovereign stoutly denied any previous knowledge of it.

The last voyage to America which Columbus made while still alive, departed from Cadiz on May 8, 1502. He hoped to find that the land converged to westward of his previous discoveries, leaving somewhere a narrow passage by which he could sail still further. He might thus be able to circumnavigate the globe and prove its spherical form. Across the isthmus, along which he vainly searched for a passage, civilization has now built the Panama Canal.

Storms and finally shipwreck on the coast of Jamaica, where he awed and subdued the natives by predicting an eclipse of the moon, forced him to abandon further exploration. After fifteen months of constant unpleasantness, a ship was obtained in which he sailed for Spain on September 12, 1504.

At Seville he heard with dismay of the illness and death of Isabella. Sick at heart and broken of body he sought in vain for Ferdinand's assistance. The man to whose kingdom he had added a new continent was always polite, but selfish, cold, and guilty of gross ingratitude. Columbus was now without supporters and without hope. For a year he languished in poverty and neglect, dying in almost complete obscurity at Valladolid on May 20, 1506, a disappointed, pathetic man.

Nor were his ashes allowed to rest in peace. To date, they have been buried five successive times and have twice followed the path across the Atlantic which he was the first to discover for the civilized world.

For seven years they lay in the vaults of the Franciscan convent at Valladolid. In 1513, perhaps realizing the enormity of his neglect, Ferdinand caused the casket to be transferred to the Grand Cathedral at Seville where a solemn mass was said before placing it in the chapel belonging to the Chartreux. In 1536 the casket was carried to the city of San Domingo on the island which Columbus had called Hispaniola. Here it remained for two hundred and sixty years until Spain ceded the island to France, stipulating that the immortal dust of the great Admiral should be transferred to Spanish soil. In December, 1795, the vault was opened and the fragments which remained were taken to Havana. After Spain's loss of Cuba, in 1898, the bones were carried back across the Atlantic to the Great Cathedral of Seville, where may they find eternal rest.

With the passing of Diego Colon, a great-grandson of Christopher Columbus, who died in 1578, the male descendents of the great discoverer became extinct. The present dukes of Verazua are descended from a sister of the last Diego, and still retain the title of Admiral.

Our chief sources of information were, for many years, Navarrete's collection of Columbian documents published at Madrid between 1825 and 1837 and the records left by Las Casas, whose résumé of the *Santa Maria's* log is still extant although there is no trace of the original. On the four-hundredth anniversary of the discovery of America, both Spain and Italy published monumental works, the one having most to do with the Admiral's flagship being "La Noa Santa Maria," published under the direction of the Royal Spanish Navy.

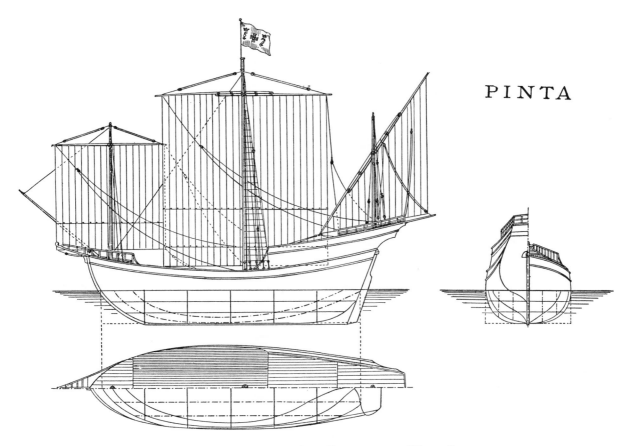

FIG. 9. LINES AND SAIL PLAN OF THE "PINTA"
From the Clark Collection of Marine Prints

THE FLEET

At the time of the Chicago "World's Fair," in 1892, replicas of Columbus' three ships were built in Spain; the *Pinta* and *Nina* at Barcelona, the *Santa Maria* at Cadiz. These ships were successfully sailed across the Atlantic, following the course charted by the great Admiral four hundred years before. The construction of these vessels was based on conscientious research in order that they might be true copies of the ships they represented. Indeed, at the time they were referred to as "exact counterparts."

The Pinta

Decked over only forward and aft, her waist being entirely uncovered, she was a small caravel of about fifty tons burden, *i.e.* carrying capacity. Her sail plan was similar to the *Santa Maria's*, namely, square rig on the fore and main masts, with a lateen on the mizen. Alonzo Pinzon commanded her crew, variously given as from eighteen to twenty-nine men.

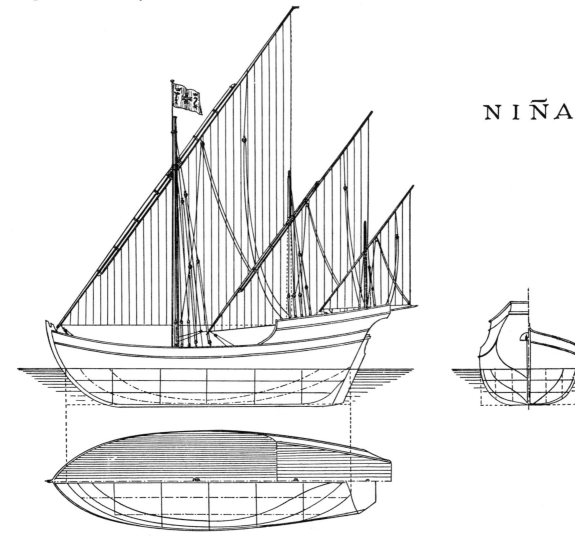

NIÑA

FIG. 10. LINES AND SAIL PLAN OF THE "NINA"
From the Clark Collection of Marine Prints

PRINCIPAL DIMENSIONS OF THE "PINTA"

Length over all	68' - 0"
Length at deck	54' - 0"
Beam	22' - 0"
Depth of hold	9' - 6"
Draft	6' - 0"
Freeboard	4' - 0"
Tons burden (metric)	50
Complement	18 (?) men
Sail area	3,000 sq. ft.
Artillery	4 falconet cannon mounted on the rail.

The Nina

She was the smallest ship of the three and, strangely enough, as has already been pointed out, the most intimately connected with the several American voyages of Columbus. She belonged to the youngest of the three Pinzon brothers, Vincent

Yanez, who commanded her on the original westward voyage. Rigged entirely with lateen sails, her appearance was strikingly like that of a Chinese junk. Her crew consisted of between eighteen and twenty-three men, the former probably being correct.

PRINCIPAL DIMENSIONS

Length over all	67' - 0"
Length at deck	55' - 0"
Beam	22' - 0"
Draft	6' - 0"
Freeboard	3' - 0"
Tons burden (metric)	48
Sail area	2,300 sq. ft.
Fore lateen yard	60' - 0"
Main " "	47' - 0"
Mizen " "	41' - 0"
Complement	18 (?) men

The Santa Maria

The ship here described is the replica which was launched at the Royal Spanish Navy Yard, Cadiz, on June 26, 1892. Although this reproduction has behind it all the thunders of official sanction, the work of various contributors to the "Mariner's Mirror" (a publication of the British Society for Nautical Research) makes Henry B. Culver believe it to contain many anachronisms.* Nor is he alone in this assertion.

Beyond a shadow of doubt the bowsprit could not have been on the center-line, the extreme position of the foremast making it necessary to ship this spar somewhat to starboard. The forecastle, the poop, and especially the transom, which is so appropriately decorated with a painting of the Holy Virgin, resemble ships of a later date than the close of the fifteenth century. The topsail is surprisingly developed for the minute sail which one could expect to find in 1492, and the sheets, instead of leading to the tops as they should, are rigged to the arms. The mainstay should unquestionably be set up to the stem head with a lanyard and some sort of crude heart. Nor should there be any ratlines on the shrouds, the tops still being reached by a Jacob's ladder fitted abaft the mast. Lifts and bowlines were probably in use as well as the forerunners of leech-lines and buntlines (then called martlets and martnets) but the braces, as shown on the plan, are much too far advanced for the rudimentary gear of Columbus' day.

The general arrangement of the sails is probably correct. To quote from the Las Casas résumé of the *Santa Maria's* log of October 24th: "I set all the sails in the ship, the mainsail with two bonnets, the fore-sail, spritsail, mizen, main topsail, and the boat's sail on the poop."

A comparison between the plans of the *Mayflower* and the *Santa Maria* will instantly show how little difference there is between the two, and how much there is to support Mr. Culver's contention that the "exact counterpart" actually incorporates many of the features of a seventeenth-century ship.

PRINCIPAL DIMENSIONS

Length over all	128' - 3"
Length of hull	94' - 0"
Load water-line	71' - 3"
Beam	25' - 8"
Depth of hold	12' - 5"

* Culver: *The Book of Old Ships*, page 75.

THE "SANTA MARIA"

Draft at bow . . . . 7' - 2"
          stern . . . . 9' - 8"
Freeboard . . . . 9' - 0"
Displacement . . . . English tons (2240 lbs.) 230
                    Metric tons 233
Tons burden 100
Sail area . . . . 5,000 sq. ft.
Complement . . . . 52 (?) men

Beside the seamen required to work the ship, there were gentlemen adventurers and officials of various sorts, the total number of men on all three ships being not far from one hundred and twenty. The officers and petty officers, who of course belong to the complement, are said to have included:

1 carpenter	1 master
1 caulker	2 pilots
1 cooper	1 surgeon
1 steward	1 quartermaster
1 master gunner	1 clerk
1 bugler	1 interpreter

HULL

This was carvel-built and of the most rugged construction. Had she been designed expressly for exploration instead of for trading, her lines might have been finer with a marked increase in speed. She had distinctly more of the cart-horse than of the hunter.

The keel was of 12" x 14" oak, sixty feet, eight inches long. To this were attached 5" x 9" double oak frames spaced eleven inches apart. Outside planking was of 3" Spanish fir.

The painting of the model made under the direction of Captain Don Antonio de la Reyna y Pidal, director of the Naval Museum at Madrid, which the Spanish government sent to England, is colorful, artistic, and plausible.

The under water portion of the hull, being covered with tallow to facilitate progress through the water, presents an ivory appearance which is very pleasing. Above the water-line the horizontal wales and vertical skids are very prominent, their function being to protect the hull when alongside a dock or when weights were hoisted on board. From the water-line to the first wale is painted black, this wale being of plain varnished wood. The second wale is painted red, and the moulding is again of varnished wood. Above the first wale, the topside has a brown appearance due to its being covered with Stockholm tar.

The spar-deck was open below the forecastle and quarter-deck, but since the Admiral's cabin was directly under the poop (and extending clear across the ship) this break in the deck was closed by a bulwark ornamented with arches and pierced by a single door and window.

Access to the forecastle and poop was by ladders on the port side, the quarter-deck being provided with an open scuttle on the center line through which a ladder descended to the spar deck.

Particular mention should be made of the wide rail caps, really billboards, which curve down from the forecastle. These serve for anchor stowage, the "bill" of the anchor catching over the inner edge so that when lashed in place it was very secure. By removing the lashing the anchor could be easily dropped.

[28]

PLATE IV

Courtesy of Science Museum, South Kensington

MODEL OF THE "SANTA MARIA" PRESENTED IN 1923 TO THE SCIENCE MUSEUM, SOUTH KENSINGTON, ENGLAND, BY THE SPANISH GOVERNMENT. THE MODEL ILLUSTRATES IMPORTANT FEATURES OF SHIP CONSTRUCTION OF THE PERIOD, MUCH OF THE PLANKING OF THE STARBOARD SIDE BEING OMITTED TO SHOW THE FRAMES. IT WAS BUILT UNDER THE SUPERVISION OF THE DIRECTOR OF THE NAVAL MUSEUM AT MADRID, FROM THE SAME INFORMATION USED IN THE DRAWING OF PLANS II, III AND IV. THE BOBSTAY HERE SHOWN HAS RECENTLY BEEN REMOVED

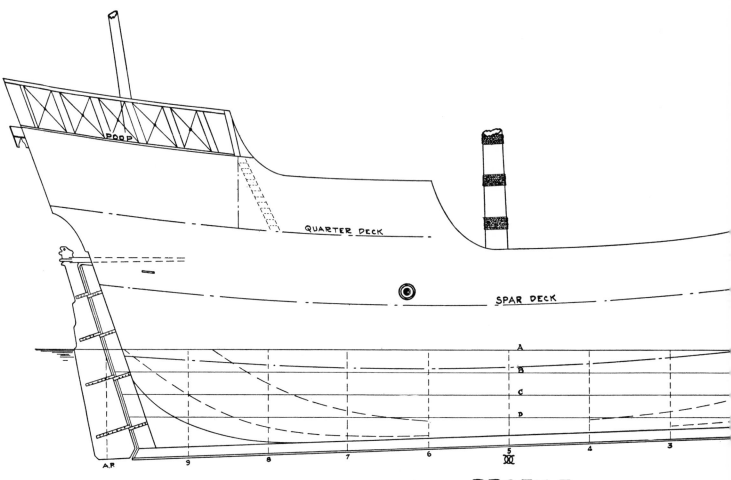

POOP

QUARTER DECK

SPAR DECK

A
B
C
D

A.P.　9　8　7　6　5　4　3

PROFILE

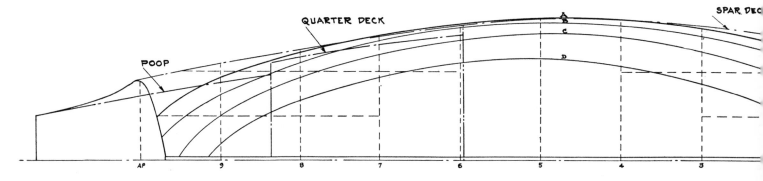

QUARTER DECK

POOP

SPAR DEC

A
B
C

D

AP　9　8　7　6　5　4　3

LINES

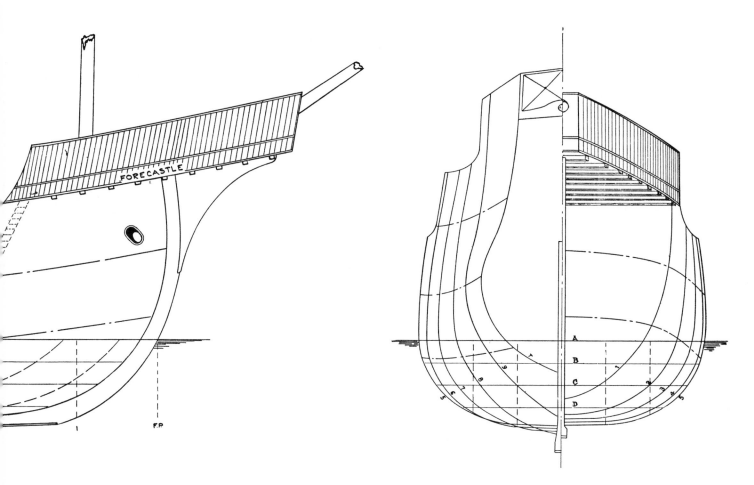

FORECASTLE

BODY PLAN

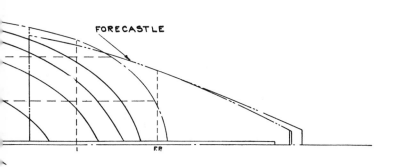

FORECASTLE

FEET

0 1 2 3 4 5 6 7 8 9 10

COLUMBUS'S SHIP
"SANTA MARIA"

DRAWN FROM INFORMATION FURNISHED
BY THE ROYAL SPANISH NAVY

F. Alexander Magoun

MASSACHUSETTS INSTITUTE OF TECHNOLOGY

CAMBRIDGE   MASS.

HALLIARD

HALLIARD

REST FOR
MAIN YARD

SAIL PLAN

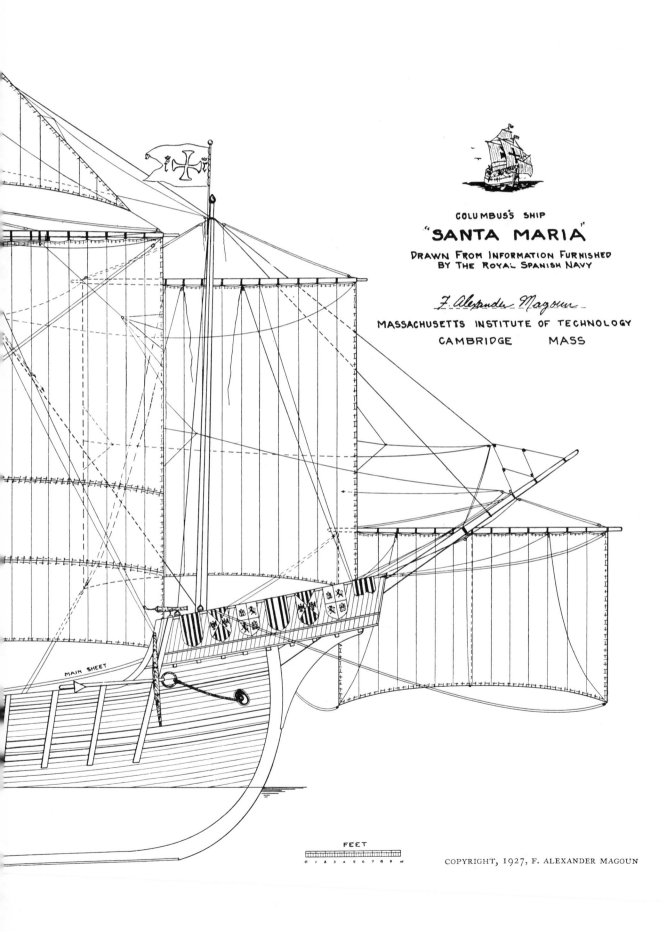

COLUMBUS'S SHIP

"SANTA MARIA"

DRAWN FROM INFORMATION FURNISHED
BY THE ROYAL SPANISH NAVY

F. Alexander Magoun

MASSACHUSETTS INSTITUTE OF TECHNOLOGY

CAMBRIDGE   MASS

MAIN SHEET

FEET

0 1 2 3 4 5 6 7 8 9 10

LOMBARDS

TWO LOMBARDIA CANNON WERE CARRIED ON THE UPPER DECK. THESE HAD A 2½ INCH BORE AND FIRED STONE SHOT OF TWO-POUNDS WEIGHT.

FALCONETS

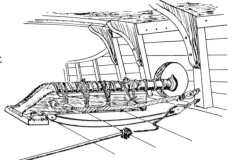

SIX WROUGHT IRON FALCONETS WERE MOUNTED ON THE RAIL THESE HAD A BORE OF ONE INCH TO AN INCH AND THREE QUARTERS AND FIRED 13 OUNCE STONE SHOT.

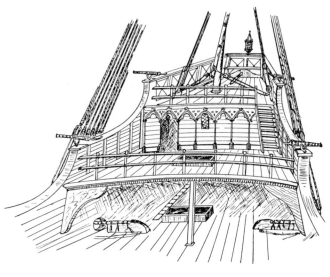

LOOKING AFT

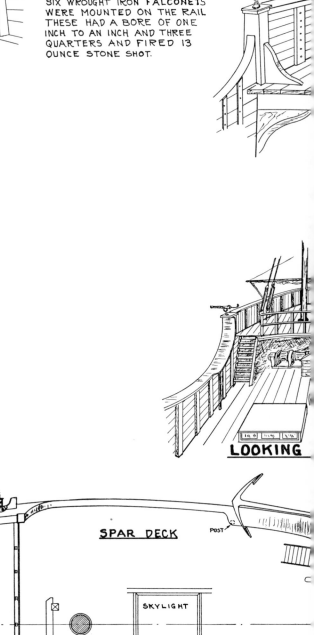

LOOKING

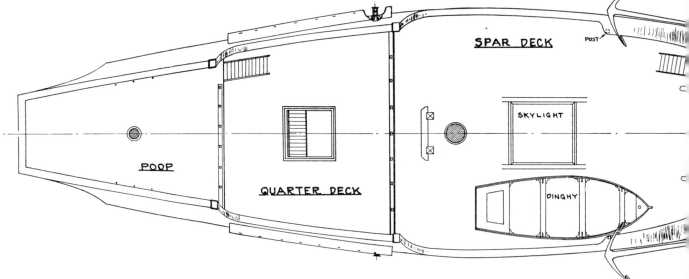

SPAR DECK

POST

POOP

QUARTER DECK

SKYLIGHT

DINGHY

DECK PLAN

STOVE

THE COOKING APPARATUS CONSISTED OF A SAND BOX ON WHICH A FIRE OF WOOD OR CHARCOAL WAS BUILT. THE UTENSILS WERE OF HAND-WROUGHT COPPER.

THE BADGE OF THE BAND OF DISCOVERERS: A WHITE FLAG WITH A CROSS OF GREEN. THE "Ҭ" AND THE "ɪ" BENEATH THE CROWNS SIGNIFY FERDINAND & ISABELLA.

THE ROYAL STANDARD OF CASTILLE QUARTERED IN WHITE AND RED WITH CASTLES IN GOLD AND WITH RED LIONS

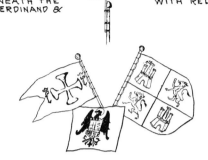

THE ESCUTCHEON OF THEIR CATHOLIC MONARCHS HELD IN THE CLAWS OF THE EAGLE OF ST. JOHN

ANCHORS   LANTERN

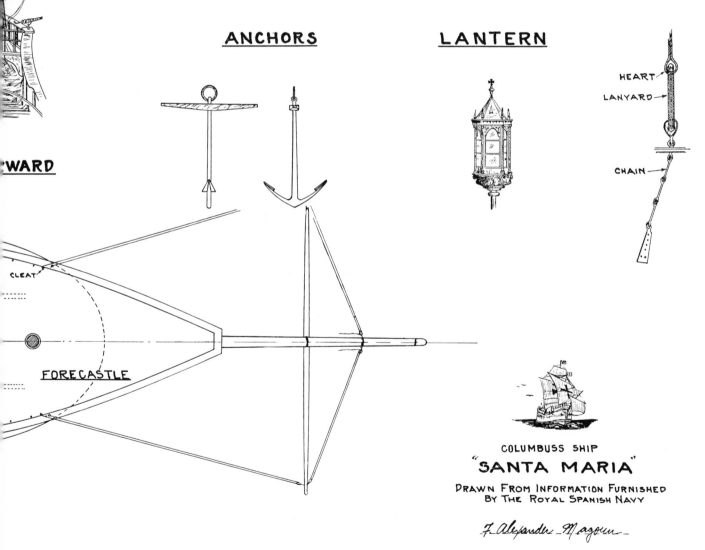

WARD

CLEAT

FORECASTLE

HEART

LANYARD

CHAIN

FEET

COLUMBUSS SHIP
"SANTA MARIA"

DRAWN FROM INFORMATION FURNISHED BY THE ROYAL SPANISH NAVY

F. Alexander Magoun

MASSACHUSETTS INSTITUTE OF TECHNOLOGY
CAMBRIDGE   MASS

The spar-deck is cut by two hatches; a large one covered by a skylight in the waist amidships, and a smaller one beneath the scuttle in the quarter-deck.

HULL FITTINGS

Steering Gear

Since the whipstaff did not come in until the sixteenth century, the *Santa Maria* was steered by means of a huge tiller which entered the ship through a hole in the transom, and was operated from the spar-deck. It was obviously impossible for the man at the tiller to see anything ahead. His orders were shouted to him by an officer conning the ship from the quarter-deck or poop when in waters impossible to navigate by means of the compass alone.

Lantern

In order that the fleet should not become separated at night, a lantern was carried on the stern of the flagship. Illumination by candles, which shone through the windows, may seem strange to us, but it served the purpose. The design of the exterior of this lantern might well be copied, for it is a most decorative affair.

Yard Rest

Projecting above the gunwales and located just forward of the mainmast were two U-shaped rests on to which the main yard was lowered when furling sail. These resemble a gigantic oar-lock or a crutch more than anything else (see Plan III).

Hawse pipe

The windlass being under the forecastle the hawse pipe led to the spar-deck. Thus, any water which entered could run aft and overboard through the spar-deck scuppers.

Chain-plates

Only the standing rigging of the mainmast was made fast outboard. The main chain-plates were consequently unique. Four brackets braced them to the hull and long-link chain made fast to the red wale held the lower hearts of the main shrouds. Those of the fore and mizen shrouds were secured to the deck inside the rail by iron fittings.

SPARS AND RIGGING

In ships of the fifteenth century the mainmast was a conspicuous feature. Its great size and height were the very culmination of the pole mast — one stick carrying more canvas than twice the area of the balance of the ship's sails. In order to strengthen the mainmast against splitting, the lower portion was lashed in seven places; an early forerunner of the iron bands found on such ships as the *Constitution* and the *Flying Cloud*.

The rake of the masts was peculiar to the period, nor was it without reason, for since the spritsail tends to raise the bow, so the forward-leaning foresail tends to depress it. The mainmast, being perpendicular to the water-line, bisects the angle between the fore and mizen to the satisfaction of the eye.

The main yard and the lateen yard, respectively sixty and sixty-four and a half feet in length, were made by splicing two suitable spars together. This gave a double strength-member in the center where the maximum stresses had to be met.

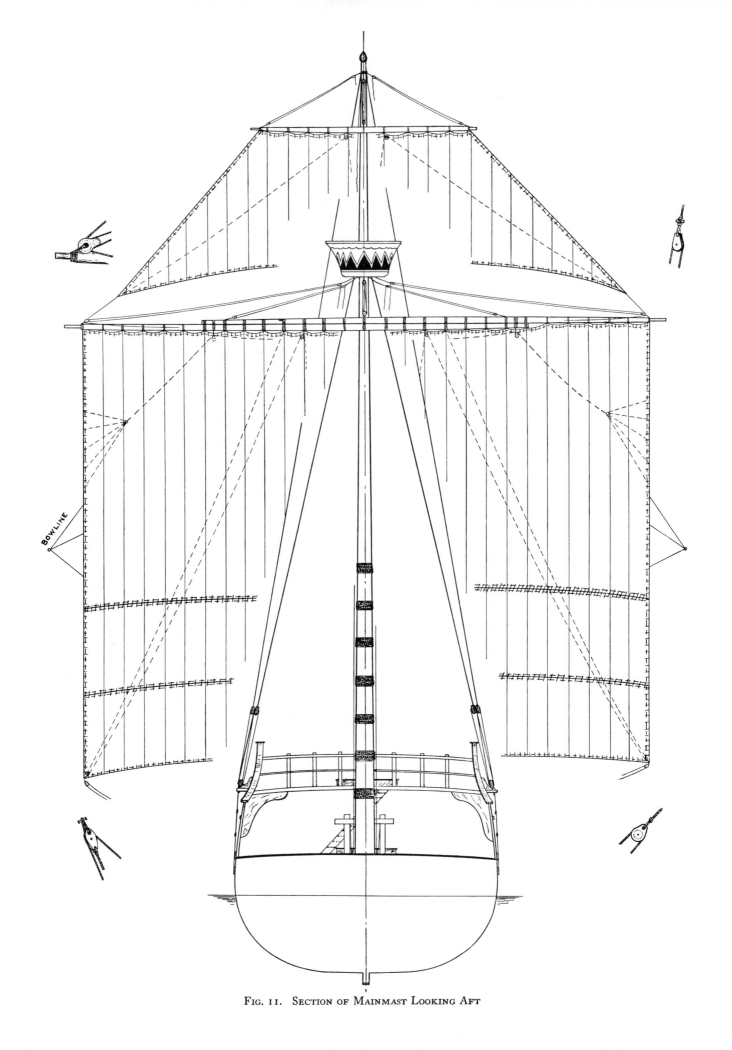

BOWLINE

FIG. 11. SECTION OF MAINMAST LOOKING AFT

A very common error on this and on much later ships (*Mayflower*, etc.) is the inclusion of a bowsprit bobstay. Indeed, the model in the Science Museum, South Kensington, London, was so equipped until this anachronism was removed in 1925. The very fact that the spritsail yard travels up and down the bowsprit makes a bobstay impossible. Nor should there be any bowsprit shrouds.

A boomkin, projecting over the stern and to which the lateen sheet led, was, however, properly braced both by a bobstay and by shrouds.

The standing rigging was set up, not with the familiar three-holed deadeye, but with hearts having a single notched hole through which the lanyard was laced. As already mentioned the two foremost shrouds and the three mizen shrouds are made fast inboard.

The description of the lead of the running rigging lends itself to tabular form:

YARD	LIFT	HALLIARD	BRACE	SHEET	
				Standing part	*Fall*
Spritsail	Forecastle		Fw'd swifter	Hull	Fore shroud
Foresail	F'c'l head via mainstay		F'c'l head via mainstay	Hull	Waist cleat
Mainsail	Posts on deck	Port rail	Poop cleat	Hull	Inboard
Main topsail	Rail	St'b'd rail	Poop via mizen		Post on deck
Lateen	Poop rail	Main top	Poop tackle	Boomkin	Poop

The topsail sheets led through sister blocks which also served for the main lifts as shown in detail at the upper left of the section at the mainmast (Fig. 11).

Bowlines from the foresail and mainsail led forward to the fore-stay and the bowsprit, from which they were belayed to cleats on the inside of the forecastle rail. There was no vang on the lateen yard. The cordage was probably of hemp.

Various dimensions for the length and diamenter of spars are given by different authorities. Those used in the preparation of these drawings were procured through the courtesy of Vice-Admiral Don Honorio Cornejo, Spanish Minister of Marine.

EQUIPMENT

Sails

Canvas had long been a well-known material by the year 1492. But instead of shortening sail with reef points, Columbus and his contemporaries did so by the

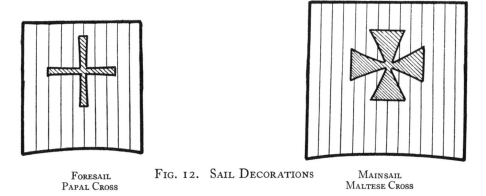

FORESAIL
PAPAL CROSS

FIG. 12. SAIL DECORATIONS

MAINSAIL
MALTESE CROSS

simple expedient of taking off a piece of canvas which had been laced through eyelets to the foot of the sail. This was called a bonnet. Sometimes, as in the case of the *Santa Maria's* mainsail, a second bonnet, properly called a drabbler, gave even further flexibility of sail area. The bonnet was cut to be from one-third to one-quarter the size of the mainsail.

Decoration of sails was still in vogue, the present popular belief being that the flagship's foresail was marked by a dark green Papal cross and the mainsail by a Maltese cross of similar color. These are an unmistakable addition to the beauty of the ship, but there being no such design on the photostats of the *Santa Maria* obtained from the Spanish Minister of Marine, they have not been included in the plans.

On models the lateen sail is usually rigged with the yard on the port side. In actual construction it was necessary to be able to move this yard from one side to the other, since the sail was of necessity on the weather side; otherwise the canvas would foul the rigging. The process of shifting the yard was a simple one. By hauling on the halliard (which led to the main top) as well as on the moutons, or tackles, at the lower extremity of the yard, it could be brought into perpendicular position parallel to the mast. It was then a simple matter to slip the lower end of the yard around to the other side of the mast.

Anchors

In 1891 the much-rusted remains of an anchor were recovered off the coast of Haiti. The opinion that it had been made in Madrid in 1450 led naturally to the conclusion that here was one of the anchors of the wrecked *Santa Maria* (some accounts say she was equipped with as many as eight anchors). Of the stock there remained nothing at all, which loss accounts for the erroneous inclusion of bands on the stocks of most models of the famous flagship. These bands were present on the replica of 1892 and are shown on the Spanish plans. They are not included here, as they constitute an anachronism.

The anchors were shipped from the fore yard-arms and stowed, as previously explained, on the "bill boards" just abaft the forecastle. The original weight of the recovered anchor is calculated as 2,300 pounds.

Windlass

This was a horizontal affair which suspiciously resembled those of the later clipper ships, both in shape and in location. Housed under the break of the forecastle, it was probably never used in connection with working the sails, but merely for weighing the anchor.

Pumps

The pumps of the *Santa Maria* were located on the spar deck and sufficiently far aft to be under the quarter-deck. In construction they were probably not very different from those of the *Mayflower*, a drawing and description of which will be found on page 60.

Implements of War

Artillery was then fearfully and wonderfully made. The two lombard cannon, carried on the spar (or upper) deck had a bore of two and a half inches, firing stone shot of two pounds weight. With the exception of the wheels which graced the gun-carriages of a few years later, these muzzle loaders were not essentially different either in appearance, operation, or method of fastening to the hull from those of even the *Constitution* herself.

The six wrought-iron falconets which were mounted on the rail, corresponded in function to the modern light, quick-firing gun. They had a bore varying from one inch to an inch and three-quarters, thirteen-ounce stone being the projectiles used (See Plan IV).

Besides these formidable weapons, she had cross-bows and arrows for use on shore, together with spears and battle axes of various sorts.

Like the Vikings, the band of discoverers carried ornamental shields along the sides of its vessel. These were of three designs: the plain gold and red stripes of Arragon; the quartered shields of Castile and Leon, with their golden castles on a red background, their red lions, rampant, on a field of white; and the bisected shields showing the black eagle of St. John holding in his claws the escutcheon of their Catholic monarchs, Ferdinand and Isabella, breaking a background of the stripes of Arragon. The arrangement of these shields may be seen on Plan III.

Instruments of Navigation

These consisted principally of: such inaccurate charts as were then available; the astrolabe, which was a primitive predecessor of the sextant; the compass, and the hour-glass. The compass was housed on the spar-deck, aft, where the man at the tiller arm could observe it and thus hold a steady course at sea.

Small Boats

The *Santa Maria* was equipped with two small boats: a large thirty-foot affair usually towed astern, and a smaller, more easily hoisted, eighteen-foot dinghy, which was carried on the spar deck.

Food

Smoked and salted beef, salt pork, rice, dried peas, vegetables, herring, and wine all appeared on the mess table of Columbus and his followers. Besides the fresh water carried in a cask on the starboard side of the spar deck (not shown on Plan IV) an additional supply was obtained from time to time by spreading canvas across the deck and catching rain.

Cooking with a charcoal fire and handmade copper utensils was possible by means of a sand-box stove such as shown on Plan IV.

Flags

From the foremast flew the swallow-tailed flag of the Band of Discoverers; a green cross on a field of white, having at the fly the initial of Ferdinand, at the pole the initial of Isabella, and each initial surmounted by a golden crown (See Plan IV).

The white and red royal standard of Castile flew from the main. It will be noted that the red lions face either with or against those on the shields along the rail, depending upon which way the wind blows. They should be shown as though climbing the mast, which they will do no matter how the flag turns.

From the mizen truck was displayed a rectangular white flag bearing the black eagle of St. John in whose claws was held the escutcheon of their Catholic monarchs, Ferdinand and Isabella.

There are various opinions as to the nature of the design flown from the mizen yard. Some say it was a crucifix, some merely a cross, but the Spanish Admiralty designate it to have been once more that of the royal standard of Castile.

Outside the door of the Admiral's cabin was a standard bearing the flag of the Band of Discoverers, an emblem conferred upon Columbus by the royal powers. This flag he carried ashore when taking possession, in the name of Spain, of the new land which he had discovered.

OPERATION

It requires no great knowledge of naval architecture to see that such a ship as this must have been an abominable sea boat. Her flat forecastle, extending as it did far out over the stem, must have hurled great quantities of spray upon the deck, instead of throwing the water off as a well-designed flare would have done. Columbus himself records in his log for September 8th that she "took in much sea over the bows."

The bluff bow and the quantity of sail area forward form a vicious circle. So much sail requires the full lines of the bow to provide sufficient buoyancy to prevent the sail from depressing her forward, and the bluff bow requires sail area well forward to keep her from persistently coming up into the wind.

That she was a "dull sailer and unfit for exploration" is entirely borne out by Captain D. V. Concas who sailed the replica across the Atlantic in 1893. The vessel pitched and rolled horribly. Her maximum speed was only six and a half knots. Yet she required only thirty-six days, as against the seventy of Columbus's fleet, in which to make the passage. Much of this difference may be accounted for by the original delay at the Canary Islands plus the superior instruments and knowledge at the disposal of Captain Concas which gave him both improved navigation, and what is more important still, the ability to "sail on, and on, and on, and on," all night as well as all day.

III

THE "MAYFLOWER"

THE defeat of the "Invincible Armada," in 1588, weakened Spain and opened the way for English colonization in America. In 1606 King James I, the successor of Queen Elizabeth, chartered two companies — the London and the Plymouth — for the purpose of making settlements which, it was hoped, would be more successful than the previous attempts of even such gifted individuals as Sir Humphrey Gilbert and his famous half-brother, Sir Walter Raleigh.

Each company was granted the right to found a colony. Each was deeded a block of land on the Atlantic Coast, one hundred miles square, with the understanding that the two settlements were to be at least one hundred miles apart.

The attempt of the Plymouth Company to establish a colony on the coast of Maine met with failure. It was the London Company which sent out in December, 1606, a party of one hundred and five men, in three small ships, who were destined to establish in Virginia the first permanent English settlement of the New World — Jamestown, named in honor of the King.

That the *Mayflower* and not the *Susan Constant* (the largest of the little Jamestown fleet) is the immortal ship of American colonization is but another example of the peculiar twists of history. The *Mayflower* owes her supremacy in the hearts of our people to a combination of many things. She had women and children aboard, which gives to her a "human interest" impossible to any expedition composed of mere men. Of equal if not greater importance is the coincidence that most American historians have been men of New England origin whose natural tendency to emphasize what took place on Cape Cod may be understood. No poet has done for the *Susan Constant* what Longfellow did for the *Mayflower* and her stern yet altogether human little band. Perhaps most influential of all was the setting aside by the Pilgrim Fathers of a day for feasting and thanksgiving; a day which has become a national institution annually reminding us of the *Mayflower*, of Plymouth Rock, and of the fortitude with which the Pilgrims saw their ship depart.

The succession of events which led up to the chartering of the *Mayflower* began in the little town of Scrooby, in Nottinghamshire, England, where a scattered congregation of Separatists, after enduring many persecutions, resolved to flee to Holland. Here they took refuge for eleven years, but, unwilling that their children should gradually adopt the language and customs of the Hollanders, turned their thoughts to the opportunities of America. They wanted to build homes where they could worship God in their own way and still be Englishmen. So these Pilgrims, as they were now called on account of their wanderings, prepared to leave Leyden for the great unknown American wilderness.

The leaders of the expedition were William Brewster and John Carver, both well advanced in years, who had the energetic assistance of two young men under thirty, William Bradford and Edward Winslow.

The *Speedwell* was the first vessel procured by the Leyden Pilgrims, and in her the originators of the enterprise embarked at Delfshaven for Southampton, England, there to join the *Mayflower*. That the *Speedwell* was intended as a permanent part of the colony's equipment may be inferred from Bradford's statement:* "A small ship [of some 60 tune], was bought, & fitted in Holland, which was intended to serve to help to transport them, so as to stay in ye cuntrie and atend upon fishing and shuch other affairs as might be for ye good & benefite of ye colonie when they come ther."

This pinnace, as vessels of her class were then called, was probably purchased some time in May, 1620. The plans of the Leyden Pilgrims were then rapidly maturing and their agreements with their "merchant adventurer" associates, who were to finance the venture, were practically concluded.

No reliable description of the *Speedwell* has ever been found, but a few facts are available from various sources. She had two masts carrying square-sails, and boasted at least three pieces of ordnance. Although bringing seventy from Leyden, her passenger list from Southampton to America was to have been thirty; the *Mayflower's* to have been ninety.

But the *Speedwell* never sailed. Her leaky condition made her entirely unfit for a trans-Atlantic voyage. This misfortune was not due to any lack of sagacity on the part of the Pilgrim Fathers, but rather to the intrigue of Sir Ferdinando Gorges and the Earl of Warwick who succeeded in stealing the Pilgrim colony from the London Virginia Company. Through agents who deliberately made the *Speedwell* unseaworthy, thus delaying the departure of the *Mayflower* from mid-summer until September, and through the duplicity of Captain Jones, who landed at Plymouth Rock instead of at the Hudson River as he was hired to do, the colony was established on the "northern Plantations" of the conspirators.†

The *Mayflower* herself was evidently chartered in London, about the middle of June, 1620. Who owned her at that time is not definitely known, the facts being that in 1609 she belonged to Christopher Jones, Richard Child, and John Moore. In August, 1622, when Captain Jones's estate was administered by his widow Joan, Child was already dead, his interest passing to Robert Child, presumably a son, and a quarter interest had been sold to some unknown buyer.‡

Other interesting information is to be found in the High Court of Admiralty Examinations which record a voyage to Norway, in 1609, when the *Mayflower* brought home 3,000 deals, 140 barrels of tar, and 42 barrels of pickled herrings. At least as early as 1616 she was engaged in the wine trade, for during that year one John Cawkin found himself in legal difficulties in consequence of his ungentlemanly conduct while under the influence of too much of the cargo. The Book of Imports into the Port of London, for the year 1620, records three days during which she discharged some 160 tons of wine. Mr. J. R. Hutchinson very reasonably advances the suggestion that much of the immunity from disease during the very unsanitary conditions of the voyage may have been due to the sterilization resulting from her alcoholic cargoes.§ The *Mayflower's* last recorded trip before being chartered by

* Bradford: *History of Plymouth Plantation*, Deane's ed., page 58.
† Ames: *The May-Flower and her Log*, page 103 *et sequentes*.
‡ "The Mayflower, Her Identity and Tonnage:" *New England Historical and Genealogical Register*, October, 1916.
§ *Ibid*.

the Pilgrim Fathers, ended on May 15th when she discharged 59 "tuns" of French wines at London.

The signatories of her charter and the terms contained therein will probably never be known. The general content, couched in the quaint if cumbersome phrases of the time, must have been to "ingage the goode ship Mayflower of Yarmouth, 9 score tuns burden, whereof for the present voyage Christopher Jones is Master," to make the trip from London "to the neighborhood of the mouth of Hudson's River in the northern parts of Virginia,"* stopping at Southampton when outward bound to complete her lading.

To prevent confusion and dissatisfaction there must have been some arrangement for freight and passage money between the merchant-adventurers and the colonists. Some had better accommodations than others. Some required more than a just share of the cubic contents of the vessel for the storage of their goods. It may be that transportation of the colonists was arranged without direct charge to any individual, a system of space allotment serving as a basis instead.

It is interesting to note that Goodwin† has calculated the cost of transportation at that time, arriving at $18. as the average charge for a first-class passage. Measured by the purchasing power of present-day currency, this represents about $150.

Unfortunately the documents left us contain almost no data whatever regarding the ship *Mayflower*. Only two explicit statements give us some clue concerning her size and rig. Bradford records that "Another (ship) was hired at London, of burden about 9 score" [tons].‡ That she had topsails is made positive by the further statement that "A lustie yonge man (called John Howland) coming upon some occasion above yᵉ grattings, was with a seele of yᵉ shipe throwne into [ye] sea; but it pleased God yᵗ he caught hould of yᵉ top-saile halliard which hunge over board, & rane out at length; yet he held his hould . . . till he was hald up."§

So little reliable information concerning the *Mayflower* is not at all surprising when one reflects that unlike Columbus, who sailed under royal patronage and returned a world hero, these Separatists were looked upon as a trivial group of religious fanatics whose departure from England was of importance only in that it removed what were considered to be some rather undesirable individuals.

In preparation for the voyage to America the ship was thoroughly overhauled at London. In those days the chartering party was expected to control and possibly even actually to undertake the fitting out. Many changes must have been made in her internal arrangements to convert what had been a merchantman, or as some authorities think, a whaler, into a ship capable of bunking roughly one hundred and twenty souls, together with supplies, furniture and other worldly goods. Bulkheads were erected. New partitions were built to furnish more cabins. Gun ports were closed to augment the cargo space.

On July 15,¶ 1620, she sailed from London, lying over at Southampton for the *Speedwell* which arrived on the 26th.

Much parleying and discontent arose among the passengers. Both attempts to improve the seaworthiness of the *Speedwell* by retrimming her produced no results. On Saturday, August 5th, the two ships weighed anchor, beating down the English

* The name was first used to designate all the eastern portion of the United States except Florida.

† Goodwin: *Pilgrim Republic,* page 320.

‡ Bradford: *History of Plymouth Plantation,* Deane's ed., page 58.

§ *Ibid.,* page 76.

¶ Old Style Calendar is here used throughout. For New Style, add ten days without change in the day of the week.

Channel until the following Thursday, when, upon consultation of the masters and passengers in authority of both ships, it was deemed wiser to put into the nearest port, Dartmouth, on account of the condition of the pinnace. Here she was unloaded and, "some leaks were found & mended, and now it was conceived by the workman & all, that she was sufficiente, & they might proceede without either fear or danger."*

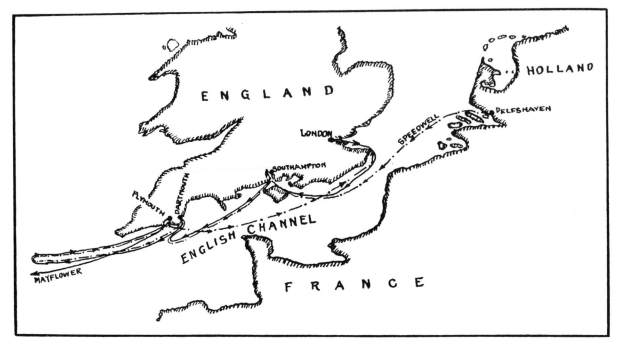

FIG. 13. THE CHANNEL COURSES OF THE "MAYFLOWER" AND THE "SPEEDWELL"

Pursued by fair winds the ships once more weighed anchor on August 23d, but before they had covered four hundred miles the *Speedwell* signalled again, whereupon the ships put back to Plymouth. Captain Reynolds emphatically maintained that the vessel was leaky and unseaworthy, the truth probably being that the leak was in his courage and the unseaworthiness in his honesty.

After some parleying, matters were finally arranged, the pinnace going back to London with eighteen or twenty of her passengers, the other twelve passengers, with part of her lading, transferring to the *Mayflower*.

Other readjustments were necessary. Christopher Martin had already proved unsatisfactory as a "governour," and in his place was elected the venerable John Carver, a merchant of some sixty years of age.

On Saturday, September 2d, the *Speedwell* departed for London. Four days later the *Mayflower* weighed anchor, at last actually embarked on a voyage which was to bring struggle, suffering and hardship to all who were on board. Yet she was freighted with the destinies of a continent.

Including the two boys born on board,† there were one hundred and four passengers besides the crew. Of the latter we have practically no reliable data, even their number being a matter of some conjecture. The names of the former have naturally received a good deal of attention and are here divided into two groups as prepared by the Massachusetts Society of Mayflower Descendents.

* Bradford: *History of Plymouth Plantation*, Deane's ed., page 68.
† Oceanus Hopkins and Peregrine White. A third child was stillborn to Mrs. Mary Allerton who survived the event by only a month.

THE "MAYFLOWER"

THE "MAYFLOWER" PASSENGERS

There were only one hundred and four (104) *Mayflower* passengers. Every one of them is included in the two lists following.

The 50 passengers from whom descent can be proved:

John Alden
Isaac Allerton
  wife Mary
  daughter Mary
  daughter Remember
John Billington
  wife Eleanor
  son Francis
William Bradford
William Brewster
  wife Mary
  son Love
Peter Brown
James Chilton
  wife ———
  daughter Mary
Francis Cooke
  son John

Edward Doty
Francis Eaton
  wife Sarah
  son Samuel
Edward Fuller
  wife ———
  son Samuel
Dr. Samuel Fuller
Stephen Hopkins
  2d wife, Elizabeth
  son Gyles (by 1st wife)
  daughter Constance
  (by 1st wife)
John Howland
Richard More

William Mullins
  wife Alice
  daughter Priscilla
Degory Priest
Thomas Rogers
  son Joseph
Henry Samson
George Soule
Myles Standish
John Tilley
  wife ———
  daughter Elizabeth
Richard Warren
William White
  wife Susanna
  son Resolved
  son Peregrine
Edward Winslow

The 54 passengers from whom we cannot prove descent:

Bartholomew Allerton
John Allerton
John Billington, Jr.
Dorothy Bradford
  (1st wife of William)
Wrestling Brewster
Richard Britteridge
William Butten
Robert Carter
John Carver
Katharine Carver
  (wife of John)
Maid servant of the Carvers
Richard Clarke
Humility Cooper
John Crankston
  son John
——— Ely
Thomas English

Moses Fletcher
Richard Gardiner
John Goodman
William Holbeck
John Hooke
Damaris Hopkins
Oceanus Hopkins
John Langmore
William Latham
Edward Leister
Edmund Margeson
Christopher Martin
  wife ———
Desire Minter
Ellen More
Jasper More
[a boy] More
Joseph Mullins
Solomon Prower

John Rigdale
  wife Alice
Rose Standish
  (1st wife of Myles)
Elias Story
Edward Thomson
Edward Tilley
  wife Ann
Thomas Tinker
  wife ———
  son ———
William Trevore
John Turner
  son ———
  son ———
Roger Wilder
Thomas Williams
Elizabeth Winslow
  (1st wife of Edward)
Gilbert Winslow

The officers and crew are an important part of any ship and emphatically deserve attention here. The number of seamen has been nowhere definitely stated, but was probably between twenty and twenty-five. That they suffered from sickness and death as well as the Pilgrims themselves is recorded by Bradford who says, "The disease begane to fall amongst them also, so as allmost halfe of their company dyed before they went away, and many of their officers and lustyest men, as ye boatson, gunner, 3. quarter maisters, the cooke, and others."* The known facts about the crew are:

Captain . . . . Christopher Jones
First Mate . . . . John Clarke
Second Mate . . . . Robert Coppin

* Bradford: *History of Plymouth Plantation*, Deane's ed., page 92.

[39]

The only petty officers mentioned are the carpenter, gunner, boatswains, quarter-master, four helmsmen, and at least two master's mates whose duties are not now fully understood. They were probably the sailing master's assistants whose work it was to keep the sails and rigging in repair.

The favorable weather of the early stages of the voyage was followed by storms, the effect of which has been described with some restraint by Capt. John Smith. "But being pestered nine weeks in this leaky, unwholesome ship, lying wet in their cabins: most of them grew weak and weary of the sea."* Lying in a bunk was the only means of keeping warm, but this expedient could hardly be considered as entirely satisfactory for the ship rolled and pitched so violently that the seams of her upper works were opened, thus allowing water to drip on to the passengers below. What incredible determination fortified these cold, wet, half-starved, seasick, overcrowded people, whose anxieties concerning the unknown wilderness ahead could only have been magnified by the perilous discomforts of the ocean!

It was during these storms that the much talked of screw was used to jack up a buckling beam. Something of the severity of wind and sea is disclosed by the fact that for days on end the *Mayflower* was forced to furl all sails, scudding before the gale under bare poles.†

The October storms, much to the relief of everybody, were followed by the usual clear, frosty, tranquil weather of November. Further rejoicing was occasioned by the birth of Oceanus Hopkins, a lusty boy whose exact date of joining the company has never been recorded. A few days later William Butten, a servant of Dr. Samuel Fuller, died. In this connection Azel Ames quotes the beautiful phrase of Goodwin: "Thus attended by the angels of life and death, the weary Mayflower neared her goal."

At daybreak on Friday, November 10th, land was sighted. Realizing that their intended destination had not been reached, "after some deliberation had amongst them selves & with yᵉ mʳ of yᵉ ship, they tacked aboute and resolved to stande for yᵉ southward."‡

But Captain Jones had no intention of delivering the colony at "the mouth of Hudson's River." Half a day's sail was sufficient to bring the *Mayflower* into dangerous shoals and breakers, probably those off what is now known as Monomoy Point. "These waters had been navigated by Gosnold, Smith and various English and French explorers, whose descriptions and charts must have been familiar to a veteran master like Jones. He doubtless magnified the danger of the passage, and managed to have only such efforts made as were sure to fail."§

Heading north again in spite of some expression of dissatisfaction by the passengers, the *Mayflower* came to anchor in Provincetown harbor sixty-seven days after leaving Plymouth (England). It was on this day, Saturday, November 11, 1620, that the "Mayflower Compact" was drawn up and signed by the forty-one male passengers of legal age who were free agents.

"In yᵉ name of God, Amen. We whose names are underwritten, the loyall subjects of our dread soveraigne Lord, King James, by yᵉ grace of God, of Great Britaine, France, & Ireland king, defender of yᵉ faith, &c., haveing undertaken, for yᵉ glorie of God, and advancemente of yᵉ Christian faith, and honour of our king & countrie,

---

* Smith: *New England's Trials*, 2d ed., 1622.

† Bradford: *History of Plymouth Plantation*, Deane's ed., page 75.

‡ Bradford: *History of Plymouth Plantation*, Deane's ed., page 77.

§ Goodwin: *Pilgrim Republic*, page 61.

PLATE V

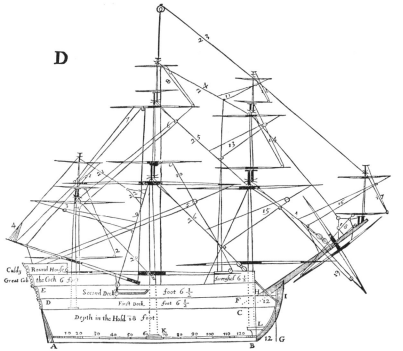

ENGLISH RIGGING-PLAN OF 1655. FROM MILLER'S "COMPLETE MODELLIST"

(1) The missen top sail Brase; (2) The missen top sail sheat; (3) The Cross jack Brase; (4) The toping lift for the missen peck; (5) The main Brase; (6) The main top sail Brase; (7) The main top sail Clew line; (8) The main top gallant Clew line; (9) The main shroud or Swifter; (10) The main top sail sheat; (11) The fore top gallant Brase; (12) The fore top gallant Clew line; (13) The fore top sail Brase; (14) The fore top sail Clew line; (15) The fore Brase; (16) The sprit sail top sail Brase; (17) The sprit sail top sail Clew line; (18) The sprit sail top sail sheat. Note that it goeth from the quarter of the sprit sail top sail yards arm to the Sprit sail Yards arm, and back to the Knee at the Boult Spirits end, and then you must measure from the Boult sprit to the fore castle, and that is your length; (19) The sprit sail Brase; (20) The missen stay; (21) The missen top mast stay; (22) The Leagues of the missen top may stay; (23) The stag staff stay; (24) The main top gallant stay; (25) The main top mast stay; (26) The main stay; (27) The fore stay. The number 14 serves likewise for the fore top mast stay, and the number 18 serves also for the Legs of the fore top may stay.

DUTCH SHIP OF ABOUT 1620. FROM FURTTENBACH'S "ARCHITECTURA NAVALIS," 1629

a voyage to plant yᵉ first colonie in yᵉ Northerne parts of Virginia, doe by these presents solemnly & mutualy in yᵉ presence of God, and one of another, covenant & combine our selves togeather into a civill body politick, for our better ordering & preservation & furtherance of yᵉ ends aforesaid; and by vertue hearof to enacte, constitute, and frame such just & equall lawes, ordinances, acts, constitutions, & offices, from time to time, as shall be thought most meete & convenient for yᵉ generall good of yᵉ Colonie, unto which we promise all due submission and obedience. In witnes wherof we have hereunder subscribed our names at Cape-Codd yᵉ 11. of November, in yᵉ year of yᵉ raigne of our soveraigne lord, King James, of England, France, & Ireland yᵉ eighteenth, and of Scotland yᵉ fiftie fourth. Anº. Dom. 1620."*

After re-electing Deacon Carver governor, this time for the ensuing year, the long-boat was sent ashore with an exploring party of fifteen or sixteen men in armor, under the command of Capt. Myles Standish. Much inconvenience was experienced in getting ashore, because only at high water was it possible to do so without wading. Many severe colds were the result.

From the anchorage just inside the tip of Cape Cod three major exploring expeditions went forth in search of a desirable site for the settlement. That of November 15th to 18th was entirely by land. Indians were seen and unsuccessfully followed for about ten miles. Buried stores of Indian corn were plundered. Game and excellent drinking water were found, but no location which appealed to the Planters.

Captain Jones was becoming impatient. He wanted to discharge his cargo as soon as possible and return to England. Accordingly the Pilgrims were informed that they must decide upon a permanent location, and that Jones "must and would" retain sufficient supplies for the voyage back to England.

But the Pilgrim Fathers were not to be hurried. Knowing the pleasure which the master of the ship found in hunting, they invited him to join the second exploring party and to act as its leader. This expedition put off in the long-boat on Monday, November 27th, the very day Peregrine White was born. Two days later the long-boat returned bringing news of more buried Indian corn, of great numbers of water fowl, and of some sort of beans.

During the afternoon of December 6th the third exploring party got away in the shallop which the ship's carpenter had been nearly a month in repairing. Two days later catastrophe threatened when their landing was met with a fierce attack by Indians which, however, did no harm.† A severe gale on the afternoon of the same day proved much more serious, breaking the shallop's mast and damaging the rudder.

In spite of these unhappy beginnings Capt. Myles Standish and his men located a harbor which offered protection for the *Mayflower* and was surrounded by land possessing the characteristics desired for the settlement. This was none other than the place called "Plimoth" on the chart made in 1616 by Capt. John Smith.‡

On Saturday, December 16th, convoyed by the shallop, the *Mayflower* left Provincetown harbor, in which one child had been born and four of the little company had died. Thus one hundred and two days after leaving England she let go her anchors within a mile of the rock which was to become the historic landing place.§

Christmas Day, not observed as a holiday by the Pilgrims because they were op-

* Bradford: *History of Plymouth Plantation*, Deane's ed., page 89. The disposition of the original document has never been traced.

† According to Azel Ames no Indians were even seen again until January 30th.

‡ Smith: *General Historie*, see map.

§ The water in shore was too shallow to allow a nearer approach.

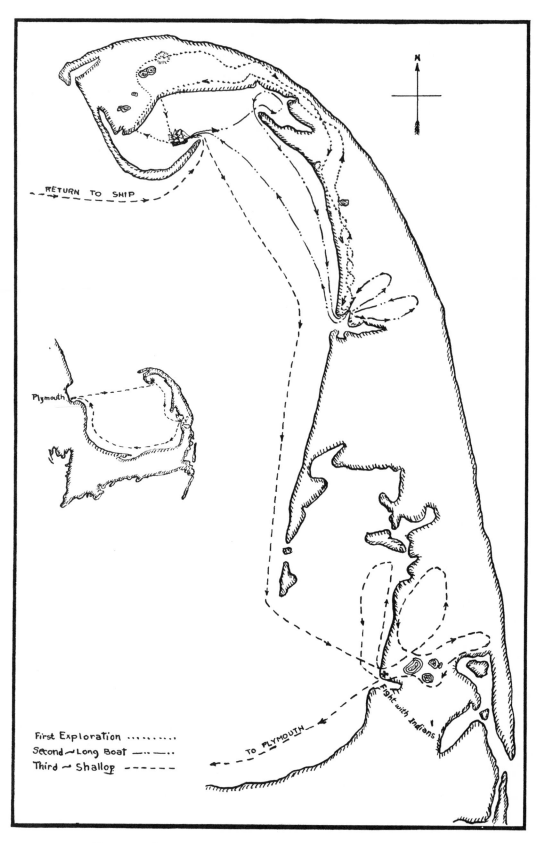

First Exploration ....
Second ～ Long Boat —.—..
Third ～ Shallop ― ― ― ―

RETURN TO SHIP

Plymouth

Fight with Indians

TO PLYMOUTH

N

FIG. 14.   ROUTES OF THE THREE EXPLORING EXPEDITIONS

posed to all saints' days, the first timber was felled. In a few weeks the town site was laid out and ground allotted. Houses were gradually erected. Ordnance was gotten ashore and mounted on a suitable platform. Friendships with the Indians were begun through the efforts of Squanto, Samoset, and Massasoit.

Over against these glimmerings of hope was the sickness on shipboard and on shore, seventeen of the Planters dying in the month of February alone. Captain Jones and his crew would have sailed away with the *Mayflower* in spite of this but, "The reason on their parts why she stayed so long, was yᵉ necessitie and danger that lay upon them, for it was well towards yᵉ ende of Desember before she could land any thing hear, or they able to receive any thing ashore. Afterwards, yᵉ 14. of Jan: the house which they had made for a generall randevoze by casulty fell afire, and some were faine to retire abord for shilter. Then the sicknes begane to fall sore amongst them, and yᵉ weather so bad as they could not make much sooner any dispatch. Againe, the Govʳ & cheefe of them, seeing so many dye, and fall downe sick dayly, thought it no wisdom to send away the ship, their condition considered, and yᵉ danger they stood in from yᵉ Indeans, till they could procure some shelter; and therfore thought it better to draw some more charge* upon them selves & freinds, then hazard all. The mʳ and sea-men likewise, though before they hasted yᵉ passengers a shore to be goone, now many of their men being dead, & of yᵉ ablest of them, and of yᵉ rest many lay sick & weake, yᵉ mʳ durst not put to sea, till he saw his men begine to recover, and yᵉ hart of winter over."†

The reasons set forth in this somewhat ambiguous paragraph of Bradford were reinforced by the fact that the *Mayflower* was totally unseaworthy at the time. Indeed she nearly capsized in the storm of February 4th, much of her cargo having by then been taken ashore and no ballast as yet put aboard to improve her stability.‡

But the last of the colonists left the ship on March 22d, to remain ashore. Seeds were already in the ground.§ The survivors of the ship's company were busy with preparations for the return voyage, setting up rigging and bending the sails.

She sailed Thursday, April 5, 1621, leaving half her passengers in peace beneath the growing grass, the other half standing on the hill with mingled emotions as the only connecting link between them and the civilized world stood out to sea. Not a single one of them went back with her.

Captain Jones hoisted his colors and fired a parting salute, doubtless answered by the guns of Captain Standish. Thus the *Mayflower* departed, leaving those grim-lipped, iron-faced, incredibly tenacious Pilgrims, alone — but unafraid.

Thirty-one days later the *Mayflower* was in England. Of her subsequent history little is known, all attempts to ascertain it being baffled by the unfortunate circumstance that nearly forty vessels, built between 1565 and 1630, were also named *Mayflower*. To distinguish the vessel of the Pilgrims from those of obscurer fame is an impossible task.

For some two years after Captain Jones's death the *Mayflower* lay idle in the Thames. An order for her appraisal, issued in May, 1624, by the High Court of Admiralty, has been unearthed, the modest result totalling £160.¶ With this appraisment the known facts concerning the Pilgrim ship end. Her ultimate fate has provoked much controversy, some authorities believing that her timbers were used in

* Demurrage.
† Bradford: *History of Plymouth Plantation*, Deane's ed., page 99.
‡ Mourt's *Relation*, Dexter's ed., page 79.
§ *Ibid.*, page 89.
¶ *High Court of Admiralty Acts*, 30:227; *Libels*, 81:167.

the construction of a barn, still standing near Beaconsfield, in Buckinghamshire, England. The people in the locality maintain that her captain, Christopher Jones, belonged to the place, and was instrumental in securing the timbers when the ship was broken up. Other equally gifted authorities are not convinced that the timbers came from A *Mayflower*, and, even admitting that, they see no reason for believing they came from THE *Mayflower*.

But she needs neither authorities, nor timbers, nor barns to keep her memory alive. The one uncertain, tedious voyage — pursued by a thousand misgivings, crowded, becalmed, storm-ridden — which the *Mayflower* made from Plymouth, England, to Plymouth, Massachusetts, has made her immortal.

ORIGINAL SOURCES OF MATERIAL CONCERNING THE SHIP
Books and Documents

Since no record, drawing, or general description of the *Mayflower* has ever been found, it is only possible to reconstruct her in terms of her time, type, and class. Original sources of material for such a study are not numerous, perhaps the best being those consulted by Mr. R. C. Anderson while preparing his model, viz. — "Fragments of Ancient Shipwrightry," in the Samuel Pepys collection of manuscripts at Cambridge (England), and "An Excellent Brief and Easy Treatise on Shipbuilding," belonging to the Scott Collection of the Institution of Naval Architects in London. Both documents give typical midship sections of 1600-1610 ships. Of equal importance is a document published in 1626, which uses the *Adventure of Ipswich* (a ship very similar to the *Mayflower*) to illustrate the method and application of tonnage measurement.

Illustrations, paintings, and old prints are more often misleading than helpful because the artist is imaginative rather than scientific. An illustration from "Architectur Navalis," published in 1629, will help to demonstrate the truth of this (See Plate V).

Present-day model enthusiasts will be doubly interested in the work of Thomas Miller, "a great Yarmouth seaman." His little book, of which several pages are here reproduced, not only gives us information concerning seventeenth-century ships, but also proves that the joys of model making were discovered long before the present time.

In studying Miller's book it must be remembered that the *Mayflower* was probably built by the year 1600 and consequently had neither spritsail, topsail, nor mizen topsail.

The Complete
MODELLIST:

SHEWING

The true and exact way of Raising the
Model of any Ship or Veſſel, ſmall or great,
either in proportion, or out of proportion.

ALSO,

The manner how to find the Length
of every Rope exactly:

AND

TABLES which give the true bigneſs
of every Rope in each Veſſel.

Together with

The Weights of their Anchors and Cables.

Performed by Thomas Miller, of great Yarmouth Seaman;
And Maſter in the Art of Raiſing the Model.

LONDON,
Printed by W. G. for George Hurlock, and are to be ſold at his
Shop at St. Magnus Church, at the hither end of London-
Bridge, near Thames-Street. 1 6 6 7.

Inſtructions for the raiſing of the Model of any Ship or Veſſel, ſmall or great.

Hen you go to raiſe the Model of any ſhip or veſſel, you muſt in the firſt place know the length of her Keel, and the depth in her Hold, and the breadth of her Beam.

First knowing the length of the Keel, take *The length of* the length of the Keel off your Scale, and place *the Keel.* it on your paper that you intend to raiſe your Model on, making two pricks one with one point of the Compaſſes, the other with the other then draw a line with your pen or penſil of black lead, as from *A* to *B.*

Then take the depth of the Hold off from your Scale with your Com- *The depth of the* paſſes, and ſet one foot in the end of the Keel line at *A*, and with *Hold from the* the other make a prick at *D*, and likewiſe from *B* to *C* : then with your *Keel to the firſt* Ruler and black lead, or pen, draw another line parallel with the Keel, *Deck* and that is the line for the firſt Deck.

Then for the height between the firſt and ſecond Deck, which appea- *The height be-* reth in the figure following, to be 6 foot and a half, then take 6 foot *tween the firſt* and a half off from your Scale, and ſet one foot of your compaſſes at *D*, *& ſecond Deck* and with the other make a prick at *E*, and likewiſe from *C* to *F*. So muſt you doe for the height between the 2d. and 3d. Deck, and ſo for the Cabin and Coch and round Houſe above that, and for the fore-caſtel all in the ſame manner, and then draw lines from prick to prick.

Then for the Stem raiſe a perpendicular line from the fore-part of *To raiſe the* the Keel to the ſecond Deck, then take two thirds of the depth in hold, *Stem.* which in the figure is 12 foot, then ſet 1 foot of your compaſſes at *B*, and with the other mark a prick at *G:* ſo likewiſe ſet 1 foot in the upper end of the line at *H*, and with the other foot make a prick at *I*, then draw a line from *G* to *I* parallel to that from *B* to *H*, then from that

outermoſt

The Fore-yard eight ninths of the Main-yard, and the Fore-top-fail-yard half that, and Top-gallant-yard half that. *Fore-yard & fore-top-fail-yard*

The Miffen-yard fomething fhorter then the Fore-yard. *Miffen-yard.*

The Sprit-fail-yard and Crof-jack-yard both one, the Crof-jack-yard half the Miffen-yard. *Sprit-fail-yard & Crof-jack-yard.*

The Sprit-fail-top-fail-yard half the Sprit-fail-yard, and the Sprit-fail top-maft almoft half the Sprit-fail-yard. *Sprit-fail- top-Maft, and top-fail yard.*

Note, *That all the fmall yards, are half the great yards from Cleat to Cleat, or from one earing of the Top-fail no another, you may have what Yard-armes you pleafe.* Note.

The Use of the Model.

IN thefe figures you fee two yards one Hoyfted, and the other Lower- *Ufe.* ed or a Portlens, the top-fail-yard alfo one Hoyfed, and the other down upon the Cape, fo muft you make in all the Models you raife: the yard a portlens gives the length of top-fail-fheats, and lifts, and tye or Jeers and Bunt-lines, and Leech-lines, or Halli-yards meafuring from the Hounds to the Deck.

The yards Hoyfted gives the length of Clew-lines, Brafes, and Clew-garnets, and Tackles, and Sheats, and Bow-lines.

In the fmall ones, is fhewed the length of Shrowds and Top-fail Halliards with Brafes, and Lifts, as in the figure *B.*

In the figure *A* is fhewed how to give a near eftimation, how many *Note.* yards of Canvafs is in a main Courfe. When you come in any Ship or Veffel, and defire to know how many yards of Canvafs is in the main or fore-Courfe: Firft, you muft know the depth of your fail, and the breadth of the Canvafs that the fail is made of, then take off fo much from the Scale as you fee the Cloth is in breadth, and place fo many cloths in the Model on the main or fore-yard, the fame depth that the fail is on, as you fee the main-Courfe in this figure: After you have fo done, then take a Fathom or two off from your fcale, and meafure every cloth up and down as you do the Ropes, and that gives you the number of yards.

Likewife

outermost line, draw the Stem to the Keel with what sweep you please running the top of your stem 3 or 4 foot above the line, as it is in the figure, then you may draw it double as you please, and the Keel likewise.

Note. And when you draw your Deck-lines, let your lower Deck-line run a foot or 2 beyond the end of the Keel aft, and so in like manner all your Decks, and then joyn them together something rounding, that the Model may have a Rake aft, and shew ship shape. You must draw your Model and Scale together at the Keel, as you see in the figure D, and note how many feet soever your Model is by the Keel, so make and *The making* divide the Scale into 15 equal parts, as is shewed, the 2 first equal parts *of the Scale.* of the Scale divide into 20 feet, 6 of those feet are one Fathom, and 12 of those feet are two Fathom. And the other 13 divisions numbred by 10, 20, 30, &c. to 130 are 10 feet a piece. By the Fathoms I measure the length of the Ropes, and also the Canvass for the sailes; and by the Scale of equal parts, I measure the Model, the larger you draw the Models of your vessels or ships, the better you may see to do your worke.

A Rule for masting and yarding by proportion, but for my part I make no use of it, because it will not hold.

The main-mast THe Main-mast must be twice and one half the length of the Beam.

The fore-Mast The Fore-mast eight ninths of the Main-mast.

Main-top-mast & top-gallant-mast. The Main-top-mast half the Main-mast, and the Main-top-gallant-mast, half the Main-top-mast.

The fore-top-Mast, & top-gallant-Mast. The Fore-top-mast, half the Fore-mast, and the Fore-top-gallant-mast, half the Fore-top-mast.

The Bolt-sprit. The Bolt-sprit, the length of the Fore-mast.

The missen Mast & missen-top-Mast. The Missen-mast, the height of the Main-top-mast from the quarter-Deck, and the Missen-top-mast half that.

Main-yard & Main-top-sail-yard. The Main-yard 6 seaven parts of the Main-mast, and the Main-top-sail-yard half that, and Top-gallant-yard half that.

The

The bignes of the Rigging for these main-masts, and main-top-mast: the fore-mast to these masts followeth in the next Page.	*Mast of 34 in.* 1 inch	*Mast of 32 in.* 2 inch	*Mast of 30 in.* 3 inch	*Mast of 29 in.* 4 inch	*Mast of 28 in.* 5 inch	*Mast of 20 in.* 6 inch	*Mast of 26 in.* 7 inch	*Mast of 24 in.* 8 inch	*Mast of 23 in.* 9 inch	*Mast of 19 in.* 10 inch	*Mast of 13 in.* 11 inch	*Mast of 12 in.* 12 inch
Penents of Tackles	8½	8	7	6½	6	5½	5	7	6	5	4	4
Runners	6	5½	5	5	4½	4	3½	5	5	4½	3½	3½
Falls of the Tackles	4	4	3½	3½	3	3	3	3½	3½	2½	2½	
Shrowds	8½	8	7½	7	6½	5	5	7	6	5	4	4
Laniards	4½	4	4	3½	3	3	3	4	3½	3¾	2½	2½
Swifters	8½	8	7½	7	6½	5	5	5½	5	4½	3¾	
Laniards	4½	4	4	3½	3½	3	2½	3½	3	3	2½	
Stay	17	16	15	14½	14	10	8	12	11½	9½	6½	6
Collar at the Stem	16	15	13	13	11	9	8	10	10	8	6	
Laniard of the stay	6	5½	5½	5	4	4	3½	4	4	3½	2½	3
Lifts	4½	4	3½	3½	3	3	2½	3	3	2½	2½	2
Lacks	9½	9	8½	8	6½	6	5	6½	6	5½	4	4
Sheates	6½	6½	6	6	5	4½	4	4½	4½	3½	2½	3
Bowlines	5½	5	4½	4½	4	4	3	3	3	2½	2½	2½
Bridles	4½	4½	4	4	3½	3½	3	3	3	2½	2	
Penents fore-brases	4	4	3¾	3½	3	3	2¾	3	3	2½	2	2½
Brases	3	3	3	3	2½	2½	2	2½	2½	2	1½	2
Clew-garnets	4	3½	3	3	2½	2½	2	3	2½	2½	1½	2
Jeers	8½	8	7	6	5½	5		6	4½	4		
Parrel Rope	6	6	5	5	4½	4	3	4½	4	3½	3	3
Brest-rope	8	7	6	5	5							
Runner of mart-lines	2½	2½	2½	2½	2	2						
Fall of mart-lines	3	2¼	2¼	2	2	2		2½	2	2	1½	
Penent of the garnet	8½	8	7½	7	6	5	4½	6	5½	5	5	4
Tye	6	5½	5	5	4½	4	3½	3½	3½	3	3	3
Fall of the garnet	4½	4	4	4	3½	3½	3	3	3	2¼	2	2

Main top mast rigging	1	2	3	4	5	6	7	8	9	10	11	12
Penent of Tackles	5	5	4½	4	3½	3	2¾	3½	3½	2½		2
Fals of Tackles	2½	2½	2½	2½	2	2	1½	2	2	1½		1½
Shrowdes	5	5	4¼	4	4	3	3	4	3½	3	2¾	2½
Laniards	2½	2½	2¼	2	2	2	1½	2	2	1½	1	1
Back-stays	5	5	5	4	3½	3	2½	4	4	3½	2	2½
Laniards	3	3	3	2½	2½	2	2	2½	2	1½	1	1
Stay	8	7	6	5	5	4½	4	5	4½	3½	3	2½
Laniard	4	4	3½	3½	3	3	2¾	3	2½	2	1½	2
Lifts	3½	3	2½	2½	2	2	1¾	2	2	1½	1	1

Note, There Bunt-lines are in bignes as followeth,

3½ 3½ 3 2½

2 2 2 2

2 2 2 1½

Note, The ships that have no jeers there tye is 4 inches, and their Halliards is 2½.

THE "MAYFLOWER"

Smithsonian Institution Model

Capt. Joseph W. Collins, long connected with the Smithsonian Institution in nautical matters, is said to have made a careful study of the seventeenth-century British merchantman shown by Admiral Paris in his "Souvenirs de Marine" before undertaking the model which was considered for many years to be the most accurate representation of the *Mayflower*.

Unfortunately the hull was constructed on the erroneous basis that the ship was of 120 instead of 180 tons burden. This, however, affects the dimensions of the hull more than it does the manner of rigging.

According to Captain Collins the *Mayflower* was a carvel-built vessel with quarter galleries and a very large, square stern containing three immense windows. He shows a succession of three quarter-decks or poops, the after one being nearly nine feet above the spar-deck. The model is "ship" rigged with one-piece pole masts like those of the *Santa Maria*.

Some dimensions of this model are:

Length knightheads to topsail	82′ - 0″
Beam	22′ - 0″
Depth	14′ - 0″
Bowsprit (outboard)	40′ - 6″
Spritsail yard	34′ - 6″
Foremast (spar-deck to truck)	67′ - 6″
Fore-yard	47′ - 6″
Fore-topsail yard	34′ - 1½″
Mainmast (spar-deck to truck)	81′ - 0″
Main yard	53′ - 0″
Main-topsail yard	38′ - 6″
Mizenmast (spar-deck to truck)	60′ - 6″
Lateen yard	54′ - 6″
Tons (burden)	120

A number of points which might provoke controversy are the open bulwarks along her waist, the sheer poles, and the vang on the lateen yard. The question of how many and what guns she carried on this particular voyage has been very happily avoided by showing the gun ports, ten in number, entirely closed.

Walter Hines Page Model

In recognition of his eminent and distinguished services, "with reference to the glorious entry of the United States of America into the war for freedom,* and in remembrance of the ties which bind historic Plymouth in unity and friendship to the American Nation," the Borough of Plymouth, England, presented a silver model of the *Mayflower* to Honorable Walter Hines Page, United States Ambassador at the Court of St. James's.

A little study will show the remarkable similarity between this and the Smithsonian model. Both have the quarter galleries, the succession of three quarter-decks, or poops, the open bulwarks at the waist, and the ten closed gun ports. Dissimilarities are to be found in the masts, those of the Page model being built up in three pieces. It also has a "bonnet" on the lateen not found in Captain Collins' model.

* The World War.

PLATE VI

Photograph by A. J. Olmstead

MODEL OF A SHIP OF THE "MAYFLOWER" PERIOD, CLASS, AND APPROXI-
MATE SIZE, BUILT BY CAPT. J. W. COLLINS, AND NOW IN THE SMITHSONIAN
INSTITUTION

PLATE VII

Photograph by A. J. Olmstead

MODEL OF A SHIP OF THE "MAYFLOWER" PERIOD, CLASS, AND APPROXI-
MATE SIZE, BUILT BY CAPT. J. W. COLLINS, AND NOW IN THE SMITHSONIAN
INSTITUTION

PLATE VIII

SILVER MODEL OF THE "MAYFLOWER," PRESENTED TO THE HONORABLE
WALTER HINES PAGE, THEN AMERICAN AMBASSADOR TO THE COURT OF ST.
JAMES'S, BY THE BOROUGH OF PLYMOUTH, ENGLAND

Reproduced by the courtesy of Mrs. Walter Hines Page

THE "MAYFLOWER"

Experts desiring to criticize adversely this beautiful product of the silversmith would inquire the reason for the mizen topmast shrouds and the lantern shown on the poop railing.

James Robertson Jack Model

After a long experience in the shipyards of Scotland, where he filled every position from apprentice boy to general manager, Professor Jack came to America to become the Head of the Department of Naval Architecture and Marine Engineering at the Massachusetts Institute of Technology. The combination of the rare books in the Institute's Nautical Museum and the excellent facilities offered by its model cutting laboratory aroused Professor Jack's interest in models of old historic ships.

That his model of the *Mayflower*, built at the same time and from entirely different sources of material, should so closely agree in the main with that of Mr. R. C. Anderson, is convincing proof of the close approximation to the original ship which rewards the careful investigator.

It is from this model that the plans contained here were started, and although differing from it in many details, the stern and the ornamental work have been copied exactly.

Pilgrim Society Model

In September, 1922, Mr. R. C. Anderson, a Vice-President of the English "Society for Nautical Research" and formerly editor of the "Mariner's Mirror," undertook for the Pilgrim Society of Plymouth, Mass., to supervise the design and construction of a model of the *Mayflower* which should be the finest thing of its kind. This was completed in 1925, the cost for manual labor alone being about $2500. Mr. Anderson gave his services.

The hull is built up exactly as the ship herself would have been, even the Spanish chestnut planking being secured with wooden trenails. Some hint of the infinite pains taken in constructing the model is contained in the 15,000 trenails necessary to secure the lower deck.

The stern and the more curved portions of the wales were cut from pieces of oak which had a suitably crooked grain; the rest of the wales are of elm. The entire hull was treated with solignum, a preservative of wood, which also gave it an antique appearance.

The equipment is complete in every detail. A double capstan, working from both the spar and the gun deck, is located abaft the mainmast. Ordnance consists of twelve brass guns: eight "minions" on the gun-deck, and four "sakers" on the spardeck. The whipstaff by which the vessel was steered is operated from the spar-deck aft, orders being shouted below through a hatch abaft the mizenmast. An attractive belfry, just at the center of the quarter-deck railing may be seen in the broadside view, as may also the ship's boat stowed on the port side, the anchor,* and the doors giving access from beneath the forecastle to the prow. The galley smoke pipe can be made out just abaft the foremast (Plates X and XI).

A unique feature is the hull decoration consisting of a series of triangles painted yellow and green, a marked contrast with the dull brown of the hull. Not knowing exactly what botanical specimen was meant by a *Mayflower*, in 1600, the stern has been ornamented by a conventionalized yellow marigold, beneath which is the ship's name supported on the tails of two dolphins.

* The anchor bands, an anachronism, have recently been removed.

The more important dimensions of this model are:

Length over all	111' - 0"
Load, water-line	90' - 0"
Beam (moulded)	26' - 0"
Draft	9' - 0"
Frame spacing	4' - 0"
Bowsprit (outboard)	36' - 0"
" (maximum diameter)	1' - 4"
" off center to starboard	2' at prow
	on center line at 23'
Spritsail yard	30' - 0"
" diameter at center	7"
Foremast, spar deck to truck	64' - 0"
" rake	1 in 30 f'w'd
" diameter at deck	1' - 3"
Fore-yard	40' - 0"
" diameter at center	10"
Fore topsail yard	18' - 0"
" diameter at center	4"
Mainmast, spar deck to truck	79' - 6"
" rake	perpendicular
" diameter at deck	20"
Main yard	50' - 0"
" diameter at center	12"
Main topsail yard	22' - 0"
" " diameter at center	6"
Mizenmast, spar deck to truck	44' - 0"
" rake	1 in 20 aft
" diameter at deck	9"
Lateen yard	48' - 0"
" diameter at center	8"
Burden	183 tons
Displacement	244 tons

As Mr. Anderson probably knows more about seventeenth-century ships than any other living man, and because there were available to him all the important references, of which he made careful study, this model is now, and probably will always continue to be, considered the authoritative attempt at reconstruction of the Pilgrim Fathers' ship.

HULL

In all probability the *Mayflower* was an old ship at the time the Pilgrims chartered her. Although there is no reason to believe that she differed materially from the merchant vessels of her time, no one can say with absolute authority what she was like, beyond Bradford's meager statement that she was a ship of about 180 tons burden. In interpreting this information it must be borne in mind that the shipbuilder measures a vessel's tonnage in various somewhat confusing ways.

Because taxes are levied in terms of a ship's carrying capacity, which obviously varies with different types of cargo, the unit of taxable tonnage measurement is in cubic feet instead of in pounds. Once the ship has been built, this value is fixed.

Gross tonnage, then, according to present British practice, is the total internal capacity below the upper deck, plus that of all inclosed deck houses above it, measured in tons of one hundred cubic feet.

Net tonnage (the modern equivalent for "tons burden") is the gross tonnage minus all spaces used for the accommodation of officers and crew, and for gear necessary in working the ship such as windlasses, the steering engine, boilers, engines and machinery.

Displacement tonnage is the total weight of the water actually displaced by the ship.

The method of measuring the net tonnage of the *Mayflower* probably was in accordance with the law of 1614 which was very simple and gave rise to the curved stem by which a vessel's rating could be considerably lowered. The straight keel on the ground multiplied by the moulded breadth, multiplied by the depth of hold, and this product divided by ninety-four gave the answer.

It has been suggested that her tonnage may have been measured by the more picturesque unit of Bordeaux wine, commonly applied to merchantmen. This amounted to about forty-two cubic feet per ton.

It was emphatically not the coal carrying tonnage adopted under the Act of Charles II (1661).

In accordance with the established principle of the times, the sum of the "rakes" of the stem and stern post should be equal to the beam.

The result of examining many prints and drawings of contemporary ships, as well as consideration of the cabin requirements of the *Mayflower*, lead the investigator to the conclusion that she could have had only a quarter-deck and poop, instead of the succession of three half-decks. These erections would generally be open at the ends and a small deck house built below them, but with the crowded conditions of the *Mayflower* it is probable that the ends of these decks were boarded up to provide shelter for the passengers and crew.

In spite of the much recorded "wetness" of the *Mayflower*, her bulwarks must have been solid instead of the open rail at first thought to be correct. In like manner careful research points to the improbability of quarter-galleries for a vessel of her size and type.

The hull must have had gun-ports, since ordnance was the "sine qua non" of seventeenth-century merchantmen. The great probability is that during the weeks of repair and alteration some of her guns were removed and stowed in the hold in anticipation of erection in the settlement's fort. This would give more space; a vital necessity, as will be shown later. Although Anderson shows guns protruding from all ports except the two flanking the rudder, he believes that twelve guns may be too many. Twelve ports are not at all unreasonable.*

There must have been a large hatch in the spar-deck, since a craft of some considerable size was hoisted in and out through it. There are several mentions of this, one being that "Monday, the 13 of November, we unshipped our shallop and drew her on land, to mend and repair her, having been forced to cut her down in bestowing her betwixt the decks; and she was much opened with the people's lying in her; which kept us long there, for it was sixteen or seventeen days before the Carpenter had finished her."†

How it was possible to provide sleeping quarters for the people known to have been on board without some of them "roosting along the spars," like sparrows on a telegraph wire, is a very considerable puzzle. As an interesting comparison, if the total area of the gun-deck were utilized for swinging hammocks, forty inches apart, as in berthing sailors on present day battleships, less than one hundred persons would be able to sleep at one time. As a further complication, it is known that some of the less important men were provided with cabins from which one would naturally infer that all the

* "The Mariner's Mirror," July, 1926.
† Mourt's *Relation*.

women and the leaders of the expedition were similarly taken care of. To the investigating spirit of a small boy we owe this information, for "there being a fouling-piece charged in his father's cabin,"* young Francis Billington shot it off; and thereby nearly blew up the ship because there was also an open barrel of gun-powder in the cabin.

Assuming that all the crew bunked in the forecastle, a recapitulation of the passenger list shows that quarters must have been provided for forty-four men, nineteen women, twenty-nine youths and boys, and ten young girls and maidens. Taking into account the cargo known to have been aboard, how was it possible to provide meals, sleeping quarters and recreation for these people in a little hull hardly over one hundred feet long? A glimpse of the exhausting life aboard the *Mayflower* is given by Bradford's remark, already quoted, that the shallop was "much opened with the people's lying in her" during the voyage.

HULL FITTINGS

Steering Gear

This was undoubtedly a whip-staff, though perhaps fitted in some less advanced form than that allowing the steersman to see forward. The mechanics of the whip-staff were very simple, being nothing more than a pivoted lever by which to pry the tiller from one side to the other. The whip-staff was capable of putting the rudder over to small angles only, much of the steering being performed by operating on the sails. When the sea was rough no man would have been sufficiently strong to hold the whip-staff against the buffeting of the waves. On such occasions steering was accomplished by means of tackles on the tiller. Thus, in many ways the whip-staff was not a very satisfactory mechanism.

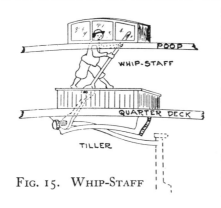

FIG. 15. WHIP-STAFF

Lantern

Only the Page model shows a lantern fixed to the stern, after the manner of that so essential to the flagship of Columbus. Because there is no mention of such a fitting in any of the *Mayflower* documents, and because it is not shown on contemporary ships, such an inclusion seems extremely unlikely, if indeed not positively improper.

Hawse Pipe

The hawse pipe led into the forecastle below the prow, which space also provided locker room in which to coil the hawser. In hoisting anchor, the hawser was taken from the pipe, through a doorway in the after end of the forecastle, and thence along the deck to the capstan abaft the mainmast.

Chain Wales

According to Anderson, the chain wales of the foremast and mizen rest on the gunwale. This location offers no direct internal bracing to resist the tremendous thrust produced by the pull of the chains and shrouds, which in effect form a toggle. Professor Jack's idea of placing them where the pressure will be taken by a deck is much the more logical.

* Mourt's *Relation*, Dexter's ed., page 43.

Galley

Cooking was done slowly and with much difficulty in a large tripod kettle which swung over a "hearth-box" in the forecastle. The galley stack, a very plain box-shaped affair, rose above the forecastle some two feet nine inches, and was probably about one foot square. The soot, which must have settled on the forecastle from this, was lessened by the use of charcoal.

Spars and Rigging

All the models of the *Mayflower* here cited are in absolute agreement as to the number and general location of the spars.

The rig of a vessel of her type would certainly be that of a three-masted "ship." At this period the bowsprit had very considerable rake. It descended from the early foremast which had raked excessively forward, and by the continued increase of this rake became the bowsprit. In order to pass the foremast, the bowsprit had to be shipped to starboard of the center line. In order that the stops might be amidships, the bowsprit was not fitted directly fore and aft but at an angle which brought its outer extremity back on to the center line. On the under side appeared a yard from which was suspended a "spritsail" or "water sail"; necessary in all those early ships. Owing to the big wave which the lee bow pushed up, tending to make the ship turn towards the direction from which the wind was blowing, these vessels were weatherly in a strong breeze. The wind pressure on the spritsail produced a force necessary to counteract this. The spritsail yard could travel along the bowsprit, making it impossible to fit a bobstay. Indeed there seems to be no reliable record of a bobstay until after the year 1670. Lack of this means of preventing the bowsprit from being pulled up by the tension of the head stays, necessitated the use of a very heavy spar which would have been heavier still had there been triangular sails or jibs.

The foremast was stepped well forward in the forecastle. In Elizabethan times it was stepped even in front of the forecastle, but by the *Mayflower* period it had moved farther aft. The topmast formed a separate spar, capable of being lowered to the deck, as this rig, introduced in Sir Walter Raleigh's time, was found to be a great advance over the old pole mast. The mainmast was similar to the foremast but somewhat taller, while the mizen was probably still a pole mast.

On the fore and mainmasts were cross yards carrying square sails which could be raised and lowered by means of ties. The shortness of the topsail yards is a noticeable feature. It was not until the latter part of the seventeenth century that the topsail yards began to approach the length of the lower yards.

The thickness of the yards was normally ¼″ for every foot of length.

Because the topsails were much wider at the foot than at the head, the reef bands were longer than the yard itself. In order to accommodate this additional width the yard arms were lengthened, and eventually the sails themselves made more nearly square.

Sails were bent to the yards by means of "robands" which passed around the spar. In those localities where there was some danger that the roband might become worn by rubbing against the mast or lower rigging, the sail was attached through holes in a long, thin strip of wood secured to the lower side of the yard.

On the mizenmast swung a lateen sail, a relic of the old Mediterranean ships which remained for many years. As yet the yard had no vang. The operation of such yards has already been discussed on page 32.

Instead of the simpler iron fittings of later years, the yards were attached to the masts by parrels. These consisted of a series of wooden balls separated by suitable flat strips and the whole strung on to ropes, thus forming an easy running collar arrangement.

The deadeyes, by which the standing rigging was secured, although now possessing the familiar three holes, were not yet circular in shape. The lacing of the lanyard is so often mistakenly performed that it merits explanation. The knot appeared always on the inboard side of the deadeye. This permitted ready examination and consequently the early detection of any weakening. It belonged at the forward hole of the upper deadeye on the starboard side of the ship, at the after hole on the port side. Thus the rigger, standing on the deck, always rove the lanyard from left to right, no matter which side of the ship he was on. The end of the lanyard was made fast with a clove hitch around the shroud. The loose end was brought down and served to the standing part.

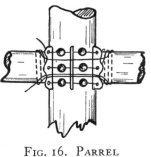

FIG. 16. PARREL

The preponderance of evidence seems to be that the ratlines of 1620 were not eye-spliced and seized at the ends, as was the case with later vessels, but were hitched in precisely the same manner as on the intermediate shrouds.

During the early years of the seventeenth century, English ships had "running backstays" which amounted to nothing but a pendant and whip. The pendant reached down to the vicinity of the top, where it terminated with a block. The standing part of the fall made fast to a timber-head. One such backstay will be found on both the fore and the main masts; there was none on the mizen.

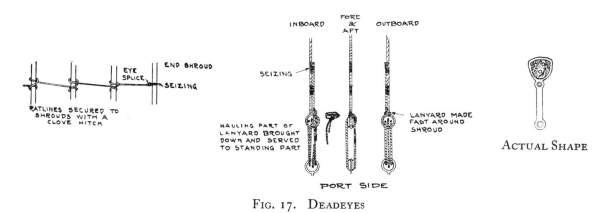

FIG. 17. DEADEYES

The topmast rigging did not secure to the truss hoop as was customary in the later clipper ships, but attached directly to the lower rigging which it tended to pull outwards. This tendency was checked by a lashing, crossing from the lower rigging of one side to the lower rigging of the other, thus offering a convenient means of taking up the slack which occurred in the rigging after a spell of dry weather, and of letting it out again when the cordage became wet (Fig. 18). All shrouds and stays were cable laid.

The series of blocks to which the fore-topmast stay attaches (Plan VI) carry a rope which thus forms a very powerful tackle. By heaving in on this rope the stay could be stretched extremely tight.

The mainstay was probably fastened by a collar which ran through a hole in the knee filling the angle between the stem and the beakhead. This collar was sufficiently

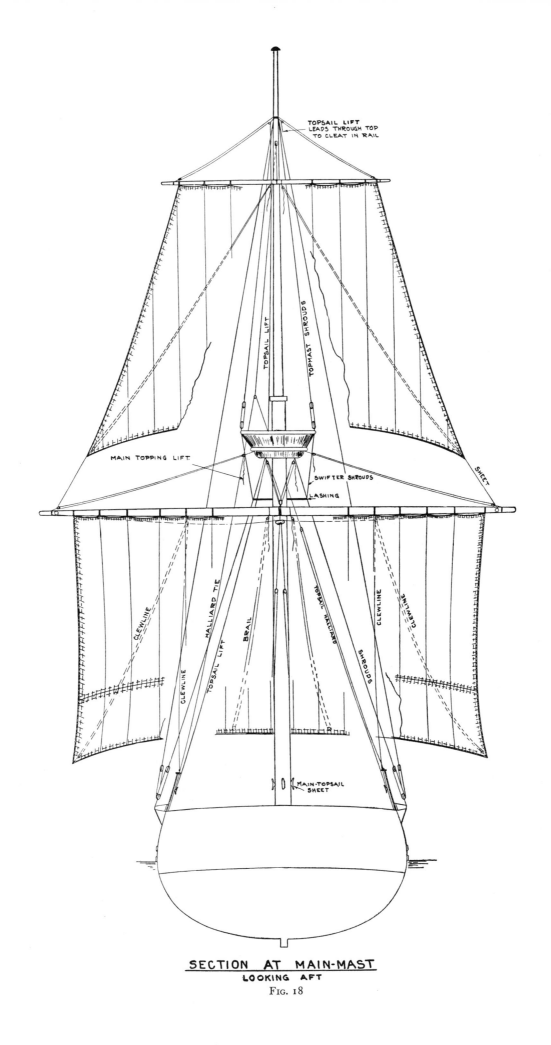

TOPSAIL LIFT
LEADS THROUGH TOP
TO CLEAT IN RAIL

TOPSAIL LIFT

TOPMAST SHROUDS

MAIN TOPPING LIFT

SWIFTER SHROUDS

SHEET

LASHING

CLEWLINE

CLEWLINE

HALLIARD TIE

TOPSAIL LIFT

BRAIL

TOPSAIL HALLIARD

SHROUDS

CLEWLINE

CLEWLINE

MAIN-TOPSAIL
SHEET

SECTION AT MAIN-MAST

LOOKING AFT

FIG. 18

long to permit the deadeye or block, which was held by a throat seizing, to come just abaft the foremast. The two parts of the collar straddled the foremast, passing under the beakhead bulkhead rail to the knee at the stem. The mainstay itself was set up either with deadeyes or with blocks, probably the former.

In most instances running rigging belayed to cleats at the bottom of the masts or inside the bulwarks, although the tremendous tangle of ropes at the bow required that many of these belay to the forecastle railing. There were no fife rails.

The method by which her yards were hoisted is not certain, since the *Mayflower* was refitted for her voyage to America at the beginning of the period of transition from the tie and halliard method to the adoption of jeers. Like other vessels equipped at the time she may have had both.

With the tie and halliard installation there were no blocks on the yard, the two ties passing over "hounds" in the cheeks of the mast. By reeving the halliard through a

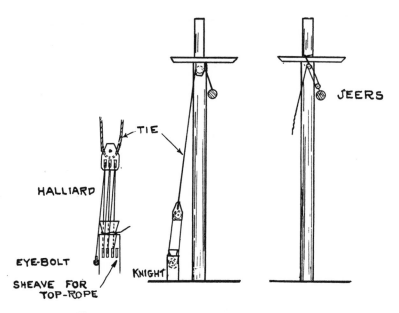

FIG. 19. METHODS OF HOISTING THE YARD

block to which the ties made fast, and thence to a series of sheaves in the "knight" timber at the foot of the mast, a powerful mechanical advantage was secured.

The introduction of jeers replaced the tie by a block on the yard and one or two blocks at the masthead. This furnished the purchase, a single hauling part coming down to the deck, in contrast with the many parts of the former halliard method. Since the English were the first to adopt jeers, in the beginning years of the seventeenth century, it seems quite probable that the *Mayflower* may have enjoyed a dual means of hoisting her yards.

Of less general importance are several details of the running rigging. The foretopsail halliard belays to starboard, the main-topsail halliard to port. Bowlines are shown on Plan VI for the starboard side only, the port side being similar. The foresail tacks carry under the bowsprit through a little fitting on the stem, and belay to the forecastle railing on the opposite side of the ship (see Plan VI, and Plan VII — Section AA). The starboard tack usually went through the hole nearest to the stem.

The spritsail clewline, here shown as single, may possibly have been double and

PLATE IX

Photograph by W. H. James

MODEL OF AN "ENGLISH MERCHANTMAN OF THE 'MAYFLOWER' PERIOD"

Built by Prof. J. R. Jack, Head of the Department of Naval Architecture and Marine Engineering, at the Massachusetts Institute of Technology, and Now Exhibited in the Nautical Museum of that Institution

PLATE X

Courtesy of Pilgrim Society, Plymouth

MODEL OF AN "ENGLISH MERCHANTMAN OF THE SIZE AND DATE OF THE
'MAYFLOWER,'" WHILE UNDER CONSTRUCTION. BUILT BY R. C. ANDER-
SON FOR THE PILGRIM SOCIETY, PLYMOUTH, MASS.

Careful examination will show the bowsprit off center to starboard; the doors leading
from the forecastle to the prow; anchor cables laid aft on the gun deck to the capstan;
the opening for the large main hatch; two bilge pumps just forward of and to each
side of the stump of the mainmast; the whipstaff just visible over the end of the poop
deck, and many other details of construction.

Photograph by E. P. McLaughlin

COMPLETED MODEL OF AN "ENGLISH MERCHANTMAN OF THE SIZE AND
DATE OF THE 'MAYFLOWER,'" BUILT BY R. C. ANDERSON FOR THE PILGRIM
SOCIETY, PLYMOUTH, MASS.

perhaps should attach one-third of the distance out on the yard instead of near the center.

EQUIPMENT

Sails

There might have been a square mizen-topsail and a spritsail-topsail carried on a little mast at the end of the bowsprit (See Plate V), but these features rightfully belong to ships of larger displacement and slightly later date than the *Mayflower*.

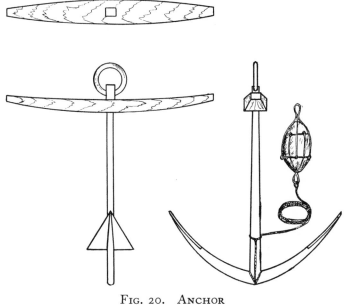

FIG. 20. ANCHOR
Scale ¼″ = 1 ft.

The holes at the lower corners of the spritsail were to allow water, which collected on the canvas from the spray, to escape when the sail was sheeted in close as shown on the Page Model (Plate VIII).

Like the flagship of Columbus, the sails had bonnets instead of reef points, the introduction of the latter occurring during the last part of the seventeenth century.

Anchors

No apparent progress had been made in the manufacture of anchors for at least one hundred years. In shape and manner of construction the anchors of the *Mayflower* were almost identical with those of the *Santa Maria*.

Because the anchor sometimes stuck on the bottom, or the hemp cables by which they held the ship were strained to the breaking point, anchor buoys were used to mark the spot beneath which the anchor lay. These buoys were attached to eighteen fathoms of line, a sufficient amount to function in water over a hundred feet deep.

When riding at anchor the cable was made fast to bitts at the end of the bowsprit. There were probably no cat heads.

Capstan

Just far enough abaft the mainmast to allow the six-foot capstan bars to clear, was located a straight, circular post which extended from the gun deck to a height of some three and one-half feet above the spar deck. Four bars were permanently installed at each deck, those on one diameter being just above the two on the other diameter.

Thus the capstan could be manned from either or both decks. On the gun deck it was used to weigh anchor; on the spar deck to handle the heavier running rigging.

Pumps

There were two bilge pumps, almost humorously similar to the wooden variety still found in the more rural barnyards, the one discrepancy being no spout for the water to flow out of. It simply spilled over the top of the pump to run across the deck, and out the scuppers. The location of these pumps was probably abreast, just forward of the mainmast on the gun deck, one pump being to starboard, the other to port of the center line by two and a half or three feet.

FIG. 21.
BILGE PUMPS
Scale ¼″ = 1 ft.

Implements of War

The *Mayflower* positively brought as many as five guns on her famous voyage of 1620. This we know from Bradford's statement that five cannon were mounted on the hill on February 21, 1621.* How many were mounted on the ship during the passage, or carried in the hold (if at all) no man can say. There must have been eight or ten guns in all — some "minions," some "sakers." The former are said to have fired a three-pound ball, the latter a four-pound ball.

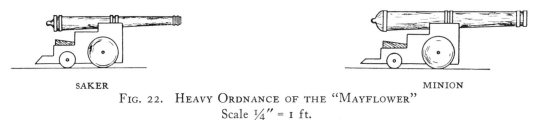

SAKER   MINION

FIG. 22. HEAVY ORDNANCE OF THE "MAYFLOWER"
Scale ¼″ = 1 ft.

There is not entire agreement between authorities in regard to size, weight, or caliber of these early brass cannon; those here shown being similar to the ordnance reproduced by Mr. Anderson.

Flags

As the *Mayflower* was an English ship she was obliged to fly the standard of England which was white with the red Cross of St. George. She would also have carried the original form of the Union Jack as decreed by James I in 1606 after the Union with Scotland. Its object was to prevent the Scotch and English ships from fighting one another as had previously been their amiable habit. This flag combined the red cross of St. George with the blue Scotch flag bearing the white cross of St. Andrew, thus impressing upon Scotch and English seamen that they were no longer to treat each other as enemies.

Small Boats

There were certainly two, probably three, small boats. The shallop has already been referred to as being stowed on the gun deck during the voyage and occasioning an exasperating delay at Provincetown Harbor due to the amount of repairing it required. It was about thirty feet long and carried a square mainsail and a jib. Some idea of her size and displacement may be had from the fact that on the day when her rudder was broken it required two stout seamen to steer her with oars while she

* Mourt's *Relation*, Dexter's ed., page 82.

PLATE XI

Photograph by E. P. McLaughlin

MODEL OF AN "ENGLISH MERCHANTMAN OF ABOUT THE SIZE AND DATE OF
THE 'MAYFLOWER'"

Designed and built under the direction of R. C. Anderson, for the Pilgrim Society,
Plymouth, Mass.

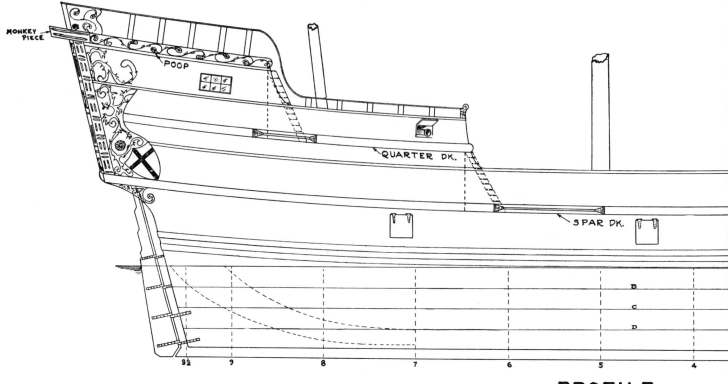

MONKEY
PIECE

POOP

QUARTER DK.

SPAR DK.

B

C

D

9½   9   8   7   6   5   4

PROFILE

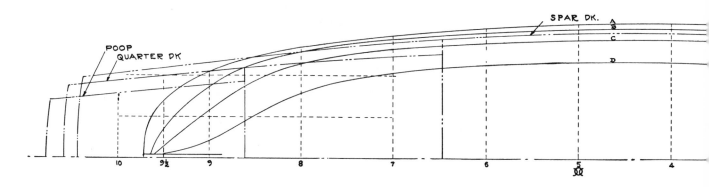

SPAR DK.
A
B
C

D

POOP
QUARTER DK

10   9½   9   8   7   6   5
                                       ⅩⅠ
                                              4

LINES

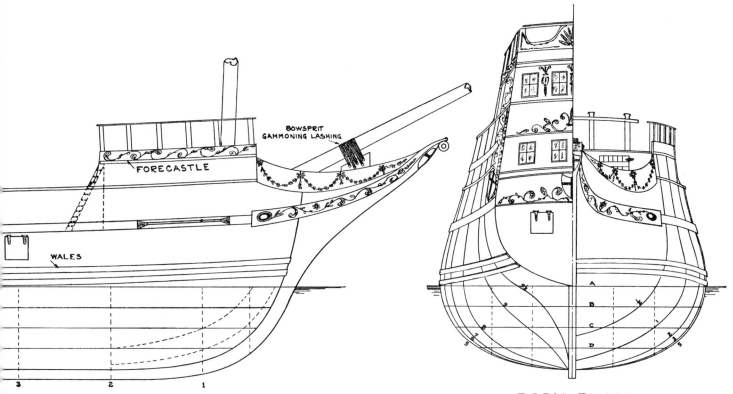

FORECASTLE

BOWSPRIT
GAMMONING LASHING

WALES

3   2   1

BODY PLAN

A
B
C
D

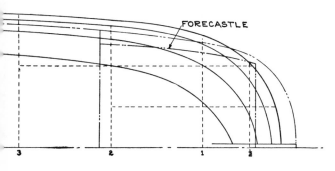

FORECASTLE

3   2   1   ½

FEET
0 1 2 3 4 5 6 7 8 9 10

THE PILGRIM SHIP
"MAYFLOWER"
AS RECONSTRUCTED FROM A STUDY
OF DRAWINGS AND MODELS OF SHIPS
OF THAT PERIOD

F. Alexander Magoun

MASSACHUSETTS INSTITUTE OF TECHNOLOGY
CAMBRIDGE   MASS.

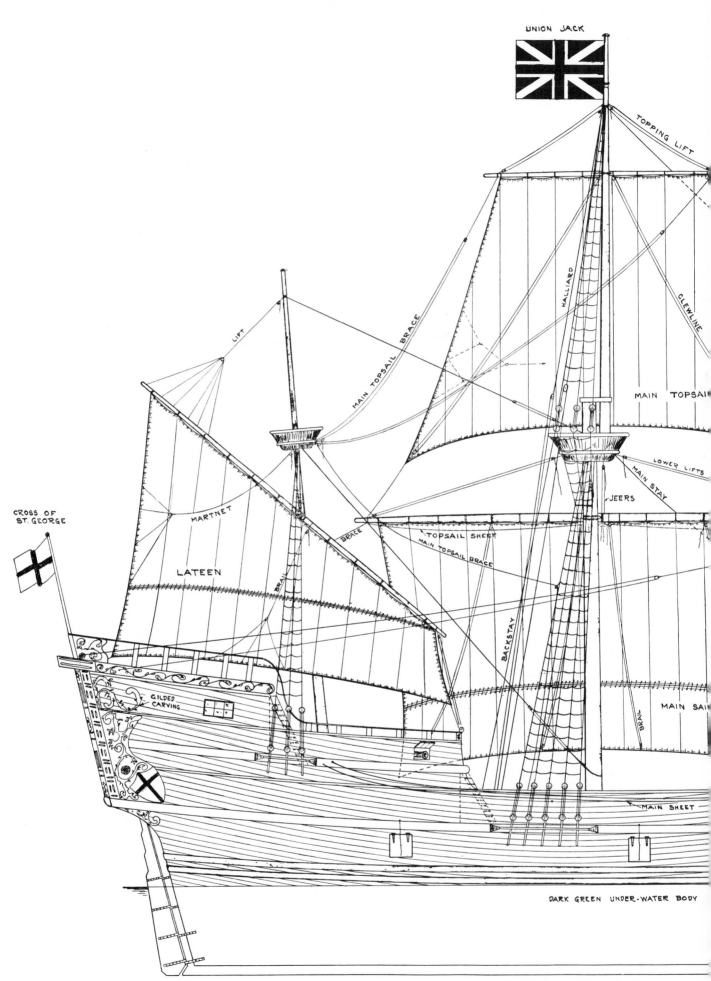

UNION JACK

TOPPING LIFT

CLEWLINE

MAIN TOPSAIL

LIFT

MAIN TOPSAIL BRACE

HALLIARD

LOWER LIFTS

MAIN STAY

JEERS

CROSS OF
ST. GEORGE

MARTNET

BRACE

TOPSAIL SHEET

MAIN TOPSAIL BRACE

LATEEN

BRAIL

BACKSTAY

MAIN SAIL

GILDED
CARVING

BRAIL

MAIN SHEET

DARK GREEN UNDER-WATER BODY

SAIL PLAN

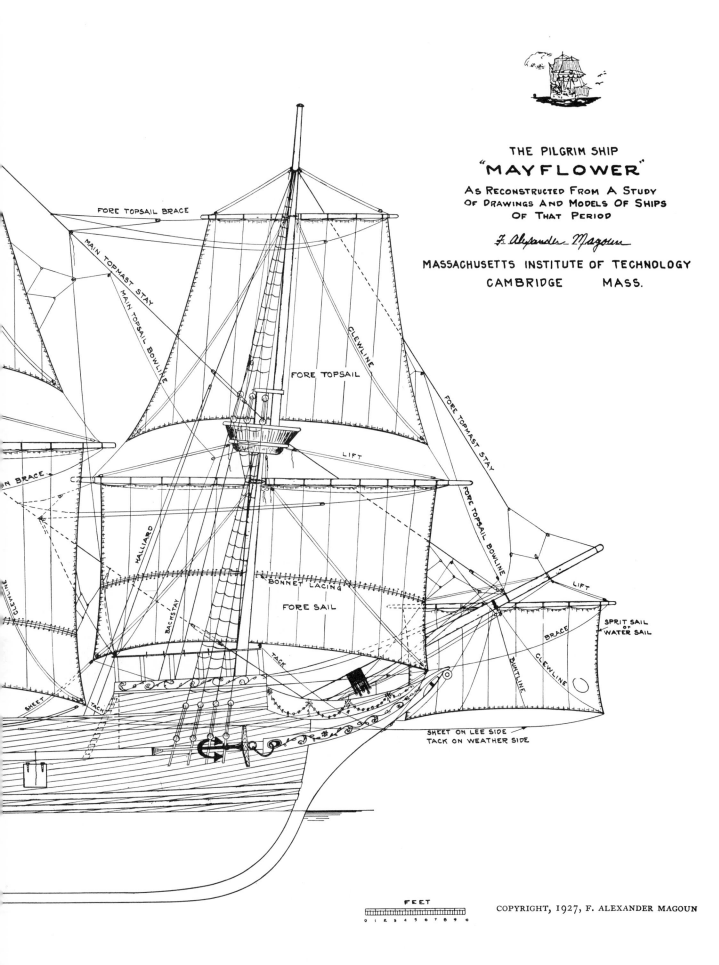

THE PILGRIM SHIP
"MAYFLOWER"
As Reconstructed From A Study
Of Drawings And Models Of Ships
Of That Period

F. Alexander Magoun

MASSACHUSETTS INSTITUTE OF TECHNOLOGY
CAMBRIDGE   MASS.

FORE TOPSAIL BRACE

MAIN TOPMAST STAY

MAIN TOPSAIL BOWLINE

CLEWLINE

FORE TOPSAIL

FORE TOPMAST STAY

FORE TOPSAIL BOWLINE

LIFT

LIFT

N BRACE

HALLIARD

BONNET LACING

FORE SAIL

SPRIT SAIL
OR
WATER SAIL

BRACE

BACKSTAY

CLEWLINE

BUNTLINE

CLEWLINE

TACK

SHEET

TACK

SHEET ON LEE SIDE
TACK ON WEATHER SIDE

FEET
0 1 2 3 4 5 6 7 8 9 0

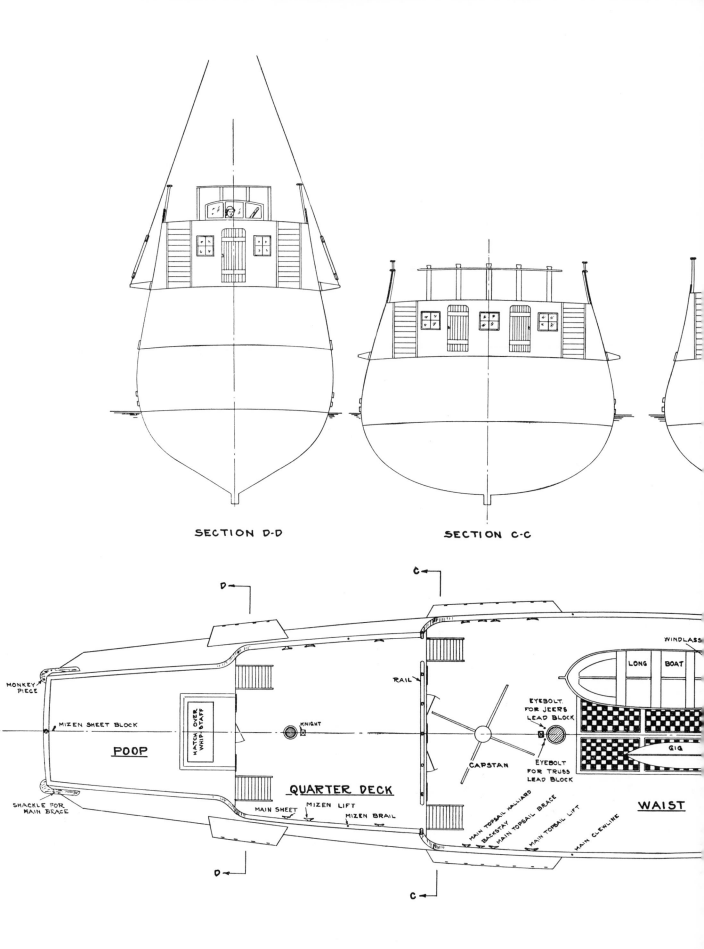

SECTION D-D   SECTION C-C

MONKEY
PIECE

MIZEN SHEET BLOCK

POOP

SHACKLE FOR
MAIN BRACE

HATCH OVER
WHIP-STAFF

KNIGHT

RAIL

QUARTER DECK

MAIN SHEET   MIZEN LIFT

MIZEN BRAIL

CAPSTAN

EYEBOLT
FOR JEERS
LEAD BLOCK

EYEBOLT
FOR TRUSS
LEAD BLOCK

WINDLASS

LONG   BOAT

GIG

WAIST

MAIN TOPSAIL HALLIARD
BACKSTAY
MAIN TOPSAIL BRACE
MAIN TOPSAIL LIFT
MAIN CLEWLINE

DECK PLAN AND SECTIONS

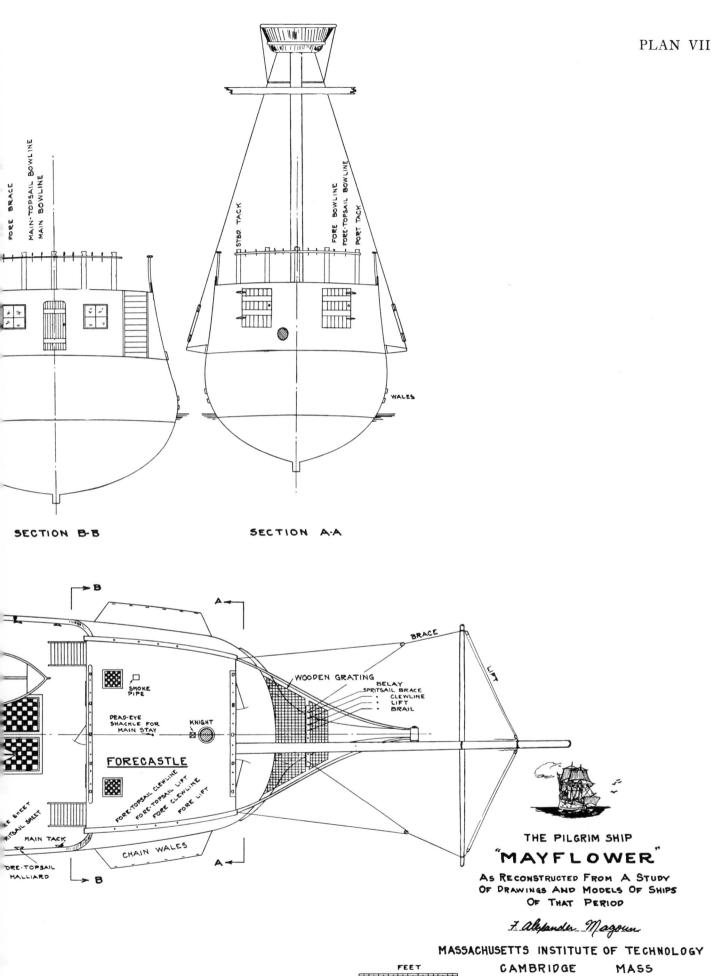

SECTION B-B

SECTION A-A

FORE BRACE
MAIN-TOPSAIL BOWLINE
MAIN BOWLINE

STBD. TACK

FORE BOWLINE
FORE-TOPSAIL BOWLINE
PORT TACK

WALES

B

A

BRACE

WOODEN GRATING

BELAY
SPRITSAIL BRACE
CLEWLINE
LIFT
BRAIL

LIFT

SMOKE PIPE

DEAD-EYE SHACKLE FOR MAIN STAY

KNIGHT

FORECASTLE

FORE-TOPSAIL CLEWLINE
FORE-TOPSAIL LIFT
FORE CLEWLINE
FORE LIFT

CHAIN WALES

E SHEET
SPRITSAIL SHEET
MAIN TACK
FORE-TOPSAIL HALLIARD

A

B

THE PILGRIM SHIP
"MAYFLOWER"

As Reconstructed From A Study
Of Drawings And Models Of Ships
Of That Period

F. Alexander Magoun

MASSACHUSETTS INSTITUTE OF TECHNOLOGY
CAMBRIDGE   MASS

FEET
0 1 2 3 4 5 6 7 8 9 10

was under sail and it was in this boat that the cannon were gotten ashore. It was undoubtedly this boat which first entered Plymouth harbor and from which the Pilgrims stepped on to Plymouth Rock. No representation of this is given here since its location on the gun deck of the *Mayflower* was out of sight.

The long-boat, lashed to the port side of the main hatch, was a smaller, but none the less useful craft. Should the anchor become fouled on the bottom and impossible to break off the ground with the capstan, it could be recovered with the long-boat. A simple log windlass, built into the forward part of the boat and rotated by thrusting levers into a series of holes, often succeeded, by a direct vertical pull on the anchor buoy line, in doing what the less direct force of the capstan could not accomplish.

That the operations in Plymouth harbor were hindered by a lack of small boats is a well-attested fact. Bradford often mentions the difficulty of getting the goods ashore for want of boats.*

Besides the shallop and the long-boat, specifically alluded to by the Pilgrim documents, there was probably a gig for the Captain, there being numerous proofs of the existence and necessity of such a boat. In the light of present laws regulating the provision of sufficient life-boats, the owners of the *Mayflower* were criminally negligent.

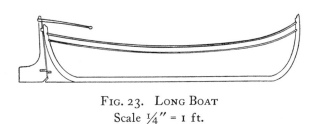

FIG. 23.   LONG BOAT
Scale ¼″ = 1 ft.

Cargo

A complete inventory of the cargo, as originally put aboard and as rearranged after the breakdown of the *Speedwell*, would be varied and curious. No such document exists, but, as with most other items, considerable light is thrown upon the problem by an investigation of the old records.

Some sixty firkins of butter were sold at Southampton to clear the port charges.† The will of William Mullins, father of the attractive Priscilla, disposes of "XXI dozen of shoes and thirteene paire of bootes wch I give into the Companies handes for forty pounds at seaven years end if they like them at that rate."‡

So far as can be discovered the only live stock aboard consisted of goats, pigs, poultry and dogs. There were neither cattle nor beasts of burden, the lack of which was sorely felt in Plymouth. The animals were probably penned on the spar deck forward, the upturned boats offering shelter for the hens. Administration of a farm, even on shore, is not always unruffled, and it would have been too much to hope that the management of live stock thus afloat could be carried on without grave difficulties. Short keep and foul weather played havoc with the "farm."

Of other items known to have been on board, a partial enumeration would include:

chairs	cooking utensils	seeds	hatchets
tables	lamps	shovels	pitch forks
beds	buckets and pails	hoes	nails
chests of drawers	lime (for mortar)	spades	chisels
trunks	blacksmith tools	axes	adz
books	clothing	saws	food stores

No plough or implement requiring the strength of a beast was brought.

* Bradford: *History of Plymouth Plantation*, Deane's ed., page 90.
† Bradford: *History of Plymouth Plantation*, Deane's ed., page 61.
‡ *Probate Act Book*, 1621-1622, Somerset House.

Food

The dietary of the Pilgrims offered far more variation than any so far chronicled in these pages: biscuits, oatmeal, butter, cheese, salt meat, smoked herring, beans, ham, onions, peas, cabbage, parsnips, and beer. The list may have been even longer.

How it was possible to cook for all those on board is another mystery. Ames offers the able suggestion that the ship's cook attended to the wants of the officers and crew, the requirements of the passengers being met by doling out food to the various families who prepared it themselves.* As he points out, the fact that so many would require food at practically the same time must have necessitated the wide use of uncooked rations, the galley being totally inadequate for the demands of even a portion of the company. Beer took the place of tea and coffee as a beverage — cold comfort that it was.

OPERATION

For the Tercentenary Celebration of 1920 an alleged replica of the *Mayflower* was built. This did not make a trans-Atlantic voyage nor were its sea-going qualities studied. Without the definite information afforded by such research, or, indeed, the complaints of the close-mouthed passengers themselves, it is obvious to the naval architect that her sea-going qualities must have been very indifferent, though somewhat better than those of the *Santa Maria*. This was proved by the rapid return which she made to England in the spring of 1621. Her passage of only thirty-one days compares very favorably with the famous fourteen day passage of Donald McKay's swiftest clipper, the *Lightning*.

The speed of the *Mayflower* under the best conditions was not far from nine knots, and though her designer knew very little as compared with modern conceptions of resistance, rigging, or stability, whole-hearted praise is well deserved by the men who brought her and her precious cargo across the stormy waters of the North Atlantic.

* Ames: *The Mayflower and Her Log*, page 198.

IV

THE UNITED STATES FRIGATE "CONSTITUTION"

ITH the Revolutionary War the religious liberty which the Pilgrim Fathers had come to America to secure was amplified to include political freedom. The vindication and establishment of this new independence were so intimately connected with the history and traditions of the frigate *Constitution* that she holds a unique place in the annals of our navy. No other ship has seen so long, so varied, or so romantic service. No other has been commanded by a succession of such brilliant, resourceful men. Not even Ericsson's *Monitor* was so far superior to anything of her type afloat. While under construction the *Constitution* was an object of ridicule; her success in battle compelled respect; her rotting timbers and rusted bolts are now a significant emblem of the past.

In 1785 there was not a single armed vessel belonging to the United States. The colonies had no navy in spite of the fact that no other organization could have been capable of earning for us a position among the nations. Quite naturally the Algerine corsairs took advantage of this situation, attacking our merchantmen with immunity and treating those on board as slaves.

The situation became unbearable, yet without apparent remedy, as the states were totally unable to pay the large ransoms demanded. These moneys were considered perfectly reasonable by the corsairs, since for three centuries they had practised piracy against the Christian nations of Europe with conspicuous success. Had there been less commercial rivalry between Holland, England, and France their united efforts could have easily put an effective stop to these barbarisms and debasing tributes; but petty jealousies between these powers made such coöperation impossible and transferred to the infantile United States the task and glory of suppressing the infamous business.

President George Washington laid the treatment of our merchantmen in the Mediterranean before Congress in 1790 with negative results. Again, in 1792, he urged the matter, this time securing $40,000. to be paid as ransom for the captives and an appropriation of $25,000. annual tribute to be paid for immunity. European complications and the hostile attitude of the Dey prevented subsequent negotiations from maturing.

More acts of piracy followed. In the fall of 1793 alone, eleven American ships were captured. Yet the resolution to equip a navy passed Congress by only a small majority. The authorization to build the ships provided that work should be discontinued in the event of a treaty being negotiated with Algiers before their completion. The bill was approved March 27, 1794.

In the absence of a Navy Department, Henry Knox, Secretary of War, was given the responsibility of securing six ships, either by purchase or by new construction. Four were to be 44-gun frigates, two were to be 36-gun frigates.

During the agitation for a navy, Mr. Joshua Humphreys, already widely known as a Philadelphia shipbuilder, not only gave enthusiastic support to the movement but advanced such sound and progressive ideas that he was eventually selected to design and superintend the construction of the frigates. Two of his letters showing how accurately his common sense was able to prognosticate the essential requirements, may well be quoted to support the wisdom of his appointment:

"From the present appearance of affairs I believe it is time this country was possessed of a navy; but as that is yet to be raised, I have ventured a few remarks on the subject.

"Ships that compose the European navys are generally distinguished by their rates; but as the situation and depth of water of our coasts and harbors are different in some degrees from those in Europe, and as our navy for a considerable time will be inferior in numbers, we are to consider what size ships will be most formidable, and be an overmatch for those of an enemy; such frigates as in blowing weather would be an overmatch for double-deck ships, and in light winds to evade coming to action; or double-deck ships that would be an overmatch for common double-deck ships, and in blowing weather superior to ships of three decks, or in calm weather or light winds to outsail them. Ships built on these principles will render those of an enemy in a degree useless, or require a greater number before they dare attack our ships. Frigates, I suppose, will be the first object, and none ought to be built less than 150 feet keel, to carry twenty-eight 32-pounders or thirty 24-pounders on the gun deck, and 12-pounders on the quarter-deck. These ships should have scantlings equal to 74's, and I believe may be built of red cedar and live oak for about twenty-four pounds per ton, carpenters' tonnage, including carpenters, smiths' bill, including anchors, joiners, block makers, mast makers, riggers and rigging, sail makers and sail cloths, suits and chandlers' bill. As such ships will cost a large sum of money, they should be built of the best materials that could possibly be procured. The beams for their decks should be of the best Carolina pine, and the lower futtocks and knees, if possible, of live oak.

"The greatest care should be taken in the construction of such ships, and particularly all her timbers should be framed and bolted together before they are raised. Frigates built to carry 12 and 18-pounders, in my opinion, will not answer the expectation contemplated from them; for if we should be obliged to take a part in the present European war, or at a future day we should be dragged into a war with any powers of the Old Continent, especially Great Britain, they having such a number of ships of that size, that it would be an equal chance by equal combat that we lose our ships, and more particularly from the Algerians, who have ships, and some of much greater force. Several questions will arise, whether one large or two small frigates contribute most to the protection of our trade, or which will cost the least sum of money, or whether two small ones are as able to engage a double-deck ship as one large one. For my part I am decidedly of opinion the large ones will answer best."

Again he writes:

"All the maritime powers of Europe being possessed of a great number of ships of the first size contemplated, and the Algerians having several, and considering the small number of ships directed to be built, the great necessity of constructing those ships in such a way as to render them less liable to be captured and more capable of rendering great services to the United States according to their number, the construction and sizes of frigates of the European nations were resorted to and their usefulness carefully considered. It was determined of importance to this country to take the lead in a class of ships not in use in Europe, which would be the only means of making our little navy of any importance. It would oblige other Powers to follow us intact, instead of our following them; considering at the same time it was not impossible we should be brought into a war with some of the European nations; and if we should be so engaged, and had ships of equal size with theirs, for want of experience and discipline, which cannot immediately be expected, in an engagement we should not have an equal chance, and probably lose our ships. Ships of the present construction have everything in their favor; their great length gives them the advantage of sailing, which is an object of the first magnitude. They are superior to any European frigate, and if others should be in company, our frigates can always lead ahead and never be obliged to go into action, but on their own terms, except in a calm; in blowing weather our ships are capable of engaging to advantage double-deck ships. Those reasons weighed down all objections."*

The ships were to be built as follows:

Constitution,	44 guns,	at Boston.
President,	44 guns,	at New York.
United States,	44 guns,	at Philadelphia.
Chesapeake,	44 guns,	at Norfolk.
Constellation,	36 guns,	at Baltimore.
Congress,	36 guns,	at Portsmouth.

For some now forgotten reason the battery of the *Chesapeake* was changed to 36 guns during her construction, making an equal division between the two types of frigates.

The reasons which Joshua Humphreys advanced for limiting construction to frigates only were well vindicated by subsequent events. The frigate is peculiarly fitted to various types of service. Its place in the fleet corresponded to that of the modern cruiser: swift enough to escape the more powerful capital ships and to do scouting service watching the movements of the enemy, yet powerful enough to defeat any armed vessel except a line-of-battle ship. The rig of the frigates was exactly similar to that of the ships of the line. The caliber of the guns was often the same. The distinguishing feature lay in the arrangement of the ordnance and in the total number of guns carried.

The word frigate has had various meanings at different times. During the sixteenth century the Mediterranean frigate was an oared vessel, smaller than a galley, and used principally for dispatch bearing. It is thought by some that during the seventeenth century the word referred to a classification predicated on the shape of the under-water body. Others hold it to have been applicable only to a certain deck arrangement. The term as we know it applies to a ship-rigged vessel used to perform the functions of a cruiser.

Line-of-battle ships were divided into four ratings: the first rate (a designation now deteriorated to the adjectival use, meaning excellent) included vessels of 100 guns or more; the second rate, 90 to 98 guns; the third rate, 64 to 84 guns, the 74's being the most common; and the fourth rate, 50 to 60 guns. First and second rates had three complete gun decks, besides which they carried cannon on the forecastle and quarter deck. Third and fourth rates were two deckers. These were handier than the three deckers. Being smaller, they made less leeway. Four could be built for less than the cost of three, making more ships available for a strategic distribution of the

* Hollis: *The Frigate Constitution,* pages 35-37.

fleet. These advantages were sufficient to outweigh the one disadvantage, that a 74 could never hope, single-handed, to engage successfully with a first rater.

Exactly the advantages just enumerated for the two-deckers applied to the frigates as compared with the 74's. They had but a single gun deck; besides which ordnance was carried forward and aft on the spar deck. The waist seldom mounted any guns.

Originally the power of a frigate was correctly indicated by the number of guns mentioned in designating her, but the invention of the carronade changed this. Thereafter the ship was still rated by the number of her long guns. The carronades were not counted. The old armament of twenty-six to thirty 18-pounders on the gun deck and six to ten long guns of smaller caliber on the spar deck could now be considerably augmented by numbers of light, rapid fire, large caliber guns. To have added more long guns would have been to prejudice the strength and the stability of the ship. To be sure, the carronade was effective only at short range, but in such an engagement it did more damage than its heavier sister. Thus the confusion arose that a 44 gun frigate often actually carried 52 cannon.

Such a ship was the *Constitution*. Yet so remarkable was the genius of Joshua Humphreys that fifteen years after she was launched she was still far superior to anything of her class afloat. Instead of the 18 pounders he chose the long 24's in spite of the fact that the few previous frigates carrying so heavy a battery had been considered unsuccessful. For this decision he was naturally widely ridiculed. Instead of the usual lighter construction he made the frames, planking, and spars fully equal in size to those of a line-of-battle ship. This was at first criticized as clumsy design, and later made the basis of the British complaint that she was not a frigate at all, but really a disguised ship of the line. The immediate effect of her successes in 1812 was that the British naval constructors cut down some of their old 74's to two decks, hoping thus to defeat the *Constitution* and the *President* with vessels of similar rating.

Immediately after the plans were prepared great quantities of live oak, hard pine, and red cedar were obtained, part of which was sent to "Hartt's Naval Yard," Boston, at which the *Constitution* was to be built. The keel of the old frigate rested on the blocks not far from where Constitution Wharf now stands.

As superintending Naval Constructor, Col. George Claghorn represented the interests of the Government, Mr. Hartley and Captain Nicholson serving as assistants. Under their inspection Paul Revere furnished the copper sheathing, composition bolts, and other brass fastenings for which he received $3,820.33; the sails took shape in a loft where the Park Street Church now stands; the anchors were forged at Hanover.

In November, 1795, just as the ship was well along toward completion, a treaty was signed with Algiers. By this agreement we paid nearly $1,000,000 to the Dey besides promising him $21,600 annually in naval stores, and a frigate which was to cost approximately $100,000. It would have been both wiser and cheaper to have completed the ships so well begun and with them to have resisted the piracy of the Dey's corsairs. Instead, work was suspended in accordance with the previous provisions of Congress.

But President Washington saw the mistake. In his Congressional Message of 1796 he said, "It is in our own experience that the most sincere neutrality is not sufficient guard against the depredations of nations at war.* To secure respect to a neutral flag requires a naval force organized and ready to protect it from insult or aggression."

The time came when the self-respect of the American nation no longer allowed forbearance, and money for the completion of the *Constitution, Constellation,* and the

* This reference was to the misfortunes our merchantmen received from both England and France.

United States was appropriated. The particular incident which served as the final straw was not connected with the Barbary pirates, but was committed by a French privateer. She destroyed an English merchantman peaceably anchored in Charleston, S. C., harbor and, still not satisfied, captured two American vessels on her way out.

Within a month the portfolio of Secretary of the Navy had been created, to which position Benjamin Stoddard received appointment April 30, 1798.

By this time the *Constitution* had been completed and was nearly ready to put to sea, though not without attendant difficulties. Colonel Claghorn had arranged for her launching on the spring tide of September 20, to which many notables were invited, including the President of the United States. She moved down the ways twenty-seven feet and refused to go farther. There she stuck in spite of the frantic application of jacks, screws and other mechanical persuasions. This unexpected obstinacy was due to the small declivity of the ways, made small because on the previous tenth of July the *United States* had suffered injury in a premature launching, the blame for which was attributed to excessive declivity of the launching ways.

Two days later a second attempt moved her an additional thirty feet, but ended in new disappointment. The part of the ways on which her stern rested had settled. There was no remedy but to rebuild them with increased declivity and more rugged support. In the meantime the excessive pressure on the keel, amidships, gave the vessel a permanent hog* which has never yet been completely removed. Indeed, before the present reconstruction this hog was determined by divers to be fourteen inches, a deflection which it is hoped will be entirely corrected before the old ship puts to sea again.

On the 21st of October, sponsored by Capt. James Sever, who broke a bottle of wine over her bow, she finally slid into the sea. It required the stimulus of outrages such as that of the French privateer to goad Congress into the appropriation of funds for fitting her out. The total cost, including $93,000. for guns and equipment, was $302,719.; the total running expenses were about $125,000. a year.

Her first officers and their annual rates of pay including the value of commuted rations were:

Captain, Samuel Nicholson $2,018
First Lieutenant, Charles Russell . . . . ——
Lieutenants, Benjamin Lee, Richard C. Beale and Isaac Hull . . 786
Lieutenant of Marines, Lemuel Clark 564
Surgeon, William Reed 804

Her complement as fixed by the Navy Department was 400 men — 22 officers and 378 petty officers, seamen and marines divided as follows:†

Commander	1	Yeoman of Gun-room	1
Lieutenants	4	Gunner	1
Lieutenant of Marines	2	Quarter Gunners	11
Sailing Masters	2	Coxswain	1
Master's Mates	2	Sailmaker	1
Midshipmen	7	Cooper	1
Purser	1	Steward	1
Surgeon	1	Armorer	1
Surgeon's Mates	2	Master-at-Arms	1
Clerk	1	Cook	1
Carpenter	1	Chaplain	1
Carpenter's Mates	2	Able Seamen	120
Boatswain	1	Ordinary Seamen	150
Boatswain's Mates	2	Boys	30
		Marines	50
			400

* The shipbuilders' antonym for "sag."
† *State Papers* (1834), Vol. XIV, page 159.

The pay of the petty officers averaged perhaps $19. a month, whereas the seamen received anywhere from $8. to $17. for the same period.

The *Constitution* first cleared for sea, under the command of Captain Nicholson, on July 22, 1798, but accomplished almost nothing in the destruction of the French privateers. Her real career began when Commodore Edward Preble ordered her canvas spread on August 14, 1803, after she had lain dismantled at the Boston Navy Yard for over two years.

The country had now reached the point where exasperation over the acts of the Algerian and Tripolitan pirates resulted in punitative action. Half measures and our cowardly acquiescence to the piratical demands of Algiers had aroused the cupidity of the Dey of Tripoli. He wanted his share of western booty, but like many examples, even in recent history, of men who had much, his greed for more caused the downfall of all.

Preble's squadron consisted of seven vessels of which the *Constitution* was the flagship. The frigate *Philadelphia* and five small ships of 16 guns or less made up the remainder of the fleet. Not one of the commanding officers had yet reached the age of thirty, but the names of such men as William Bainbridge, Isaac Hull, and Stephen Decatur show of what stuff they were made. That the crew of the flagship soon discovered what could be expected of the "Old Man," is related by the then Midshipman Charles Morris.

"We had nothing of interest on the passage until near the entrance of the Straits of Gibraltar, when, upon a very dark evening, with very light winds, we suddenly found ourselves near a vessel which was evidently a ship of war. The crew were immediately but silently brought to quarters, after which the Commodore gave the usual hail, 'What ship is that?' The same question was returned; in reply to which the name of our ship was given, and the question repeated. Again the question was returned. Again the question was returned instead of an answer, and again our ship's name given and the question repeated, without other reply than its repetition. The Commodore's patience seemed now exhausted, and, taking the trumpet, he hailed and said, 'I am now going to hail you for the last time. If a proper answer is not returned, I will fire a shot into you.' A prompt answer came back, 'If you fire a shot, I will return a broadside.' Preble then hailed, 'What ship is that?' The reply was, 'This is His Britannic Majesty's ship *Donnegal*, eighty-four guns, Sir Richard Strahan, an English Commodore. Send your boat on board.' Under the excitement of the moment, Preble leaped on the hammocks and returned for answer, 'This is the United States ship *Constitution*, forty-four guns, Edward Preble, an American Commodore, who will be damned before he sends his boat on board of any vessel.' And, turning to the crew, he said, 'Blow your matches, boys.' The conversation here ceased and soon after a boat was heard coming from the stranger, and arrived with a lieutenant from the frigate *Maidstone*. The object of this officer was to apologize for the apparent rudeness which had been displayed. He stated that our ship had not been seen until we had hailed them; that it was, of course, very important to gain time to bring their men to quarters, especially as it was apparent we were not English, and they had no expectation of meeting an American ship of war there; and that this object had induced their delay and misrepresentation in giving the ship's name. The excuses were deemed satisfactory, and the ships separated.

"This was the first occasion that had offered to show us what we might expect from our commander, and the spirit and decision which he displayed were hailed with

PLATE XII

UNITED STATES FRIGATE "CONSTITUTION"

From a water-color, by an unknown American artist, owned by a Boston collector

From a Line Engraving in the Peabody Museum, Salem

pleasure by all, and at once mitigated greatly the unfriendly feelings which the ebullitions of his temper had produced."*

By the civilian unacquainted with the problems of provisioning a fleet 3,000 miles from a home port, of keeping that fleet at sea without adequate means of reconditioning the ships, and of successfully maintaining a blockade against such a port as Tripoli in spite of adverse winter winds, the accomplishments of Commodore Preble can never be understood or appreciated.

At the very beginning of hostilities the impetuosity of Bainbridge lost the *Philadelphia* to the Tripolitans. In chasing a zebec into Tripoli he ran too far inshore in unfamiliar waters, grounding the bow on a submerged rock, in spite of the fact that the sounding lead showed six fathoms of water at the time. Frantic efforts to float her off failed. The yards were braced aback, cannon were run aft, anchors were dropped, fresh water was pumped overboard, even the foremast was cut away with no success. Nine enemy gunboats came out and captured her easily. A few days later a northwest gale lifted the ship off, whereupon the pirates proceeded to fit her out for their own uses. For the next eighteen months they employed the unhappy crew of the *Philadelphia* under horrible conditions of slavery.

The brunt of the war against Tripoli was carried by the smaller vessels, the *Constitution* serving principally as a mother ship. On board her Commodore Preble planned his campaign and arranged the details of such daring exploits as that by which Stephen Decatur was able to burn the *Philadelphia*.

In a small ketch, which had been captured from the enemy, sixty-four men,† including eleven officers, sailed into the harbor of Tripoli the night of February 16, 1804. With them was a Maltese pilot, Salvadore Catalano, who was familiar with the harbor and whose reply to a challenge from the *Philadelphia* allayed all suspicion until the last moment. Most of his comrades lay crouching in the bottom of the boat with mingled emotions while the pilot represented the ketch as a Maltese trader which had lost its anchors in the terrific storm just passed, and requested permission to tie up alongside for the night. The request was granted and a line thrown to him. Then, not forty yards from the batteries on shore and under the very muzzles of the gunboats in the harbor and the loaded long 24's of the *Philadelphia*, the Americans swarmed over her bulwarks. The Moors were panic stricken. Twenty minutes later, lit up by the flames which were consuming the *Philadelphia* and splashed by a barrage from forts and gunboats, the ketch pulled out of the harbor, under the power of sixteen long oars. Even the guns of the *Philadelphia* added to the din, their charges going off one by one as the heat of the conflagration reached them. Not one of Decatur's men was scratched. Lord Nelson described the undertaking as "the most bold and daring act of the age."

In three of the five direct attacks made on Tripoli between July 25th and September 4th the *Constitution* took active part. The fighting was bloody, hand to hand conflict of the most strenuous sort, for though the American squadron had only some 1060 men, they succeeded in vanquishing 25,000 Moors. Instance after instance of the intrepidity and daring of the Americans are available. A lieutenant, a midshipman, and nine sailors boarded a gunboat having a crew of thirty-six. The lieutenant was wounded eleven times but after killing fourteen of the enemy he captured the ship without the loss of a man.

On the morning of August 28th the *Constitution* attacked alone. Preble report-

---

* Commodore Charles Morris, U. S. N.: *Autobiography*, page 21.
† Morris: *Autobiography*, page 25.

ed to the Secretary of the Navy, "We continued running in, until we were within musket shot of the Crown and Mole batteries, when we brought to, and fired upwards of three hundred round shot, besides grape and canister, into the town, Bashaw's Castle, and batteries. We silenced the castle and two of the batteries for some time. At a quarter past six, the gunboats being all out of shot and in tow, I hauled off, after having been three-quarters of an hour in close action. The gunboats fired upwards of four hundred round shot, besides grape and canister, with good effect. A large Tunistan galliot was sunk in the mole — a Spanish seignior received considerable damage. The Tripoline galleys and gunboats lost many men and were much cut."*

Not a man on the *Constitution* was hurt during any one of the assaults on Tripoli.

In September, Commodore Preble was relieved by Commodore Barron, who brought with him two frigates, the *President* and the *Constellation*. Barron maintained the blockade so effectively laid down by Preble, but illness soon forced him to relinquish his command to Captain Rodgers. He chose the *Constitution* as his flagship.

In May, 1805, a treaty was drawn up in her cabin. When it was signed on June 3d, the war against Tripoli was over. But Rodgers was not yet satisfied. He moved his fleet to an anchorage off Tunis where by vigorous diplomacy he negotiated a treaty ending tribute forever.

That assurance might be "doubly sure," part of the squadron remained in the Mediterranean to keep a watchful eye on the pirates. It was 1807 before the *Constitution* returned home to be dismantled at the New York Navy Yard, and laid up for another two years. Commodore Rodgers commanded her again in 1810 but transferred his flag to the *President* which he considered the faster vessel. Isaac Hull, formerly first lieutenant on the old frigate, now became the captain.

She made a number of unimportant coastwise voyages and then carried the new American minister, Mr. Barlow, to France. This mission, which included transferring Mr. Russell from France to his new position at the Court of St. James's, was not to be accomplished without some firm delicacy, since the English were blockading the entire French coast. The British Commodore endeavored to delay the landing at Cherbourg without success, as Hull ignored him. Later, in Portsmouth harbor, another incident helped to precipitate the war which came soon after.

During the evening of November 13, 1811, when Captain Hull was known to be absent at London, a boat came alongside the *Constitution* to report that one of her sailors had just deserted to a British frigate, the *Havannah*. Next morning the English captain refused to give the man up without an order from the admiral, Sir Roger Curtis, who, in turn, refused to surrender him on the grounds that the sailor claimed to be an Englishman and as such demanded protection. Subsequent investigation proved the deserter to be a galley helper who had been confined for a petty theft, but who escaped through an open port.

Before a week passed a deserter from the *Havannah* swam to the *Constitution* declaring himself to be an American. The officers on our frigate were elated. "A boat was immediately sent to the *Havannah* to reciprocate the politeness of the preceding evening, and the next morning we had the satisfaction of assigning the same reason and the same testimony for refusing a demand for his restitution from the captain and admiral."†

Another incident showing to what an extent both officers and sailors were capable

---

* Hollis: *The Frigate Constitution*, page 109.
† Com. Charles Morris: *Autobiography*, page 44.

of going in this business of impressing seamen is quoted from "Naval Scenes in the Last War," a pamphlet written by Moses Smith, sponger of number one gun under Captain Isaac Hull. This pamphlet was found in the library at Harvard University by Rear Admiral Elliot Snow (C. C.), U. S. N., and has been reprinted in the "Golden Book" for October, 1927.

"About this time the *John Adams* arrived at Annapolis from a foreign cruise, and from her men we learned of a striking case of heroism, which is worthy to be told. A coloured seaman belonging to New York had been pressed into the English service, and when the *Adams* was lying off their coast, he got an opportunity to come on board of her as one of a boat's crew, sent with an officer upon some errand. Thinking now his time had come to escape from the British, he determined if possible not to return. Accordingly, as he stood upon the deck of the *Adams*, he suddenly seized a boarding axe, and in presence of the crew, cut off the fingers of his right hand at a single blow. Then with his left hand holding up the bloody weapon, he exclaimed,

" 'Now let the English take me, if they want me.'

"However, disabled as he was, they took him back, our officers having no power to interfere. If patriotism be anything but a name, then surely this noble African deserved a better fate. There are exalted qualities often concealed beneath a darkened skin."

On the recommendation of Captain Hull the ship was thoroughly overhauled after her return home. Because there were no drydocks yet available, vessels were "hove down" for cleaning and repairing the bottom. To do this all moveable weights were put ashore and the ship careened in shallow water, first to one side, then to the other. The work was carried out under the direction of "Jumping Billy" Haraden, formerly sailing master on the *Constitution*, who understood her requirements so well that by giving her less ballast and a better sailing trim he greatly improved her speed.

Thus she was exceptionally well prepared for the war declared against Great Britain on June 18, 1812, which is chiefly responsible for her glorious history. This second conflict with our mother country was brought about by our inability to remain neutral toward both France and England, and by the illegal action of the British in not only searching our ships, but impressing our seamen. There is no doubt that most navies of that period included many foreigners, their numbers depending upon the difficulty of securing seamen at home. We were probably no exception to this rule, particularly during the war with Tripoli, but a clear distinction exists between persuading a foreigner to enlist and forcing him to serve against his will.

In spite of the tremendous difference in the number of ships at the disposal of the combatants we had several advantages. England was occupied by much more important military matters in France. Although we possessed not one single line-of-battle ship, the frigates we did have were far superior to those of any other navy afloat. Our seamen fought with enthusiasm instead of being driven to fight. Our officers applied themselves to the intelligent study of tactics and strategy instead of following Lord Nelson's dictum, "Never mind manoeuvers, always go at them." Science usually wins.

No American officer showed more sagacity than Isaac Hull. His command sailed from Washington Navy Yard three days after war was declared, but being not yet fully equipped, anchored off Annapolis to receive men and stores.

After clearing the Capes, Captain Hull laid his course for New York where he expected to join Commodore Rodgers. Light contrary winds made his progress up the coast extremely slow. About two o'clock on the afternoon of Friday, July 17th, four ships were sighted to windward heading toward the New Jersey coast. Naturally supposing them to be the American squadron, the *Constitution* made to join this little fleet. A fifth sail appeared in the middle of the afternoon which eventually turned out to be the *Guerriere*. The wind died down leaving all six ships becalmed well out of range of each other and entertaining various erroneous ideas. The British thought the *Guerriere*, Capt. J. R. Dacres, another American frigate; Captain Dacres mistook his comrades for the American fleet; Hull had no misgivings about the squadron but, uncertain of the newcomer, altered course to investigate her.

At seven-thirty Hull cleared for action, and three hours later displayed the code signals for half an hour without reply. When dawn came the *Constitution* and the *Guerriere* had unexpectedly drifted within range, Captain Dacres making signal this time with one rocket and two guns. No reply. Fearing that he had fallen into the hands of Commodore Rodgers, he made haste to draw off as speedily as possible under the existing conditions.

Captain Hull no longer entertained any delusions. The British ran up their colors and gave chase, quite successfully at first since they seemed to have a bit more wind. The action began at five o'clock when the British opened fire. Hull had provided for a return of such attentions by cutting away the taffrail so that two twenty-four pound guns might fire directly aft from the spar deck in addition to the two guns he had ordered trained through the windows of his cabin. So much rake had been given to the stern that the guns fired through the stern ports could not be worked with safety and their use was given up.*

The conduct of this resourceful skipper under such apparently hopeless conditions has been dramatically recorded for us by a member of the crew.

"Captain Hull came aft, coolly surveyed the scene, took a match in his hand, and ordered the quarter-master to hoist the American flag. I stood within a few feet of Hull at the time. He clapped the fire to my gun, No. 1, and such a barking as sounded over the sea! It was worth hearing. No sooner had our iron dog opened his mouth in this manner, than the whole enemy opened the whole of theirs. Every one of the ships fired directly toward us. Those nearest kept up their firing for some time; but of course not a shot reached us then, at the distance we were.

"Captain Hull gave up the match to the captain of the gun, and we kept blazing away with our stern chasers. The shots we fired helped to send us ahead, out of the reach of the enemy. There was little or no wind; but we resolved to save ourselves from capture, or sink in the conflict. We soon found, however, that we made but slow work in getting ahead."†

Every detail which might assist escape was carefully attended to. Twenty-three thousand gallons of fresh water were pumped overboard. All the sails were wet down to close the texture of the canvas that it might catch every breath of air. Various combinations of sails were tried in order to secure the maximum result (see page 93). Seeing the British furl all sails on the frigate *Shannon*, which was then taken in tow by all the small boats of their entire fleet, seemed for a few minutes about to decide the action in favor of the enemy, but it suggested to Lieutenant Morris the expedient by which the *Constitution* ultimately made good her escape.

Continuing the story in the words of gun-sponger Moses Smith:

"Hull called Lieutenant Morris to him and said calmly, 'Let's lay broadside to them, Mr. Morris, and fight the whole! If they sink us, we'll go down like men!'

* Morris: *Autobiography*, page 52.
† Moses Smith: *Naval Scenes in the Last War*.

PLATE XIII

United States Frigate "Constitution" escaping from a British
Fleet, July 18, 1812

From a painting on copper by J. Font, Port Mahon, Minorca

United States Frigate "Constitution" engaging H.M.S. "Guerriere"

From a water-color by François Roux, owned by Hermann F. Clarke

"We were off Little Egg Harbour, on the New Jersey shore, at the time stretching in toward the Delaware Bay. The enemy had drawn in between us and the land, so that the prospect was they might cut us off from the Capes.

"Mr. Morris now spoke to Captain Hull: 'There is one thing, sir, I think we'd better try.'

" 'What's that?' replied Hull.

" 'Try to kedge her off,' said the lieutenant."*

The ship was floating in twenty-five fathoms of water. The launch and the first cutter were put overboard and sent ahead with a kedge, to which was secured nearly a mile of rope — every available piece of rigging or hawser from five inches upward that could be found on board. Some controversy has arisen as to the nature of this kedge, but the preponderance of evidence clearly indicates that it was an anchor, not a kind of large umbrella which could be opened.† The idea that any such contrivance could offer sufficient resistance by which to move the ship is in itself absurd.

By dropping the anchor and heaving in the hawser the *Constitution* was slowly pulled ahead. The Chief of the Bureau of Engineering, U. S. N., has recently estimated that forty horse-power was thus exerted to propel the ship. As soon as the British discovered the source of energy which was moving her they were quick to imitate. Indeed they even devised a superior method, for by attaching an anchor to each end of the hawser which was passed through a hawse pipe on each side of the bow, the crew could warp the ship ahead continuously, one anchor being carried forward while the other was holding on the bottom. All that was necessary was a periodic reversal of the capstan.‡

In spite of this the *Constitution* was not overtaken. All night long her crew labored. Not a man slept, except at his post on deck during the few minutes of his relief.

Sunday morning all the British vessels were to leeward. Both sides tacked; the one hoping to escape, the other to overtake. An American merchantman hove in sight to windward whereupon the nearest English frigate displayed the American colors as a decoy. Captain Hull immediately hoisted the Union Jack.

When the wind came by which the *Constitution* was able to make good her escape, Captain Hull resorted to another stratagem, often wrongly attributed to some Yankee merchant skipper. Being to windward, the squall struck him before it reached the Englishmen. It was powerful enough to roll the *Constitution's* huge side well over into the water. Hull immediately let all his gear go by the run, hauling up the sails by the brails and clewlines apparently in the utmost confusion as if it were impossible to carry a yard of canvas. Observing this, the enemy hastened to get everything shipshape before the gust should reach them. But no sooner had they furled their sails than Captain Hull ordered his courses and topsails set. The ship surged forward, opening the distance to the opposing frigates before they were able to comprehend what had happened. Hull was not only a naval officer — he was an experimental psychologist.

The coolness and resourcefulness with which the American commander proceeded made it possible for him to get his boats aboard even when his ship was making a speed of ten knots. No sailor would have supposed it possible. The British squadron cut all its boats adrift and after abandoning the chase spent several days cruising about to pick them up.

* Moses Smith: *Naval Scenes in the Last War.*

† *United States Naval Institute Proceedings,* May, 1927.

‡ James: *Naval History,* page 371.

A month later the *Constitution* and the *Guerriere* met again, this time without additional company to spoil their tete-à-tete. They sighted each other about two o'clock in the afternoon and soon were manoeuvering for reconnaissance and advantage. What these rousing moments meant to the officers and men of our young navy cannot be related with more interest or authority than by an eyewitness.

"'Sail ho!'

"'Where away?' inquired the lieutenant in command.

"'Two points off the larboard bow, sir!' was the reply.

"Hull had now come on deck. His first order was to a midshipman:

"'Mr. German! take the glass and go aloft. See if you can make out what she is.'

"German was soon above us, looking intently in the direction named.

"'What do you think?' asked Hull, with animation.

"'She's a great vessel, sir! Tremendous sails.'

"'Never mind,' coolly added Hull. 'You can come down, sir! Mr. Adams,' addressing another officer, 'call all hands. Make sail for her!'

"But before all hands could be called, there was a general rush on deck. The word passed like lightning from man to man; and all who could be spared, came flocking up like pigeons from a net bed. From the spar deck to the gun deck, from that to the berth deck, every man was roused and on his feet. All eyes were turned in the direction of the strange sail, and quick as thought studding-sails were out, fore and aft. The noble frigate fairly bounded over the billows, as we gave her a rap full, and spread her broad and tall wings to the gale.

"The stranger hauled his wind, and laid to for us. It was evident that he was an English man-of-war, of a large class, and all ready for action. In one of her topsails we read these words: 'NOT THE LITTLE BELT'

"We understood this to mean that the ship we were now approaching was not the *Little Belt* which had been previously attacked. But we knew that very well; and subsequent events proved that they might have saved themselves the trouble of telling us of it. We saw it was the vessel we wanted to meet, not the *Little Belt*, but the big *Guerriere*, of thirty-nine guns.

"As we came up she began to fire. They were evidently trying to rake us. But we continued on our course, tacking and half-tacking, taking good care to avoid being raked. We came so near on one tack, that an eighteen-pound shot came through us under the larboard knight-head, striking just abaft the breech of the gun to which I belonged. The splinters flew in all directions; but no one was hurt. We immediately picked up the shot, and put it in the mouth of long Tom, a large gun loose on deck — and sent it home again, with our respects.

"Another stray shot hit our foremast, cutting one of the hoops in two. But the mast was not otherwise injured, and the slight damage was soon repaired.

"Hull was now all animation. He saw that the decisive moment had come. With great energy, yet calmness of manner, he passed around among the officers and men, addressing to them words of confidence and encouragement.

"'Men!' said he, 'now do your duty. Your officers cannot have entire command over you now. Each man must do all in his power for his country.' "*

Finally disgusted, Hull determined on closing with the enemy.

"Why don't you fire?" he asked.

* Moses Smith: *Naval Scenes in the Last War.*

PLATE XIV

UNITED STATES FRIGATE "CONSTITUTION" ENGAGING H.M.S. "GUERRIERE"

From a French aquatint by Gerrin, after Garneray, in the Macpherson Collection

UNITED STATES FRIGATE "CONSTITUTION" ENGAGING H.M.S. "GUERRIERE"

From a painting by Thomas Birch at the Naval Academy, Annapolis

PLATE XV

UNITED STATES FRIGATE "CONSTITUTION" ENGAGING H.M.S. "GUERRIERE"

From an engraving by Tiebout, after Birch, in the Macpherson Collection

UNITED STATES FRIGATES "CONSTITUTION" (RIGHT) AND "RARITAN" (LEFT) OFF RIO JANEIRO

Note the President Jackson figurehead. From a lithograph after a drawing by Martinet.
From the Macpherson Collection

"We can't get our guns to bear, as she now lies," was the answer.

"Never mind, my boys!" he said to the men, "you shall have her as close as you please. Sailing-master! lay her alongside!"

Just before four bells both sides opened a heavy broadside fire and with it came relief to the American crew, who up to now had impatiently held their fire at the command of the self-possessed Captain Hull. Ten minutes later the mizenmast of the *Guerriere* went over the side, which occasioned the immortal exclamation of an American gunner, "By God, we've made a brig of her! Next time we'll make her a sloop!"

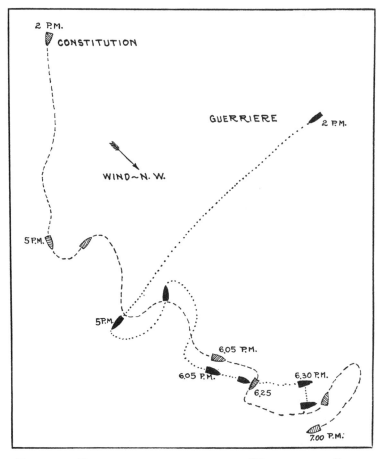

FIG. 24.   ENGAGEMENT BETWEEN THE "CONSTITUTION" AND
THE "GUERRIERE" AUGUST 19, 1812

Constitution, Capt. Isaac Hull, U. S. N.; displacement, 1576 tons; complement, 456 men; losses, 7 killed, 7 wounded; armament, 55 guns; broadside, 684 pounds.

Guerriere, Capt. James R. Dacres, R. N.; displacement, 1338 tons; complement, 272 men; losses, 15 killed, 63 wounded; armament, 49 guns; broadside, 556 pounds.

Latitude 41° 30′ north; longitude 55° 0′ west.

"As an intended insult, the English had hoisted a puncheon of molasses on their main stay, and send out word:

" 'Do give the Yankees some switchel. They will need it, when they are our prisoners.'

"But we made a very different use of this molasses from what they intended. Our shooting at hogsheads in the Chesapeake Bay, was now turned to good account. We soon tapped their sweet stuff for them, in a way which they little thought of. The Yankee shot tasted the English molasses, and not the Yankee lips. We made the decks of the *Guerriere* so slippery, that her men could hardly stand! They had more switchel prepared for them than they knew what to do with." *

With the loss of a mast the English lost the ability to manoeuver their ship, and consequently any hope of victory. The *Constitution* could now sail across her bow, firing raking broadsides which did fearful execution. So close did she sail that the enemy's jibboom fouled in the starboard rigging of her mizenmast. An attempt was made by Lieutenant Morris to lash the *Guerriere* in this disadvantageous position, but he was shot before he could accomplish it. Nor was it necessary, for as soon as the ships separated the other two masts of the Englishmen toppled over, rolling her gun deck ports almost under water. Hull then retired to inspect his ship for injuries, reeving new braces where necessary. Later, two anchor-stocks were fastened on to the foremast making it as good as new where a stray shot had done some damage. At seven o'clock he was back in the enemy's lee, prepared to continue the fight. Knowing that it was hopeless to do so, Dacres fired a gun to leeward in token of surrender. A few minutes later the prisoners had been removed to the *Constitution*, and the *Guerriere* set on fire. At a distance of about three miles Captain Hull hove to and awaited the results.

"Hundreds of eyes were stretched in that one direction, where the ill-fated *Guerriere* moved heavily on the deep. It was like waiting for the uncapping of a volcano — or the bursting up of a crater. Scarcely a word was spoken on board the *Constitution*, so breathless was the interest felt in the scene.

"The first intimation we had that the fire was at work was the discharge of the guns. One after another, as the flame advanced, they came booming towards us. Roar followed roar, flash followed flash, until the whole mass was enveloped in clouds of smoke. We could see but little of the direct progress of the work, and therefore we looked more earnestly for the explosion — not knowing how soon it might occur. Presently there was a dead silence; then followed a vibratory, shuddering motion, and streams of light, like streaks of lightning running along the sides; and the grand crash came! The quarter deck, which was immediately over the magazine, lifted in a mass, broke into fragments, and flew in every direction. The hull, parted in the center by the shock, and loaded with such masses of iron and spars, reeled, staggered, plunged forward a few feet, and sank out of sight."†

In this action there was equality neither in strength, nor seamanship, nor damage inflicted. Every initial and every subsequent advantage belonged to the *Constitution*. Here also she earned the sobriquet so often applied to her. While yet on the ways she had been criticized by English officers as "nothing but a clumsy pine box." Observing that some of the enemy's shot struck her side, and failing to penetrate, fell into the sea, a sailor shouted, "Her sides are made of iron!" Henceforth she was to be affectionately known as "Old Ironsides."

The political effect of this engagement was widespread and immediate. A great and enthusiastic banquet was held in Faneuil Hall, Boston, on September 5, in honor of the officers and crew. The victory gave a once more united front to the States, some of which (particularly Massachusetts) had so far disapproved the war as to threaten secession. It stimulated Congress to a new appreciation of the Navy. It sobered the English into a new respect for their opponents.

Much of the success of the *Constitution* was due to the excellent discipline maintained on board and to the spirit of her crew. Moses Smith, the sponger of number

* Moses Smith: *Naval Scenes in the Last War.*
† Moses Smith: *Naval Scenes in the Last War.*

one gun, already quoted, relates the following incident which took place some time prior to the opening of hostilities with England.

"An order from the lieutenant:

" 'Lay aloft there, men! Take in two reefs!'

"No quicker said than done. Every man was at his post in an instant, and the sails were in proper shape.

"My station, it will be recollected, was on the fore-top, and there I was busily employed with the rest of my gang, when an awkward shipmate next to me made a bungling piece of work of it, leaving his part of the sail somewhat loose.

" 'Who's that lubber?' cried Lieutenant Reed from below.

"No answer.

" 'Larboard fore-yard there! what awkward chap is that?'

"All silent.

"Seeing me next to him, the lieutenant then ordered me to pass his name.

"Still not a word. A sailor never informs against his shipmate.

" 'Down here, every one of you!' shouted Reed.

" 'Who was that scamp on the larboard side?' asked he of one of us, as we reached the deck.

" 'Don't know, sir,' muttered out the man.

"This was too much for the lieutenant. His wrath rose at once, and considering it as a conspiracy to defeat the discipline of the ship, he dealt alike with all. The whole gang of us took a flogging for our supper."

Another reason for her success was the constant drilling at the guns to which her crew had been subjected. Target practice was not then considered necessary by many naval officers. Captain Hull had his own ideas. During a week's delay at Annapolis, after the repairs which had been made at the Washington Navy Yard, he busied his crew with daily exercises intended to perfect the gun crews.

Among other methods he anchored a hogshead a mile off in the water and fired at it as a target. The crew soon made close work of it. After they had practised sometime, Hull gave a knowing look as he passed along —

"I'll risk you now, my boys!" said he. "If it were an enemy's boat you had there, you'd cut it all to splinters."

The next exploit of our remarkable frigate was under the command of Commodore William Bainbridge, previously referred to as Captain of the *Philadelphia*. He relieved Hull at the Boston Navy Yard on September 15, 1812, much to the dissatisfaction of the crew. They did not yet realize the incredible luck of their ship. The log records many cases of discipline — until after the action with the *Java* which took place off the coast of South America on December 29th.

Two sails were sighted to windward, one of which proved to be a large frigate

At one-thirty Commodore Bainbridge described a circle, the better to have a look at her, laying his course off-shore in order to draw away from the enemy's consort.* For two hours they sailed on parallel courses, the Englishman gradually overhauling his quarry. At noontime both ships displayed their colors, the *Constitution* hoisting the Stars and Stripes both to the main truck and the mizen peak, with a jack at the foremast truck.

At one-thirty, Commodore Bainbridge decided to close, manoeuvering in such a way that the *Java* was obliged to come smartly on to the port tack to avoid being raked. He opened the action at two o'clock by firing a broadside at the *Java* while she

---

* Later found to be an American merchantman recently captured and subsequently retaken.

was still a mile away, his tactics throughout the action being to keep out of range of the enemy's carronades until she had been sufficiently weakened by his long 24's. Three times the *Java* tried to cross the *Constitution's* bow in order to rake her. Three times "Old Ironsides" fired a broadside and came about to the other tack under cover of the smoke. The British commander, Captain Lambert, tried unsuccessfully to board his adversary, losing his foremast in the attempt. Between three o'clock and five minutes of four every mast and spar of the *Java* was shot away excepting the

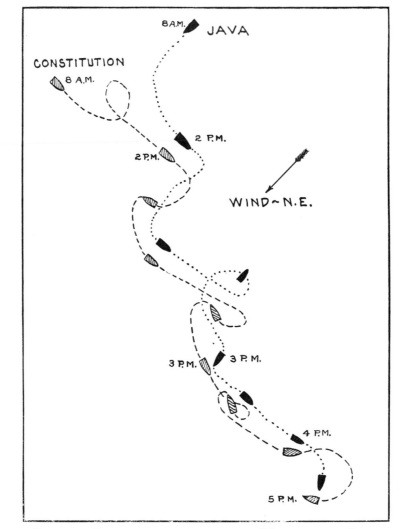

FIG. 25. ENGAGEMENT BETWEEN THE "CONSTITUTION" AND
THE "JAVA," DECEMBER 29, 1812

Constitution, Commodore William Bainbridge, U. S. N.; displacement, 1576 tons; complement, 475; losses, 12 killed, 22 wounded; broadside, 654 pounds.
Java, Captain Henry Lambert, R. N.; displacement, 1340 tons; complement, 377 or 426; losses, 48 killed, 102 wounded; broadside, 576 pounds.
Latitude 13° 6′ south; longitude 31° 0′ west.

lower mainmast and the stub of the bowsprit. In the resulting wreckage it was almost impossible to man any of the guns.

In imitation of Captain Hull's example, Commodore Bainbridge then drew away to overhaul his rigging and make any necessary temporary repairs. Three-quarters of an hour later he was back again to find what gallant efforts the *Java* had made to

PLATE XVI

UNITED STATES FRIGATE "CONSTITUTION" ENGAGING H.M.S. "JAVA." PLATE I
From an aquatint by R. and D. Havell, after N. Pocock, in the Macpherson Collection

UNITED STATES FRIGATE "CONSTITUTION" ENGAGING H.M.S. "JAVA." PLATE II
From an aquatint by R. and D. Havell, after N. Pocock, in the Macpherson Collection

PLATE XVII

United States Frigate "Constitution" Ready for Launching, May 27, 1858,
After Repairs at Portsmouth, N. H.

United States Frigate "Constitution" as she Appeared while
Serving as a Receiving Ship

This photograph was made about 1905. Courtesy of the Commandant, Navy Yard, Boston, Mass.

renew the action; a sail set on the stump of her mainmast and as many guns cleared for action as possible. This could not possibly have been more than a brave gesture. The odds were too great. She surrendered at half past five.

This action is comparable to that with the *Guerriere* in almost every respect. The *Java* was also a 38-gun frigate; she was inferior to the *Constitution* in every respect except speed; she was so badly damaged that the only possible course was to sink her. On both occasions the officers and crews treated each other with consideration, respect, and generosity as soon as the conflict had been decided, a conspicuously different attitude from that taken by many subsequent historians of both nationalities.

In Bainbridge's victory another similarity between this and the previous action cannot be over-estimated. Like Hull, he had drilled his crew incessantly at the guns. The *Java* had been at sea for six weeks during which time her men had fired but six broadsides, all blank cartridges. In the five weeks which the *Constitution* had been cruising, her gun crews had fired not only blank cartridges, but also at a target. The log of "Old Ironsides" records many such entries as "beat to quarters, exercised the men at the great guns," "drilled with musketry," "exercised the guns, blank cartridges, and afterward firing at a mark." Thus, our sailors worked automatically, yet with sufficient individuality to make impossible the crippling of a gun through the wounding of any member of its crew. This was resourcefulness and perfection, unequalled by any other navy in the world. The Americans prepared in every possible way: the English tried to meet with courage alone, the unbeatable combination of courage plus skill.

A second and less well-known escape from a superior British force occurred on April 3, 1814, under the command of Capt. Charles Stewart. While sailing from Portsmouth to Boston, two 38-gun English frigates were sighted directly to windward and less than four miles away. An action could be avoided by making for Salem harbor, but since nobody aboard was familiar with the channel between Baker's Island and the Misery, the only possible course lay around Halfway Rock and into Marblehead. There was some question as to the accomplishment of this without being first cut off. Prize goods to the amount of $10,000 were thrown overboard. Spare spars and provisions were similarly disposed of in order to lighten her. Even the casks of "spirits" were started. This final loss secured success. By noon she was safely squared away toward Marblehead and the protecting guns of Fort Sewall. The *Constitution* was thus saved, but prevented from putting to sea until the following winter when stormy weather made the British blockade ineffectual.

One more naval victory remains to be chronicled: the capture of the *Cyane* and the *Levant*. The withdrawal of the British 50-gun frigate *Newcastle* from the immediate environs of Boston harbor, in December, gave to Captain Stewart the opportunity of putting to sea for which he had waited so long. The early part of February found him off the coast of Portugal, and in spite of having learned of the peace at Ghent on at least two separate occasions, his enthusiasm for action was not in the least deterred. Both officers and men wished to repeat the successes of previous crews.

With the same peculiar presentiment by which Columbus is said to have accurately prophesied the discovery of land "within a day's sail," Stewart one morning assured his men of a fight before the following night. A sail was sighted at two o'clock the next afternoon. Soon another was seen a bit to westward of the first. Pursuit was in order.

The *Cyane* altered course to join the *Levant* and ask for instructions, Captain Douglas being the senior officer. Meanwhile the *Constitution*, with studding-sails set, had broken her main royal-mast and was delayed by the necessity of repairing the damage. At five o'clock she opened the action by firing her bow guns at the *Cyane*.

The English strategy of this part of the engagement was the deferring of action; that of the Americans, the crippling of the *Cyane* before her consort could render assistance. Neither side was completely successful in carrying out its plan. Real fighting commenced shortly after six o'clock when broadsides were exchanged at a range of 300 yards although mist and the dense smoke from the guns rendered visibility difficult. Finding himself abreast of the *Levant*, with the *Cyane* luffing up astern of him intending to deliver a raking broadside, Captain Stewart fired his guns at the former, and under cover of the resulting smoke braced his yards aback, went astern,

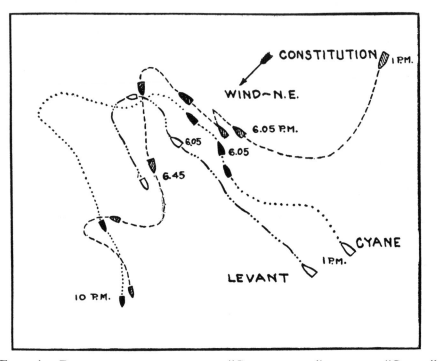

FIG. 26.   ENGAGEMENT BETWEEN THE "CONSTITUTION" AND THE "CYANE"
AND THE "LEVANT" FEBRUARY 20, 1815

Constitution, Capt. Charles Stewart, U. S. N.; displacement, 1576 tons; complement, 451 men; losses, 6 killed and 9 wounded; armament, 54 guns; broadside, 704 pounds.

Cyane, Capt. Gordon T. Falcon; complement, 180 men; armament, 34 guns; broadside, 454 pounds.

Levant, Capt. George Douglas; complement, 140 men; armament, 21; broadside, 309 pounds.

The *Cyane* and the *Levant* lost 19 killed and 42 wounded.

Latitude 30° 44′ north; longitude 14° 39′ west.

and delivered a heavy fire into the *Cyane*. Shifting his yards to fill the sails once more he then pulled ahead to fire two broadsides at the stern of the *Levant* as she was turning to go to her companion's assistance. This was marvelous seamanship.

Realizing with what effect Stewart could attack the *Levant* in this position, Captain Falcon sailed directly between the two, allowing his senior officer to draw away in order to repair damages. Falcon then turned to port so that he might sail before the wind. Stewart took advantage of this by coming sharply about for another raking broadside at the *Cyane's* stern. When she luffed, he was directly astern of her port quarter which position gave him such an advantage that, being already badly shot to pieces, the first enemy ship surrendered.

The hull had been pierced a number of times near the water-line, five carronades had broken loose and were cavorting over the deck with the terrific destruction of a juggernaut, many of the crew were disabled, and the main- and mizenmasts were about to topple overboard.

The next hour was spent in removing all her officers to the *Constitution*, putting fifteen marines aboard the *Cyane* to guard the crew, and preparing to finish off the *Levant* which, unmindful of the surrender already accomplished, was even then seeking to renew activities against her antagonist.

At ten minutes of nine the two ships passed within fifty yards on opposite tacks. An exchange of broadsides was followed by another manoeuver across the enemy's stern by the *Constitution*, with the usual deadly results. Beginning now to suspect his position and that of the *Cyane*, Captain Douglas attempted to escape, but too late. The pursuit lasted barely thirty minutes.

With remarkable ability Captain Stewart had succeeded in fighting two ships separately, in continually raking both of them, and in avoiding being raked himself.* He had the advantage of the weather-gauge at the opening of the action, of always knowing that any ship seen in the fog and smoke was an enemy, and that either antagonist alone was inferior. His guns were also capable of outranging the enemy. His decision to close was probably predicated on the greater opportunity thus offered to subdue both ships.

This was the last and the most valiantly uproarious fight of the *Constitution*, the one argument palliating its sanction by both factions after the treaty of peace was known to have been concluded, being the assertion that there was no way of knowing whether or not the governments involved had accepted the treaty. That this was considered sound logic at the time is clear, because the treaty provided thirty days for the cessation of hostilities after the document had been signed. No odium whatever was attached to Captain Stewart's action nor to the later attempt of the British fleet to capture him at Fort Praya on March 12th.

Here, the *Constitution* lay at anchor in a light fog when three large ships were observed in the offing. Stewart was shaving at the time, but as soon as his lieutenant reported to him he ordered the anchor up. This was soon superseded by the order to cut the cable and get under way with all haste. Fifteen minutes later the ship was standing out to sea, closely followed by her two prizes, the *Cyane* and the *Levant*. Naturally this attempt to escape attracted the attention of the incoming squadron which forthwith gave chase. It proved to be the two 50-gun frigates *Leander* and *Newcastle*, built expressly to overpower the American variety, accompanied by a smaller ship of 40 guns.

The chase grew hot, so hot that it was necessary for the *Cyane* to tack away from the other two in order to escape at all. An hour later the *Levant* did the same thing. The enemy should have concentrated on the *Constitution*. Instead they altered course in a body after the *Levant*. To the fog which caused this we are indebted for the preservation of "Old Ironsides." The *Levant* was recaptured. Both the *Cyane* and the *Constitution* escaped.

While the victories of the War of 1812 were by no means confined to the *Constitution*, she "drew the first blood," and succeeding in obtaining such a large share of the successes that her name is symbolic of that struggle. Her naval triumps were all ac-

* Three hours after the action the *Constitution* was in fighting trim again.

complished in a period of twelve years, but what she did then has made her worthy of preservation for centuries.

For the next six years she was laid up, putting to sea again in 1821 for patrol work in the Mediterranean. This was monotonous, unromantic business which ended when she went out of commission at the Boston Navy Yard, July 19, 1828. The Navy had no further use for her. She was reported unseaworthy by a board of inspection and survey, which also recommended that she be broken up and sold. Oliver Wendell Holmes, then only a young law student at the Dane Law School, protested in three ringing stanzas which swept the country and which still preserve her.

On June 24, 1833, she entered the new drydock at Boston Navy Yard, the first frigate ever to be docked in the United States. President Martin Van Buren himself came to see her old captain, Isaac Hull, direct the ceremony. Josiah Barker took charge of the reconstruction which was so well performed that another twenty-five years elapsed before she had to be rebuilt.

"In December, 1848," according to President Charles W. Lyons, S. J., of Georgetown University, "the *Constitution* set out on a cruise that took her to the Mediterranean, where she cruised mostly along the Italian coast. At that time the Pope had left Rome because of troubled times, and was receiving shelter at the hands of the King of Naples.

"Captain Gwynn extended an invitation to the King of Naples and Pope Pius IV to visit the *Constitution*, then lying in the Bay of Naples. The invitation was accepted, and these dignitaries were rowed to her in a boat manned by the captains of the other warships in the harbour, of which there were many — French, Russian, English, Spanish, and American.

"This is the first and only known instance of a sovereign pontiff being on American territory — for such was the deck of 'Old Ironsides.'"

In 1858 she was hauled out at Portsmouth, N. H., and entirely renewed.

The Navy Department decided to transfer her to the Naval Academy in 1860, for instructing the midshipmen, where she was commissioned on August 1st and for a month commanded by Lieut.-Commander David D. Porter, soon to be famous in other connections.

During the Civil War she was towed from Annapolis to Newport to prevent her capture by the Confederates. There she remained as a training ship until the end of the war when she put to sea again, commanded by Commander George Dewey, afterward the Admiral at Manila Bay.

In 1878 she transported goods to LeHavre for the Paris exhibition. On the way home she ran aground but was gotten off and docked at Portsmouth, England, with the assistance of her old enemies.

Her last commission ended in December, 1881, when she paid off at New York, after which she served at Portsmouth, N. H., as the receiving ship. Here she was docked and again rebuilt in the summer of 1897. She was now one hundred years old, in observance of which a tug towed her back to Boston, her birthplace, where the entire North Atlantic fleet celebrated her arrival on September 21, 1897. The *Constitution* has never left the Boston Navy Yard since.

In 1907 extensive repairs were made on her interior and rigging, but it was deemed unsafe to dock her. New cannon were cast, the battery on the spar deck being mistakenly made exactly similar to the cannon on the gun deck. The henhouse-like structure which had covered her top sides during her days as a receiving ship was removed, new masts and spars, and a caulked deck replacing shingles and clapboards and window panes. Part of her former glory was restored for a time. She once could withstand the artillery of enemy vessels, but the microscopic organisms and the slow chemical changes which attack all things gradually destroyed her again.

At noon on June 16, 1927, flying the flags of 1812 from her stub masts, she was dry docked in exactly the same dock facing Bunker Hill Monument which she had been the first to enter almost exactly ninety-four years earlier. Every precaution was taken that she should not fall apart in the process. Over two hundred internal shores were erected. Steel cables made a truss to stiffen her bow and stern. Special sliding cradles provided a surface for her to rest upon. Three divers made certain that all was as it should be below, because her structural condition was far worse than in 1907.

On shore, Secretary of the Navy Wilbur, half a dozen Admirals, Governor Fuller of Massachusetts, Mr. John L. Nicholson, the ninety-one year old grandson of the *Constitution's* first commanding officer, and two great granddaughters of Joshua Humphreys, her designer — Miss Letitia A. Humphreys and Miss Susan Carson — watched the rotted hull warped slowly across the sill of the dock when Naval Constructor John Lord, U. S. N., gave the command, "Stand by the winch." For the first time in the western hemisphere a rotting hulk, which had lain in the water for thirty years, was being docked. It was an occasion of patriotic significance, of technical difficulties, and of historic importance.

At a pier just down the water front lay one of our most modern cruisers with immaculate paintwork and shining brass. The U. S. S. *Memphis,* but recently returned from Europe with Col. Charles A. Lindbergh, hero of the air, afforded an excellent basis of comparison between the cruiser of the present day and that of one hundred and thirty years ago.

	Constitution	*Memphis*
Length over all	204' - 0"	555' - 6"
Beam	44' - 8"	55' - 4"
Draft	22' - 6"	14' - 3"
Speed	13½ knots	33.7 knots
Horse Power	600*	90,000
Displacement	2,200	7,500
Armor	21¼" oak	2" steel
Guns	30 long 24-pounders	12 - 6" guns
	22 - 32 lb. carronades	4 - 3" anti-aircraft
Range	1200 yds.	23,000 yds.
Complement	475	424
Launched	1797	1924

Immediately after her docking a service was held in the Old North Church from whose spire Paul Revere caught the gleam of the lantern that sent him forth on a midnight ride, and within whose walls Captain Nicholson lies buried. Here, prayer was offered in thanksgiving for the glowing memories of "Old Ironsides," and in the hope that the American nation might appreciate the spiritual significance of her rebuilding.

This time she is to be restored and fitted out exactly as she was in 1812, so far as funds, materials and exhaustive research make possible. When the work is completed about twelve per cent of the original material will still remain in her hull.

* Sail power estimated by Bureau of Steam Engineering U. S. N.

RECAPITULATION*

1794-1797	Under construction at Hartt's Shipyard, Boston.
1798	Congress votes March 27 to fit her out for sea.
1798-1801	Cruising in West Indies.
1801-1803	Laid up at New York.
1803-1806	Flagship, Mediterranean squadron, Tripolitan War.
1806-1810	Cruising in Mediterranean and West Indies.
1811-1812	Cruise to Europe. Repairs at Washington Navy Yard.
1812-1812	War with Great Britain.
1812	July 17, escapes from squadron of seven British ships.
	August 19, captures frigate *Guerriere*.
	December 29, captures frigate *Java* and five smaller vessels.
1813	Overhauled at U. S. Navy Yard, Boston.
1814	February-April, captures *Picton* and three smaller vessels.
	Escapes into Marblehead from two larger frigates.
	Blockaded at Boston for eight months.
1815	February 20, captures *Cyane* and *Levant*.
1815-1821	Laid up at U. S. Navy Yard, Boston. Repaired.
1821-1828	Flagship, Mediterranean squadron.
1828-1830	Laid up at Boston. Condemned by naval commissioners. Saved by poem of Oliver Wendell Holmes.
1833-1834	First ship to enter new dry dock at Boston, June 24, 1833. Repaired. Difficulty over figurehead representing Andrew Jackson.
1835-1838	Flagship, Mediterranean squadron.
1839-1841	Flagship, Pacific squadron.
1842-1843	Flagship, Atlantic squadron.
1844-1846	Cruise to East Indies, Pacific Ocean and Coast of Brazil.
1848-1851	Flagship, Mediterranean and African squadron; visited by Pope Pius IX.
1851-1852	Laid up at New York.
1852-1855	Flagship, Mediterranean squadron, for last time.
1855-1860	Laid up at the U. S. Navy Yard, Portsmouth, N. H., until reconditioned as a school ship.
1860-1871	School ship for midshipmen at Annapolis, Md. (and Newport, R. I., during Civil War).
1871-1875	Hauled out and rebuilt at U. S. Navy Yard, Philadelphia.
1876-1878	Training Ship at Philadelphia yard.
1878-1879	Last cruise in foreign waters. Carried to Havre, France, United States exhibits for Paris Exposition.
	Ran aground at Swanage Point, England. Salvaged with aid of English Navy.
1879	May 24, arrived home in New York.
1879-1881	Training ship for apprentice boys.
1882-1897	Laid up at the U. S. Navy Yard, Portsmouth, N. H., serving part of the time as receiving ship.
1897	October 21, arrived at Navy Yard, Boston, for celebration of her 100th birthday.

* From a compilation by Rear Admiral Elliot Snow (C.C.), U.S.N.

PLATE XVIII

UNITED STATES FRIGATE "CONSTITUTION" IN DRY DOCK
NUMBER ONE, AT THE UNITED STATES NAVY YARD,
BOSTON, JUNE, 1927

UNITED STATES FRIGATE "CONSTITUTION" JUST AFTER ENTERING DRY DOCK NUMBER ONE
AT THE BOSTON NAVY YARD, JUNE 16, 1927

Amidships can be seen the cribbing over which run the cables temporarily installed to keep the hull from falling to pieces when the dock was pumped out. Previous to docking, all possible weights were put ashore. Courtesy of the Commandant, Navy Yard, Boston, Mass.

PLATE XIX

BOW VIEW OF THE UNITED STATES FRIGATE "CONSTITUTION"
From a photograph made May 17, 1927. Courtesy of the Commandant,
Navy Yard, Boston, Mass.

VIEW OF THE STARBOARD QUARTER GALLERY OF THE UNITED STATES FRIGATE "CONSTITUTION"
From a photograph made May 17, 1927. Courtesy of the Commandant, Navy Yard, Boston, Mass.

THE UNITED STATES FRIGATE "CONSTITUTION"

|---|---|
1897-1900	Permanently on exhibition at the U. S. Navy Yard, Boston.
1900	February 14, repairs authorized by Congress. Money to be donated. Response only a few hundred dollars.
1905	Navy recommends using decaying hull for target. Popular sentiment aroused to prevent this.
1906	Congress votes $100,000 for repairs and restoration.
1907-1908	Topsides restored. New spars, etc., but vessel not docked.
1909-1925	On exhibition at the U. S. Navy Yard, Boston.
1925	March 4, Congress authorized restoration, money to be raised by popular subscription.
1925-1927	Campaign for funds. For the first time a complete set of plans of the ship are commenced.
1927	June 16, docked for complete reconstruction in same dock she was the first to enter, June 24, 1833.

It is expected that the *Constitution* will not only be able to spread her canvas and put to sea, but that she will actually do so, visiting ports on both coasts, and even on the navigable rivers, that the nation may imbibe anew the spirit and the history of the Republic in its early days. As a ship of war she is useless. As an emblem of freedom and the indomitable character of our forefathers she is invaluable.

HULL

The advantages of Humphreys's design cannot be overestimated. In every instance his balance between the conflicting claims of speed, armament, and protection was adjusted to a nicety. The lines of the hull show something of the bluff bow of the *Mayflower* period, but the fineness of the run and the shape of the midship section give her a greater beauty and better speed.

For many years a tracing at the Bureau of Construction and Repair in Washington, made from a copy by William Doughty, has been considered to be correct. The present reconstruction was begun on that assumption, but when it was found that the ship is 15″ deeper than the plan shows, and divers measuring her keel found it to be 157′-10″ long instead of the 147′ shown on the plan, the opinion that possibly the Bureau tracing is only a preliminary drawing "cribbed" from some French design,* gained weight. This explanation is made the more plausible by the fact that the scale of Mr. Humphreys's plan corresponds fairly closely to 9/32″ equals 1 foot and not to the 1/8″ equals 1 foot scale used by the Navy. It is dated 1794 and is therefore positively not a finished plan made from the mould-loft offsets. Nothing else could be absolutely correct.

The lines on Plan VIII were made by applying half-breadths lifted from the decks of the ship herself, to the sections shown on Humphreys's plan which had first been relocated to agree with the actual length of the keel. No correct set of lines is now available, but before the ship is undocked her offsets will be measured and an accurate plan made. Although inadequate for the use of a mould loft, it is believed that Plan VIII is so close to the truth that any error would not be perceptible at the scale shown.

The question of "displacement" is one which again needs explanation. The actual weight of the water displaced was 2,250 tons. This figure corresponds to the measurement used for the size of warships at the present time, but not in 1812. "Measure from the fore part of the main stem to the after part of the sternpost above the

* Humphreys himself says he followed French practice.

upper deck; take the breadth thereof at the broadest part above the main wales, one-half of which breadth shall be counted the depth; deduct from the length three-fifths of such breadth; multiplying the remainder by the breadth and the product by the depth; divide by 95: the quotient is the tonnage."*

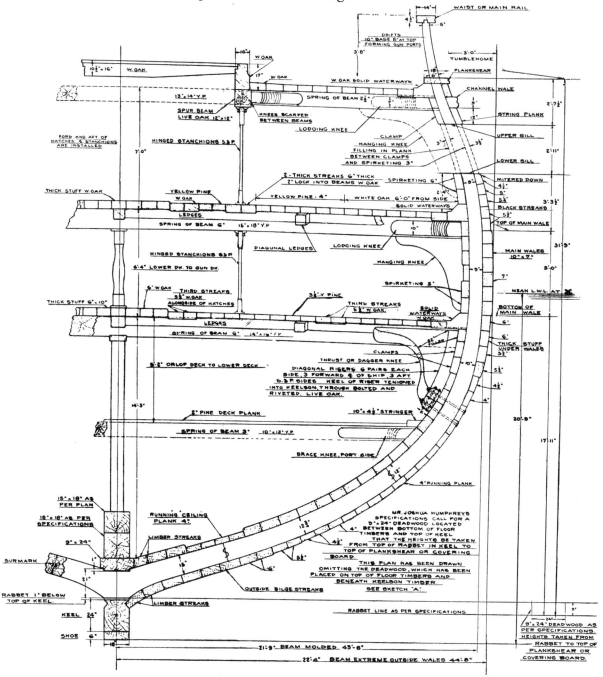

FIG. 27. MIDSHIP SECTION OF THE UNITED STATES FRIGATE "CONSTITUTION"
From a plan drawn by Lieut. John A. Lord (C.C.), U.S.N., reproduced by the courtesy of the Commandant, Navy Yard, Boston, Mass.

The whole question of the tonnage of the *Constitution*, as compared with that of her adversaries, is one which is surrounded by controversy. British authors claim that our rules gave a smaller answer than theirs; American authors claim that the English

* Quoted by Hollis: *The Frigate Constitution*, page 8. He does not give his authority.

rules produced a result fifteen per cent smaller. The discussion is really fruitless, because no such rule could possibly give a sound basis of comparison. The real criterion can be found only in the lines, namely the weight of the water displaced.

The rugged construction of the hull appears at once on studying Figure 27. This

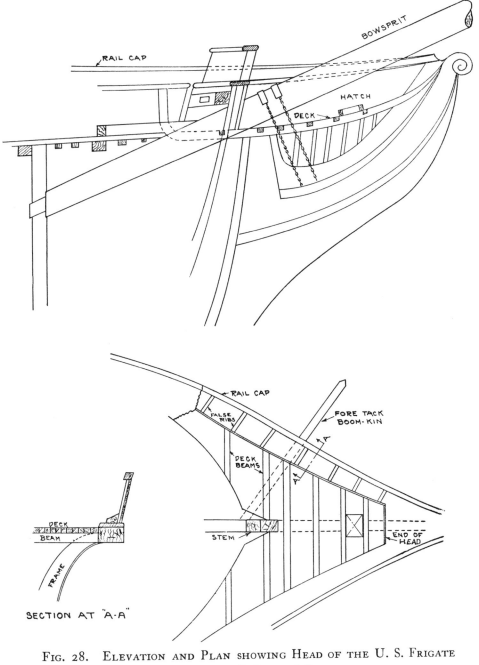

FIG. 28. ELEVATION AND PLAN SHOWING HEAD OF THE U. S. FRIGATE
"CONSTITUTION." SCALE $\frac{1}{16}''$ = 1 FT.
Reproduced by courtesy of the Commandant, Navy Yard, Boston.

plan was drawn by Lieut. John A. Lord (C. C.), U. S. N., in charge of the reconstruction, from Humphreys's specifications of 1794. It shows the oak keel, 18″ x 24″, capped by a 6″ shoe, the live oak frames 15″ thick at the keel, the heavy 15″ x 18″ yellow pine beams beneath the gun deck, the live oak knees 10″ thick, and the 7″ x 10″ oak planking at the water-line reinforced by 5″ spirketing on the inside of the frames. There is no space between the frames as on a steel ship. They form a continuous vertical section over which the outside planking is a longitudinal covering.

During the repairs made on "Old Ironsides," at the Boston Navy Yard, in 1833, "a piece of timber 9 feet long, 27 inches wide, 14 inches thick, and weighing 1,460 lbs., was removed from her. On breaking it up, in it were found 364 pounds of iron, and 163 pounds of copper. Never did ship bear a more appropriate name than 'Old Ironsides.'"

Many other details such as the small head room between the berth deck and the gun deck are apparent. Indications of the twelve diagonal live oak risers which strap the hull, three forward and three aft of the midship section on each side of the ship, can be found. An appreciation of the stiffness and strength afforded by this construction as well as by the thrust knees can be gained only from an inspection of the ship herself.

The exceptionally broad beam which Humphreys gave to his frigates increased their stability and afforded a better angle for staying the masts. In accordance with the old rule that the tumble-home be one inch per foot of moulded depth, her topsides curve inwards for a distance of thirty inches.

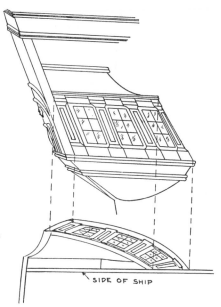

FIG. 29. QUARTER GALLERIES, U. S. FRIGATE "CONSTITUTION"

Scale 1/16" = 1 ft.

In order to provide for the crew toilet facilities which would discharge directly into the ocean, a platform was built out beyond the forward end of the spar deck, triangular in shape, and terminating at the stem. This was called the "head" and furnished the generic name for space on modern ships devoted to similar purposes. Access was had through an opening in the bulwarks on each side of the bowsprit. One of these apertures may be seen clearly in Plate XXIII. By building a curved falsework between the knuckle of the head and the bow, the objectionable flat surface found on the Santa Maria was avoided and the formation of spray in a seaway was reduced. The construction of the head, the manner in which it forms a smooth projection from the bow, and its exact location relative to the bowsprit and stem can best be understood through the medium of Fig. 28 and Plates XVIII and XIX.

More ornamental than the head, but offering a similar service to the Commodore, were the quarter-galleries. Leading directly from his cabin as they did, through the windows he was able to con the ship forward without going on deck, an advantage which must have saved him many steps.

An extraordinarily detailed and complete model of the Constitution, belonging to the Bureau of Construction and Repair, has been the source of much enlightening information during the present restoration. Its accuracy is far superior to that of the model belonging to the Peabody Museum, Salem, Mass., which was used in 1907 (see Plate XXVI). The Salem model was made by a sailor who had served aboard the Constitution. Though probably correct diagrammatically, like most such examples it is not reliable as to dimensions. Two photographs of the Bureau model will give an even more concrete form to any impressions gained from the drawings (Plates XX, XXIV).

PLATE XX

STERN VIEW OF THE BUREAU OF CONSTRUCTION AND REPAIR
MODEL OF THE UNITED STATES FRIGATE "CONSTITUTION"

Courtesy of the Commandant, Navy Yard, Boston, Mass.

STARBOARD QUARTER GALLERY AND SIDE OF THE BUREAU OF CONSTRUCTION AND REPAIR MODEL
OF THE UNITED STATES FRIGATE "CONSTITUTION"

Courtesy of the Commandant, Navy Yard, Boston, Mass.

Just forward of the mainmast is an immense hatch 40' - 5⅝" long by 14' - 0" wide (Plan X). The hatch allowed the small boats to be stowed on the gun deck during an action, removing the danger of wounds and loss of life which flying splinters would have caused had the boat stowage been struck by a shell. Of less importance, from the viewpoint of the naval officer, was the increased protection given to the boats.

Above the copper bottom, the outside hull was painted entirely black with the exception of the conventional white band between the gun ports. The ports themselves and the rail cap were black. The inside of the bulwarks was entirely white, matching the color of the deck erections. Dirty hands would soon have spoiled the appearance of the fife rails, which were consequently yellow, and the hammock berthing covering, which was consequently black.

Hull Fittings

Steering Gear

On the spar deck, just forward of the mizenmast, is the double steering wheel. In a heavy sea one man, or even two, would be entirely inadequate to hold the wheel of so large a ship. The double wheel allowing four men to work, not only provided for such contingencies, but also made double the power available to lay the wheel over while in action. In this way the course could be altered much more rapidly, a vitally important factor in any battle and often so under more ordinary conditions. The tiller rope was carried on a drum between the two wheels. From here it led below to a watch tackle on each side of the long tiller, the installation differing from the standard gear of the later clippers in that the tiller was longer and a deck below, and there were two wheels instead of one (See Fig. 44).

Hawse Pipes

Two hawse pipes on each side made it easily possible to have four anchors out at once. The pipes led to the gun deck, along which the 8" diameter hawser first used, and the chain cables of later times were carried aft to be stowed in the locker amidships. Quite obviously such large ground tackle could not readily be carried way aft and around the capstan, as was done on the *Mayflower*. Instead, a special rope called a "messenger" was used. This endless rope was formed into a long loop, with many short pieces spliced to it at intervals along its entire length. A few turns were taken around the capstan with the messenger and the loop carried forward so that it lay alongside the hawser. As many of the small ropes on one part of the loop as possible were then tied to the anchor cable. The crew hove round on the capstan while some of their mates untied the "stops" or shortropes, where the hawser went through the hatch to the stowage locker below. Others made fast the "stops" to the forward end of the cable as it came through the hawse pipe. The messenger went round and round endlessly until the anchor was hauled up and catted.

Figurehead

The original figurehead of the *Constitution* was made by Skillings Brothers and represented Hercules, the emblem of strength. This was ruined by a shot during the siege of Tripoli and replaced by a figure of Neptune which in turn gave way to a plain billet called a fiddle head by reason of its resemblance to the end of a violin. During the reconstruction of 1833, Captain Jesse D. Elliott, Commandant of the Boston Navy Yard, roused great opposition by insisting on replacing the billet with a figure of Andrew Jackson, President of the United States. The objection of the then Republican city of Boston was not shared by the Navy Department which readily approved Captain Elliott's suggestion. Handbills, newspaper threats, and anonymous letters did not deter the Commandant in the least. The figurehead was made, installed, and a marine guard posted to see that no harm befell it. As though this were not enough, the *Constitution* was moored between two lines of battleships to make undetected approach the more difficult. Yet, in spite of all these precautions, on the night of July 2, 1834, during a heavy thunder storm, the noise of which covered the sounds of his saw, Samuel W. Dewey severed the head from the body and carried it off in a bag. He accomplished this without any suspicion on the part of the nearby sentry, and successfully escaped in spite of the unexpected difficulty of having his row boat filled with water from one of the ship's scuppers.

The damage was later repaired in New York by Mr. L. S. Beecher who had made the original. For over forty years the wooden effigy of Andrew Jackson watched the bow wave of the *Constitution*, a roll of papers in his right hand, the left inserted between the edges of his coat after the most approved Napoleonic style.

At the present time there is no figurehead to seemingly support the bowsprit of "Old Ironsides," and because so many living people think of her stem as terminating with a fiddle head, or mindful of the experiences of Captain Elliott, or for whatever reasons may be more correct, the Navy Department has decided to make no change.

Hammock Stowage

Surmounting the rail cap, approximately abreast of the fore and main channels, is a projection for the stowage of the sailors' hammocks. It consists of iron fittings, which hold the network provided for the hammocks, and also support the canvas cover which served to keep the interior dry. Then, as now, canvas hammocks were useful during an action to plug holes made in the side of the ship by enemy shells. Each morning the hammocks were brought up from below, aired, and stowed.

SPARS AND RIGGING

The remark has been made that the frigates were clipper-rigged. The truth is that the clippers were frigate-rigged. Although their full lines prevented the development of the high speeds later attained by merchantmen, the frigates represented the ultimate development of the square rig.

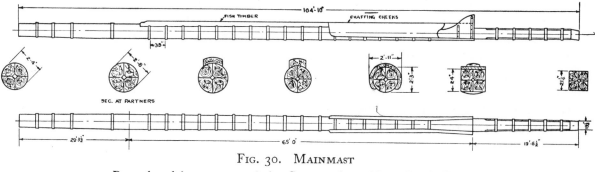

FIG. 30. MAINMAST

Reproduced by courtesy of the Commandant, Navy Yard, Boston.

Humphreys gave to his masts a greater diameter than was the standard practice. This not only enabled them to stand up under more canvas, but lessened the chances of a mast being carried away either by a direct hit or by the cutting away of the rigging. The *Constitution* was never dismasted in action.

Because the wood at the center of a tree is about twenty per cent stronger than the sapwood near the bark, the lower masts were built up from four heart sections cut from four trees. These were bound together by iron hoops, a hole in the center allowing ventilation. The fish timbers were to protect both spars and masts when the former were hoisted or lowered.

In addition to the three masts there was a spankermast, a ten inch member erected directly abaft the mizenmast and used to carry the boom, gaff, and rings for the spanker sail.

DIMENSIONS OF MASTS

	Length Over All	Diameter	Head
Foremast	94' - 0"	2' - 7"	16' - 0"
Topmast	56' - 0"	18½"	7' - 0"
Topgallant	28' - 0"	11"	
Royal	20' - 0"		
Mainmast	104' - 10"	2' - 8"	19' - 6½"
Topmast	62' - 10"	18½"	10' - 0"
Topgallant	32' - 0"	12"	
Royal	21' - 0"		
Mizenmast	81' - 0"	21½"	13' - 6"
Topmast	48' - 0"	14½"	7' - 0"
Topgallant	23' - 6"	9"	
Royal	20' - 0"		

DIMENSIONS OF SPARS

	Length Over All	Diameter	Yard Arm
Fore Yard	81' - 0"	18"	3' - 3"
Topsail	62' - 2"	12½"	5' - 3"
Topgallant	45' - 0"	9"	3' - 6"
Royal	28' - 0"	7"	1' - 2"
Main Yard	95' - 0"	22½"	4' - 0"
Topsail	70' - 6"	15½"	4' - 6"
Topgallant	46' - 0"	9¾"	4' - 0"
Royal	30' - 0"	8"	1' - 4"
Cross-Jack Yard	75' - 0"	14"	3' - 3"
Topsail	49' - 0"	9½"	4' - 0"
Topgallant	32' - 0"	7½"	2' - 6"
Royal	20' - 0"	6"	1' - 0"

Rake: foremast, $\frac{9}{16}$" per ft.; mainmast, $\frac{9}{16}$" per ft.; mizenmast, $\frac{15}{16}$" per ft.

	Length	Diameter		Length	Diameter
Bowsprit	65' - 4"	2' - 8¼"	Spanker mast	53' - 0"	10"
Jib-boom	49' - 0"	14"	Spanker boom	55' - 0"	15"
Flying Jib-boom	52' - 0"	12"	Spanker gaff	40' - 0"	14"
Spritsail yard	60' - 0"	14"			

At the time of writing, all the above figures, particularly those relating to diameter, had not been definitely settled. They are not, however, much at variance with the dimensions which will ultimately be adopted as final.

The lower masts and the top-masts were held together by caps and by tops. The sizable platforms built on the lower trestle-trees, called "tops," were used not only in the handling of rigging, but also as a station for riflemen during an action. It was from a top that a sharpshooter killed Lord Nelson at Trafalgar, and that Captain Lambert was mortally wounded in the action between the *Constitution* and the *Java*.

The cap served only as a strength member to hold the parts of the mast together, and incidentally provided a roller through which a stay passed to the deck below (See

Plan IX). Although apparently of rather insignificant dimensions, as compared to other parts of the vessel, the main lower-mast cap with its iron strapping, rollers, and leather collar weighed over a ton.

The function performed by the top in holding the topmast and lower-mast together was accomplished by the trestle- and cross-trees in the case of the topmast and topgallant mast. "Bolsters" reinforced the trestle-trees where they flanked the timber, and were mitered over the cross-trees to give them additional support. This

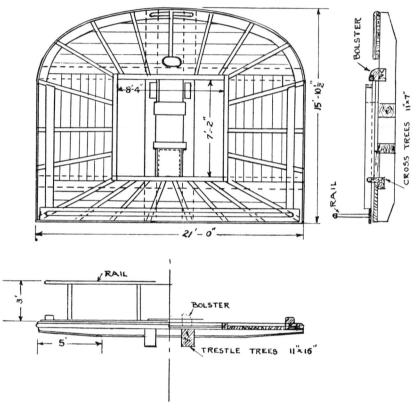

FIG. 31. MAIN TOP

strengthening assisted the cross-trees in holding the topgallant shrouds, one of which started from the top and secured just below the truck; the other two of which started just below the topsail yard and secured at the spreader above the topgallant yard.

The spritsail yard, although having outlived most of its influences as a sail-carrying spar, had not yet given way to outriggers. Its chief use was to give a purchase to the rigging of the jib-boom.

The large head sails and the pull on the bowsprit and jib-boom from the standing rigging demanded that the bobstays be heavy and the martingale well braced. In order to satisfy this requirement the *Constitution* had a double martingale boom or "dolphin striker" as it is more familiarly called.

The number of spars on the masts has probably varied at different times and is at present the subject of considerable discussion. Did she, or did she not, have skysails? The Navy says "No," in support of which Lieutenant Lord has collected much evidence. Since his decision, now approved by the Bureau of Construction and Repair, is final, there will be given here only some of the evidence which has caused many previous artists and model makers to include these spars.

The sail plan drawing by Charles Ware, in 1817, for the *Constitution*, shows sky-sails. The existing spar plan also shows them, but specifies the absolutely absurd di-ameter of 2½ inches for the skysail yards. This might be ample for a catboat — not for a frigate.

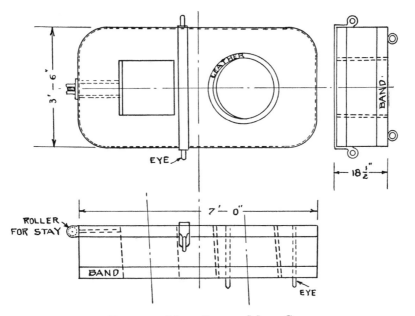

FIG. 32. MAIN LOWER-MAST CAP

Extracts from her log book quoted by contemporaneous publications in connection with Isaac Hull's escape from the British fleet refer to skysails. Saturday, July 18, 1812. . . . "The frigate astern hoisted American colors as a decoy; we immediately hoisted English colors, got royal studdingsails fitted. At 11 A.M. took in skysails."

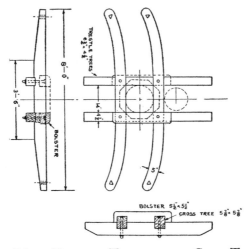

FIG. 33. MAIN TOPMAST TRESTLE- AND CROSS-TREES

Again, quoting the log for Sunday, July 19 . . . "At 2 got shifting backstays on the top-gallant mast, and set them well up; took in gaff-topsail and mizen-topgallant staysail. At ½ past 2, set the mizen-topgallant and main royal staysails and main sky-sails."*

* *Naval Monument*, page 4, Boston, 1816. (The accompanying engraving shows no skysails.) See also Roosevelt: *War of* 1812, page 87; Morris: *Autobiography*, page 54.

The parrels for the lower spars consisted of nothing but two turns of heavy hemp rope; those of the topsail, topgallant, and royal yards were wooden semi-circular crutches closed by a leather-covered rope.

The painting of the masts and spars divides itself into three parts.

   White — lower masts   *Black* — spanker boom and gaff
       mast heads   lower yards
       bowsprit   topsail yards.
       jib-boom   *Natural* — topmasts (except at heads)
       flying jib-boom   topgallant yards
       tops.   royal yards
                    all yard arms.

Booms, not found on any of the ships previously discussed, appear on the *Constitution* in connection with the working of the tacks of the foresail and the braces of the

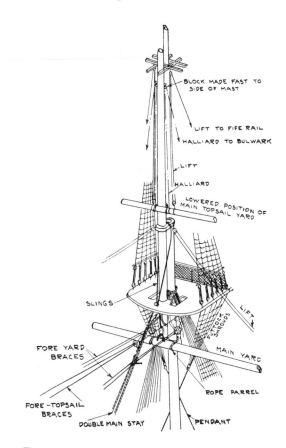

FIG. 34. DETAILS OF THE MAINMAST RIGGING

mainsail. The fore tack boomkins project on each side of the stem from below the middle of the head (See Plate XXII).

The standing rigging was made much heavier than would have been necessary for a merchantman, due to the certainty that part of it would be shot away in action. This aggravated the weakness of the channels which was a particular shortcoming of the *Constitution*. The necessity of dodging the gun ports made it difficult to give them proper bracing and many of her commanding officers complained of the weakness of these particular members.

Any looseness of the standing rigging was dangerous, since it allowed the masts to "whip" when the ship rolled and might cause their rupture. Means of taking in or

PLATE XXI

Main Top, Looking Forward, of the Model of the United States Frigate "Constitution," Built by Dr. Karl Vogel

Main Top, Looking Aft, of the Model of the United States Frigate "Constitution," Built by Dr. Karl Vogel

slacking off the hemp ropes (whose length changes with the weather) had to be provided. For this reason the futtock shrouds of the fore- and mainmasts attached to pendants leading to hearts and a lanyard at the deck (those of the mizenmast attached directly to the lower shrouds). For the same reason the main topmast and topmast preventer stays, as well as the lower mizen stays, instead of being made fast to the masts, were passed over rollers and led to the deck below where they were held by a lanyard reeved through tremendous thimbles. The main topgallant and topgallant preventer, and the mizen topmast and topgallant stays made fast to the tops in a similar way, afer passing over rollers higher up on the masts.

Sailors could quickly go aloft by means of the ratlines on the shrouds and topmast shrouds, points above the topmast cap being reached via a Jacob's ladder on the after side of the topgallant mast.

The bowsprit shrouds, four in number on each side, passed through an eye on the spritsail yard (now really nothing but an outrigger) and thence to the catheads. The first and third bowsprit shrouds could be tightened by a tackle, the second by a lanyard reeved through deadeyes, the inner shroud only by resplicing the end.

The running rigging was exceedingly complicated and difficult to master, yet so thoroughly drilled were the sailors that all sails, including the studding sails, could be set in five minutes. Topsails could be reefed in two minutes from the command "lower away to belay the topsail halliards." This performance seems incredible to us but was even beaten before the old ship went out of commission. About 1850 ships were able to send up the lower yards and topmasts and cross topgallant yards in less than five minutes. The spars swayed aloft in such an exercise weighed about fifteen tons and the sails not far from one ton.

Men were sometimes killed in drills of this sort, but not always in vain, for on accomplishing the right thing at exactly the right time depended the entire safety of the ship in battle and on many other occasions. Such skill made possible the magnificent handling of the *Constitution* in the battle with the *Cyane* and the *Levant*.

The belaying plan for all three fife rails, the port pin-rails, the cleats on the fore and main-masts, and the spider hoop on the mizen will be found on Plan X. In studying these a number of facts must be kept in mind.

The course yards were suspended from the caps by slings.

The fore and main topsail halliards were double, one part belaying to each rail. The mizen topsail halliard was single and belayed to port. The watch tackles for the topsail halliards made fast to the channels as shown on Plan X.

Halliards belaying to port: fore royal, main topgallant, mizen royal.

Halliards belaying to starboard: fore topgallant, main royal, mizen topgallant.

The ties for these halliards were made fast to the tops. The topsail halliards needed no ties as their ends were made fast to the yards from which the rope led to a block fitted on the side of the mast and down to the watch tackle hooked into the channels. To clarify the information contained on Plans IX and X, details of the main top, main yard, and main topsail yard are shown below.

Explanation of all the details pertaining to running rigging would require a text book by itself. Consequently no attention has been given here to the studding sail gear which does not differ materially from that used on the later clippers. One remaining point which should be discussed concerns the clewlines used to furl the courses. These could be hauled up either from the fife rail, or from the cleat at the base of the mast, or from both.

The hard laid hemp of the standing rigging varied in size from 1½ inches to 12 inches in circumference. Some idea of the complexity of the cordage may be had by

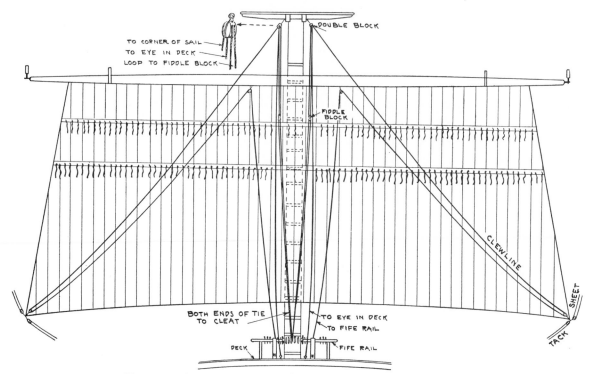

FIG. 35.   ARRANGEMENT OF CLEWLINES FOR THE COURSES

a perusal of the following extract from the table of running rigging made for the 1927 restoration.

STANDING RIGGING, HARD LAID HEMP

Item	Circumference	Item	Circumference
Mainstay	12 inches	Topmast backstays	9 inches
Forestay	12	Topmast stays	8
Pendants	9½	Topgallant backstays	5
Fore and main shrouds	9½	Topgallant stays	4
Mizen shrouds	7	Royal stays	2½

RUNNING RIGGING, SOFT LAID HEMP

Mainmast	Gross Length	Circumference
Truss tackles	260 feet	2¾ inches
Jeer fall	350	4½
Pendant tackles	1200	3¼
Lifts	470	3½
Braces	608	4
Tacks	400	4¾
Sheets	400	4¼
Clew garnets	400	3
Main bowline	120	3¼
Reef tackles	350	2½
Buntlines	530	2¾
Leechlines	432	2½
Clew jiggers	520	2
Top burtons	1060	3
Topsail tye halliards	1440	3¼
" lifts	360	4½
" braces	600	3¼

Topsail sheets	368	5
" clewlines	540	3
" bowlines	300	2¾
" buntlines	360	3
" reef tackles	476	3½
" clew jiggers	520	2¼
" lift jiggers	300	2½
" bunt jiggers	210	2½
" tacks	550	3
Topping lift	400	3
Braces	360	3
Topgallant mast rope	510	4
" lifts	270	3¼
" braces	600	2
" halliards	350	2½
" sheets	450	4
" clewlines	400	2¼
" buntlines	400	2¼
" bunt whip	180	2
" lift jiggers	240	2¼
Royal yard rope	380	3
" lifts	240	2¾
" braces	480	2¼
" sheets	380	2¾
" clewlines	400	2

MISCELLANEOUS

	Gross Length	Circumference
Best bower anchor cable	720 feet	22½ inches
Messenger	600	14
Gun breeching (each)	24	7
Outhaul tackles (each)	60	2½
Wheel rope		3
Cat falls		4½

EQUIPMENT
Sails

Because the courses were necessarily reefed in action the area of the topsails was made greater than it would otherwise have been. Furthermore they were provided with four rows of reef points instead of the three bands more customary in merchant practice. The canvas was 22 inches wide and varied in weight from the 18-ounce staysails to the 12-ounce royal. There were some thirty-odd sails in all, studding sails, jibs, staysails, spanker, and regular square sails. In detail they were:

Flying jib	Main topsail	Middle staysail
Outer jib	Main topgallant sail	Mizen topgallant staysail
Fore topgallant staysail	Main royal	Spanker
Fore topmast staysail	Main top staysail	Mizen gaff topsail
Fore sail	Middle staysail	Fore studding sail
Fore topsail	Main royal staysail	Fore topmast studding sail
Fore topgallant sail	Mizen topsail	Fore topgallant studding sail
Fore royal	Mizen topgallant sail	Main studding sail
Main staysail	Mizen royal	Main topmast studding sail
Main sail	Mizen staysail	Main topgallant studding sail

It will be seen that all spars on the fore- and mainmasts carried studding sails except the royals. There were no studding sails whatever on the mizenmast.

In order to replace spars lost either in action or a storm, a few spare members were carried on the spar deck.

Anchors

Instead of being hoisted from a yard arm, as was done aboard the *Santa Maria* and the *Mayflower*, the anchors of the *Constitution* were hoisted in from a beam called the cathead, after the capstan had drawn it to the surface of the water. The stock was made of two pieces of oak, bound together by iron bands. The remainder of the anchor was wrought iron, the total weight being 5,600 pounds.

In port the anchor could swing from the cathead but the motion of a ship under sail would very soon have torn it loose from such a position. At sea, therefore, anchors were always taken aboard and lashed to the deck, in spite of which they were sometimes washed away (see log of *Fly-ing Cloud*, page 111). On the *Constitution* the forward spar deck port was used through which to house the anchor (see Plan IX). The forward gun deck port, although here shown with a long 24-pounder protruding, usually had no gun, and was invariably used as a bridle port when anchoring the ship.

FIG. 36. ANCHOR

Capstan

Abaft the mainmast is a double capstan similar in principle and usage, but different in construction from that of the *Mayflower*. It could be worked from either or both the spar and the gun deck. The drum on the gun deck was used to hoist the anchor with the aid of a "messenger," as already described. The spar deck drum was used in connection with the heavier running rigging, and if necessary, to warp the ship alongside a dock. The capstan bars were removable, a rack for their storage being provided along the waist bulwarks on the spar deck and at some convenient place on the gun deck. A photograph of the gun deck showing the capstan will be found reproduced on Plate XXIV.

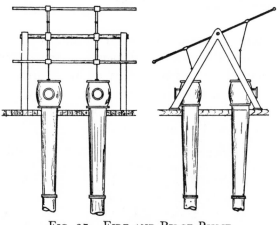

FIG. 37. FIRE AND BILGE PUMP

Pumps

Two units of fire and bilge pumps, each worked by long handles after the manner of early fire engines, flanked the mainmast: one forward, one abaft of it. These were double plunger pumps, for by installing a pair of cylinders to each pump the down-stroke of one plunger corresponded to the up-stroke of the other. Each motion

PLATE XXII

GᴜN PᴏRT ᴏN ᴛHE UNITED STATES FRIGATE "CᴏNSTITUTION"

Bᴏᴡ VIEᴡ ᴏF ᴛHE UNITED STATES FRIGATE "CᴏNSTITUTION"

From a photograph made about 1910.   Courtesy of the Commandant, Navy Yard, Boston, Mass.

PLATE XXIII

SPAR DECK OF THE UNITED STATES FRIGATE "CONSTITUTION," LOOKING FORWARD FROM ABAFT THE FOREMAST

Note the adjustable lashing securing the main topmast and the main topmast preventer stays. The double mainstay, which straddles the foremast, may be seen made fast to the bow. Attention is also called to the sheaves in the fife-rail posts and to the entrance to the "head" seen at the left. Courtesy of the Commandant, Navy Yard, Boston, Mass.

SPAR DECK OF THE UNITED STATES FRIGATE "CONSTITUTION" LOOKING FORWARD

The double steering wheel can be seen just forward of the mizenmast. In 1907 the mizen fife-rail was omitted and long 24's instead of carronades were incorrectly placed on the spar deck. Courtesy of the Commandant, Navy Yard, Boston, Mass.

of the handle pumped water from one piston or the other. The forward installation consisted of but two cylinders, the after installation (shown in Fig. 37), was double, and therefore had four cylinders.

Implements of War

For centuries the chief weapon on land or sea has been the gun. Its principal naval function has always been the same: to defeat the enemy by disabling his men and by sinking his ships.

The long 24-pounders of the *Constitution* were cast-iron, the trunions being cast of a piece with the gun. The carriage, of elm, ran on four solid wheels. Elevating the gun was accomplished by levering up the breech and sliding in a wedge called a "quoin" upon which the breech rested. Training the weapon was accomplished by

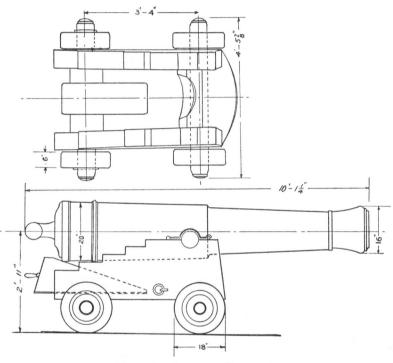

FIG. 38. LONG 24-POUNDER

revolving the carriage laboriously with a kind of crowbar. The damage to the deck planking can be imagined. The recoil was taken by a heavy rope, called a breeching, which attached to the knob of the breech, was reeved through ring bolts in the carriage, and was made fast to bolts in the ship's side. After recoil the gun was run out again by tackles.

The long gun possessed one great advantage: it could outrange the carronade, and if well operated had a chance of crippling the enemy before coming to close quarters. Crude estimates of the range could be made with the aid of a sextant, either by measuring the angle to the top of the enemy's mast, or by using the ship as a base from the two ends of which angles to the enemy at the apex of the horizontal triangle thus formed were measured simultaneously. These measurements were necessarily rough and practically all actions were fought out at close range where the exact distance was unimportant.

Long 24-pounders were very heavy, securing the maximum range possible by the use of a large bursting charge and a long barrel. The bore was nearly six inches in diameter; the length, ten feet. On a charge of six pounds of powder the range was

1200 yards at two degrees of elevation. The gun crew numbered from six to fourteen men, since under various conditions portions of the crew had to be called away to trim sails, extinguish fires, repel boarders, etc.

In order that spray or rain might be kept out of the gun-deck, shutters were provided which closed the gun-port effectively. The upper half of the shutter could be raised by a cord passing inboard through a hole above the port. The lower half could be easily pushed down from within, or drawn up again by another cord. Hooks secured the two halves in the closed position. Thus the shutters could be closed without running the guns in, as was necessary with such arrangements as that found on the *Mayflower*. Two round glass ports in the upper half of the shutter allowed the admission of light when the weather conditions made it desirable to exclude wind or water.

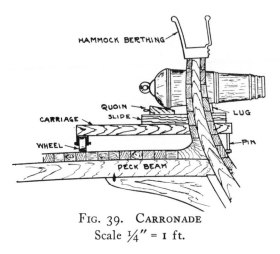

FIG. 39. CARRONADE
Scale ¼″ = 1 ft.

The carronade, so called because it was first made at Carron, Scotland, in 1774, was a much lighter gun, throwing a heavy missile for a shorter distance. It had no trunions, but was secured to a sliding piece of timber by lugs on its under side. A bolt which ran along a slot in the carriage kept this timber in place. Elevation was accomplished as with the long gun or by means of a quoin or wedge. A 32-pound carronade measured 4′ to 4′ - 8″ long with a 6½″ bore, weighed about 2,000 pounds, fired a 32-pound shot with two pounds, ten ounces of powder, and in extreme necessity could be worked by as few as two men. The range, with one degree of elevation, was 380 yards.

The advantage of the carronade lay in its lightness. This made it available for locations where a heavier gun would have been prejudicial to the stability of the ship. Since it threw a much larger projectile than a long gun of the same weight, it did correspondingly more damage at the short ranges then usual in battle.

Figure 39 is taken from a sketch made in 1835 by Naval Constructor Samuel Hartt, and now to be found in an "Inspection Return of Ordnance" made at the United States Navy Yard, New York, during September of that year.

To date, the exact dimensions of the 32-pound carronades carried by the *Constitution* have not been unearthed. Those of her sister ship, the *United States*, are known, however, and although varying from gun to gun, the table below is representative of a fair average.

Diameter of bore	6½″	Extreme diameter at breech	1′- 5¾″
Length of gun	4′ - 8″	Extreme diameter at muzzle	0′-10¼″
Length, pompellion to center of lug	2′ - 9″	Length of lug	0′- 8″

THE UNITED STATES FRIGATE "CONSTITUTION"

The carriage was a forty-five degree quadrant swinging around a pin fixed to the outside of the hull. Thus the entire strength of the frames and planking was utilized to hold the carronade in place. The bottom of the quadrant just cleared the bottom of the gun-port across which it swung by means of the two wheels at the inboard extremity of the carriage.

In action, at short ranges, rapidity of fire was the thing to be striven for since precision in aiming the piece was unnecessary. As a matter of fact, little attention was paid to aiming in any navy except our own where the gunners were clever enough to fit pieces of pipe along the barrels of the long guns through which they sighted at the enemy. Hence the greater accuracy of their fire.

The powder exploded by means of a flint-lock, but matches were always lit and kept in readiness. After the piece recoiled, it was sponged out, the sponge being in effect a rammer covered with sheepskin. A cartridge was then put in, followed by a wad. Both were rammed home until the gun captain could feel the cartridge strike against the priming wire which he was holding in the touch hole. A ball and a second wad were rammed in. Meanwhile the captain pierced the cartridge with his wire and the firing mechanism had been adjusted. The gun was now run out, all ropes being carefully laid so as to clear after the explosion came. Immediately following the recoil, the gun captain covered the vent with his thumb in order to smother the sparks, and the process was repeated. Under good conditions a round a minute could be fired.

By way of comparison the secondary battery of a modern warship can fire once every seven seconds; the sixteen-inch guns approximately once in twenty seconds until the guns become too hot to work.

Then, as now, the higher the guns were above the water the more efficiently they could be worked, especially in rough weather. With the sailing ships, a vessel sometimes heeled over so far that her lee guns could not be trained at all.

The first battery installed on the *Constitution* consisted of twenty-eight long 24-pounders on the gun-deck and ten long 12-pounders on the quarter-deck. These guns were made in England, the main-deck battery serving in 1812 against the country which had manufactured it. Preble altered the spar-deck battery, in 1804, by the addition of six 24-pounders which he used against Tripoli. This battery was the basis of her rating as a 44-gun frigate. Later 42-pound carronades were substituted, but being too heavy, Hull replaced them with 32-pound carronades.

Her battery during the War of 1812 consisted of thirty long 24-pounders on the gun-deck, sixteen 32-pound carronades on the quarter-deck, six 32-pound carronades on the forecastle, with one long 18-pounder and two long 24's in reserve as bow-chasers.

The following is a correct account of ammunition expended on board the *Constitution* in the action with the *Guerriere*:*

24-pound round shot	300	24-pound canister shot	40
32-pound round shot	236	32-pound canister shot	60
18-pound round shot	10	24-pound double lead shot	47
32-pound stand of grape	140		
24-pound stand of grape	120	Total number of shot	953

Amount of gunpowder, 2,376 pounds

Since then her battery has undergone many changes. When she went back to Annapolis, after the Civil War, she had but seventeen guns in all. In 1900 she had none.

* This memorandum was taken from the *Log Book of the Constitution*, by R. F. Dunn.

[101]

It is now proposed to correct the long 24's cast at the Boston Navy Yard and placed not only on her gun deck, but also on the spar deck in 1907, by manufacturing carronades for the upper battery.

Ammunition consisted of solid shot, shrapnel, canister, bar-shot, and chain-shot.

Beside the cannon she carried small arms for the marines, and boarding-pikes for boarding an enemy, or for discouraging any such attempt on his part. These long poles, surmounted by a bayonet-like piece of wrought iron, were placed in convenient racks where a few specially detailed members of every gun crew could reach them immediately on hearing the warning whirs of a large watchman's rattle. One of these pikes is now in the Nautical Museum at the Massachusetts Institute of Technology.

Flags

The ensign, known as the Fort McHenry Flag, was made under the direction of Commodore Barry and General Striker by Mrs. Mary Pickerskill, and is the navy ar-

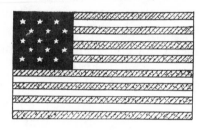

rangement of stars. The flag consisted of fifteen stars, white in a blue field, with fifteen stripes alternate red and white. The blue field rested on the fifth red stripe, and was the national flag during the War of 1812, and continued without change in design until the year 1818. The field was square, as shown, not oblong as at the present time.

Ordinarily the ensign was displayed only at the peak, as shown on Plan IX. In action and on occasions when the ship was "dressed," it was flown from all the masts.

At the mainmast was flown either the broad pennant, or the commission pennant, depending upon the circumstances. When the Commodore was aboard, the broad pennant at the mainmast truck signified his presence and marked the vessel as a flagship. Exactly the same thing is done today. The design shown below of the Jack or Broad Pennant is the type flown by ships of the United States Navy during the War

FIG. 40. ENSIGN
Scale ⅛" = 1 ft.
Size 16'-0" x 9'-6"; 4 required; one each for gaff, fore, main, and mizenmasts.
Size 4'-0" x 2'-4½"; three required for boats.
Size 2'-6" x 1'-5¾"; two required for boats.

FIG. 41. BROAD PENNANT
Scale ⅛" = 1 ft.
Size 12'-0" x 5'-0"; one required.

FIG. 42. COMMISSION PENNANT
Scale ⅛" = 1 ft.; one required

of 1812. Fifteen stars are arranged in a thirty-inch circle with a large center star for the Commodore. The width at the beginning of the swallow-tail is 3'-5" which is 7'-0" from the end.

Any vessel in commission, not a flagship, displays the Commission pennant from the mainmast. The design of this flag remains unchanged today. It is forty feet long, five and one-sixteenth inches high at the pole. The thirteen stars on a field of blue are followed by a red and a white stripe which end in a long swallow-tail.

PLATE XXIV

BUREAU OF CONSTRUCTION AND REPAIR MODEL OF THE UNITED STATES FRIGATE "CONSTITUTION"

Courtesy of the Commandant, Navy Yard, Boston, Mass.

GUN DECK OF THE UNITED STATES FRIGATE "CONSTITUTION," LOOKING FORWARD

At the right may be seen the lower part of the capstan and the handles of the pumps.

From a photograph made March 8, 1925

PLATE XXV

Model of the United States Frigate "Constitution," Built by Dr. Karl Vogel

THE UNITED STATES FRIGATE "CONSTITUTION"

Small Boats

Some frigates carried as many as twelve small boats, the number on men-o'-war at that time being more than those provided for merchantmen. The *Constitution* had at least four: three nested on the main hatch, one slung from the davits at the stern where it was well lashed in order to prevent it from swinging (See Plate XX). These boats were quite as large as many of the small boats used in the navy today.

The reason for placing no guns along the waist can now be appreciated, as they would interfere with getting the boats over the side.

The boats carried by the *Constitution* when first commissioned were probably: one pinnace, 24 feet long, 7 feet broad, and 2 feet 8 inches deep; one long boat, 33 feet long, 9 feet broad, and 4 feet deep; one jolly boat, 22 feet long, 6 feet 6 inches broad, and 2 feet 4 inches deep; one barge, 33 feet long, 7 feet broad, and 2 feet 6 inches deep.

Berthing

Staterooms for the officers were provided in the after part of the ship. Here they were near the steering wheel and therefore the center of control of the vessel. The Admiral's cabin was on the gun deck, not in the lower dampness of the berth deck.

All the crew slept in hammocks. Each man was allowed a space twenty-two inches wide by eight feet long in which to swing his hammock from the beams under the gun deck. That they remained healthy at all, sleeping near the water-line in such a dark, close, unventilated hole where the clear distance between decks was less than five feet, seems incredible. No wonder the daily sick list averaged twenty-four men.

Under present naval regulations the hammock hooks are spaced twenty inches apart, in a dry, well-lighted deck where the air is continually changed by artificial ventilation, but it is seldom that the hammocks are hung closer than every other hook.*

Commanders of the *Constitution* who were especially thoughtful of their men, allowed them to sleep on the gun deck where the ventilation was much better, due both to the greater head-room and to the large gun ports which could be opened when the weather permitted.

Something of the conditions under which the crews of the frigates must have lived may be imagined by comparing the sizes of the *Constitution* and the *Memphis*, given on page 83, with that of their crews. It should also be remembered that the *Constitution* enjoyed no canned goods, no distilled water, and no meat kept fresh by artificial refrigeration.

Food

The ration fixed by Congress, in 1801, for each man left nothing to the imagination of the cook, and prohibited the enlistment of orthodox Hebrews.

Sunday — 1¼ pounds beef, 14 ounces bread, ½ pound flour, ¼ pound suet, ½ pint spirits.

Monday — 1 pound pork, 14 ounces bread, ½ pint peas, ½ pint spirits.

Tuesday — 1 pound beef, 14 ounces bread, 2 ounces cheese, ½ pint spirits.

Wednesday — 1 pound pork, 14 ounces bread, ½ pint rice†, ½ pint spirits.

Thursday — 1¼ pounds beef, 14 ounces bread, ½ pound flour, ¼ pound suet, ½ pint spirits.

Friday — 14 ounces bread, ½ pint rice, 4 ounces cheese, 2 ounces butter, ½ pint molasses, ½ pint spirits.

* *General Specifications, United States Navy*, 1917.
† Not specified whether cooked or uncooked.

Saturday — 1 pound pork, 14 ounces bread, ½ pint peas, ½ pint vinegar, ½ pint spirits.

The two standbys were the bread and the spirits, butter being an obvious luxury. The amount of whiskey for six months has been estimated by Ira Hollis as fully one hundred barrels.*

Modern vessels are equipped with evaporators which turn great quantities of salt water into fresh, by a process of distillation. The *Constitution* had no such apparatus, but her tanks had a capacity of 48,600 gallons.

The frigates necessarily remained at sea for long and uncertain periods. For this reason space was allotted in the hold for the stowage of six months' provisions, one-half the period anticipated by both Columbus and the Pilgrim Fathers.

OPERATION

The function of a warship is to meet and to destroy enemy merchant shipping and war vessels of equal or inferior strength. The three most important elements of a man-o'-war are speed, armament, and protection. No one vessel can be superior in all three. More or larger guns mean less displacement available for propulsion and armor; heavier protection means fewer guns and less speed. The frigate emphasized the speed element at the expense of artillery and protection just as the modern cruiser does. A clever designer, such as Joshua Humphreys, comes nearer to a realization of all three elements in one ship than is possible to the mere imitator.

The *Constitution's* superiority in guns, for a ship of her type, has already been discussed, as has the unusually heavy construction of her sides. Her superior sailing qualities now require enumeration.

She could be worked within eleven points of the wind; she steered, scudded, lay-to and rolled easily; and although not very dry in a seaway, close-hauled she beat everything she sailed with. These excellencies must not be construed as comparing her to a modern *de luxe* passenger liner, for on one trans-Atlantic voyage she rolled so heavily as to part some of her chain plates and to pitch a 24-pounder out through one of the forecastle ports.

The ballast of one hundred and forty tons originally put aboard was later reduced to seven tons with an improvement in her speed, beside the tonnage thus made available for other purposes. She then logged thirteen and one-half knots.

Frigates usually went into action under topsails, topgallant-sails, jib, and spanker. The courses and the royals were furled. In heavy weather the topgallant sails were also furled and possibly a reef taken in the topsails. The clews were stopped to the yards so that the sail would not break loose should the sheets be shot away. Tubs of water were placed in the channels as a precaution against fire. The decks were wet down and sanded to prevent the men from slipping in the pools of blood.

The procedure for single ships discovering an enemy, expressed in brief, would read:

Prepare for action, beat to quarters, and, if at night, stow the hammocks, and light the decks. Unship the bulkheads, clear the batteries both sides, put on the hatch-gratings and tarpaulins, open the magazine, and wet the passage, sand down the decks, light the matches, filling the tubs with fresh water for the men. Get up spare breechings and tackles, as also a sufficiency of shot, shells, grape, and wad. Rig the pumps, place shot plugs at the mainmast, sling the yards and gaffs, rack the ties and halliards aloft, stopper the topsail-sheets. Have luffs, pendant-tackles, hawsers, and fighting-

* Hollis, *The Frigate Constitution*, page 21.

PLATE XXVI

MODEL OF THE UNITED STATES FRIGATE "CONSTITUTION"

Presented to the Salem East India Marine Society, in July, 1813, by Commodore Isaac Hull, and now in the Marine Room at the Peabody Museum, Salem. It is this model to which so much importance was attached during the reconstruction of 1907.

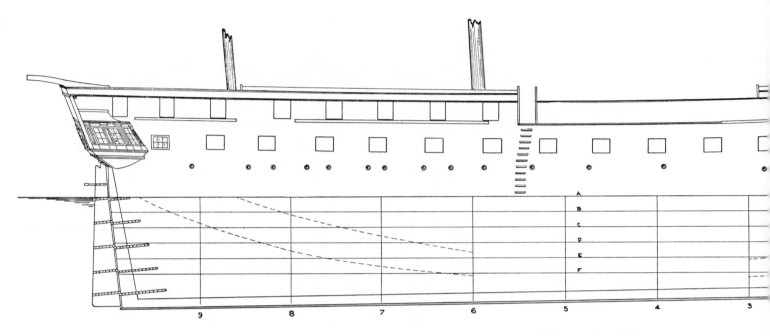

SHEER PLAN

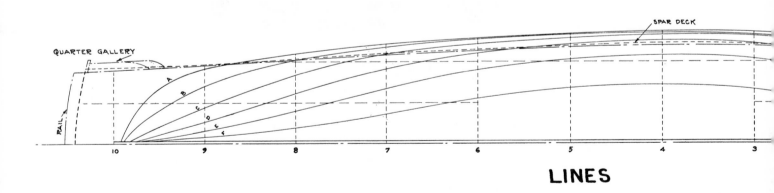

LINES

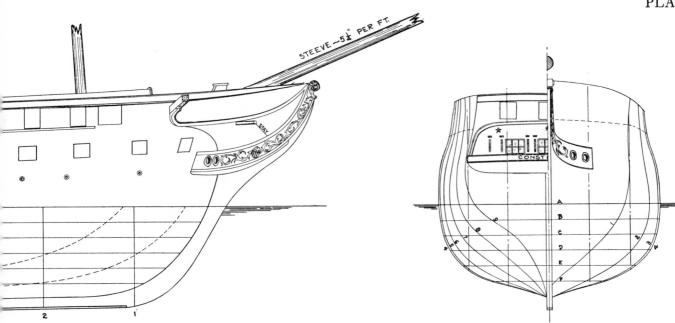

STEEVE –5¼" PER FT.

BODY PLAN

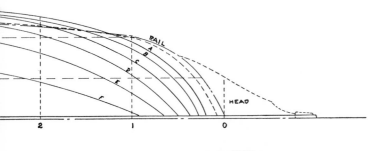

FEET

U.S. FRIGATE

"CONSTITUTION"

DRAWN FROM THE OFFICIAL PLANS FOR
THE 1927 RESTORATION LENT THROUGH THE
COURTESY OF THE COMMANDANT, NAVY YARD, BOSTON

F. Alexander Magoun

MASSACHUSETTS INSTITUTE OF TECHNOLOGY
CAMBRIDGE   MASS.

COPYRIGHT 1927 BY F.A.M.

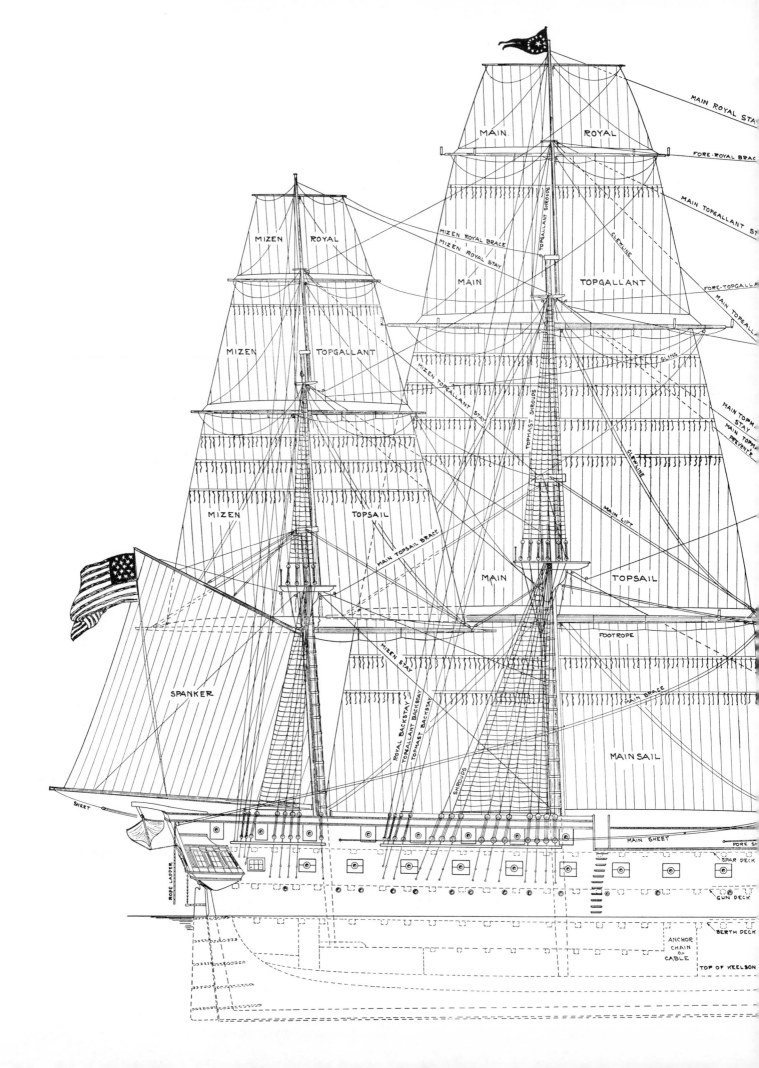

MAIN ROYAL STA

FORE-ROYAL BRAC

MAIN TOPGALLANT ST

FORE-TOPGALLA

MAIN TOPGALLA

MAIN TOPM.
STAY
MAIN TOPM.
PREVENT.

MIZEN ROYAL BRACE
MIZEN ROYAL STAY

MAIN ROYAL

MIZEN ROYAL

MAIN TOPGALLANT

CLEWLINE

MIZEN TOPGALLANT

SLING

MIZEN TOPGALLANT STAY

MIZEN TOPSAIL

TOPMAST SHROUDS

TOPGALLANT SHROUDS

TOPMAST SHROUDS

CLEWLINE

MAIN LIFT

MAIN TOPSAIL BRACE

MAIN TOPSAIL

FOOT ROPE

MIZEN STAY

MAIN BRACE

MIZEN

MAIN

SPANKER

ROYAL BACKSTAY
TOPGALLANT BACKSTAY
TOPMAST BACKSTAY

SHROUDS

MAIN SAIL

SHEET

MAIN SHEET

FORE S

SPAR DECK

ROPE LADDER

GUN DECK

BERTH DECK

ANCHOR
CHAIN
or
CABLE

TOP OF KEELSON

U.S. FRIGATE
"CONSTITUTION"

DRAWN FROM THE OFFICIAL PLANS FOR
THE 1927 RESTORATION LENT THROUGH THE
COURTESY OF THE COMMANDANT, NAVY YARD, BOSTON

F. Alexander Magoun

MASSACHUSETTS INSTITUTE OF TECHNOLOGY
CAMBRIDGE   MASS.

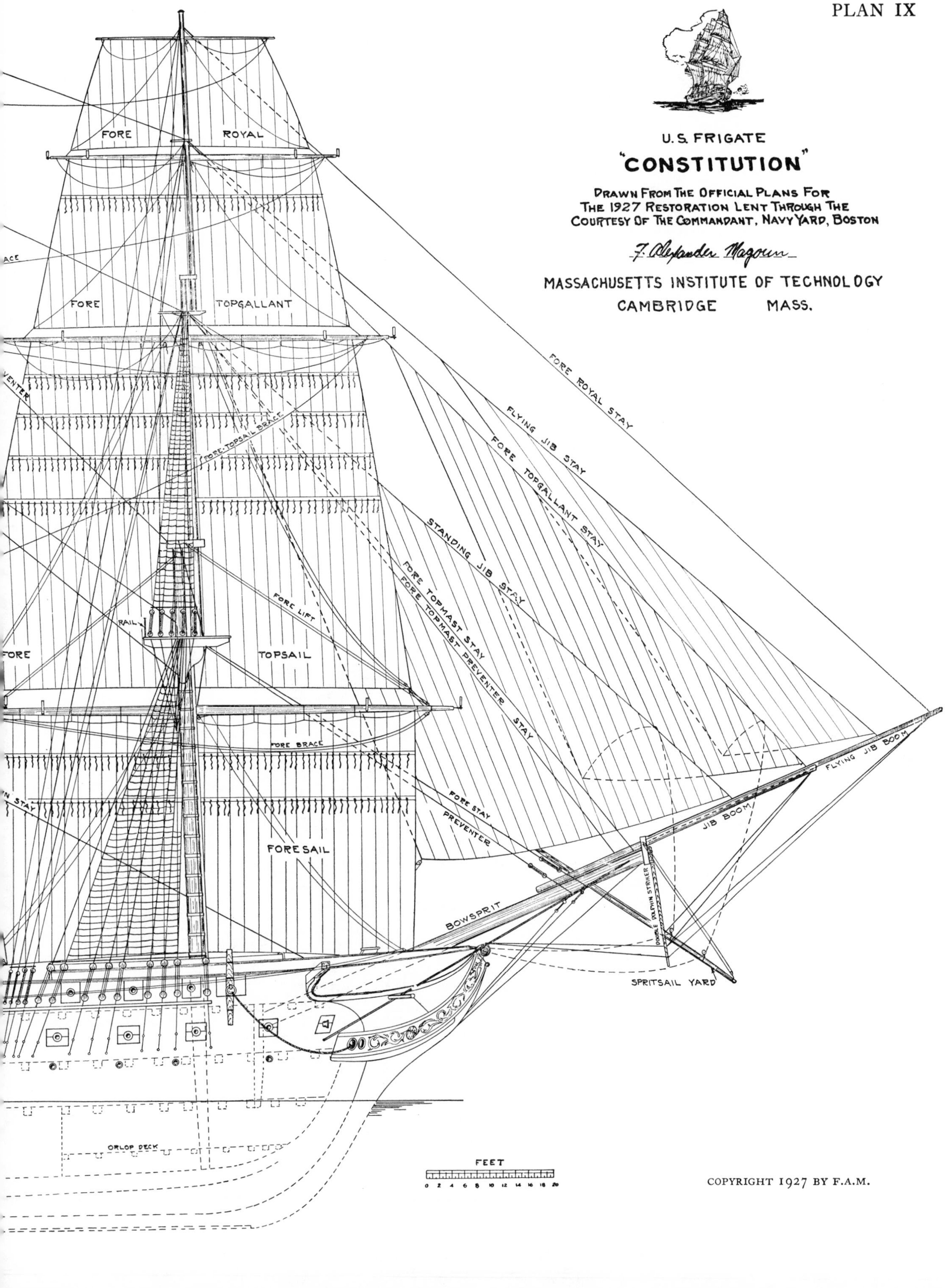

FORE   ROYAL

ACE

FORE   TOPGALLANT

VENTER

FORE TOPSAIL BRACE

FORE LIFT

RAIL

FORE

TOPSAIL

FORE BRACE

N STAY

FORESAIL

FORE ROYAL STAY

FLYING JIB STAY

FORE TOPGALLANT STAY

STANDING JIB STAY

FORE TOPMAST STAY

FORE TOPMAST PREVENTER STAY

FORE STAY
PREVENTER

BOWSPRIT

FORE DOLPHIN STRIKER

FLYING JIB BOOM

JIB BOOM

SPRITSAIL YARD

ORLOP DECK

FEET
0 2 4 6 8 10 12 14 16 18 20

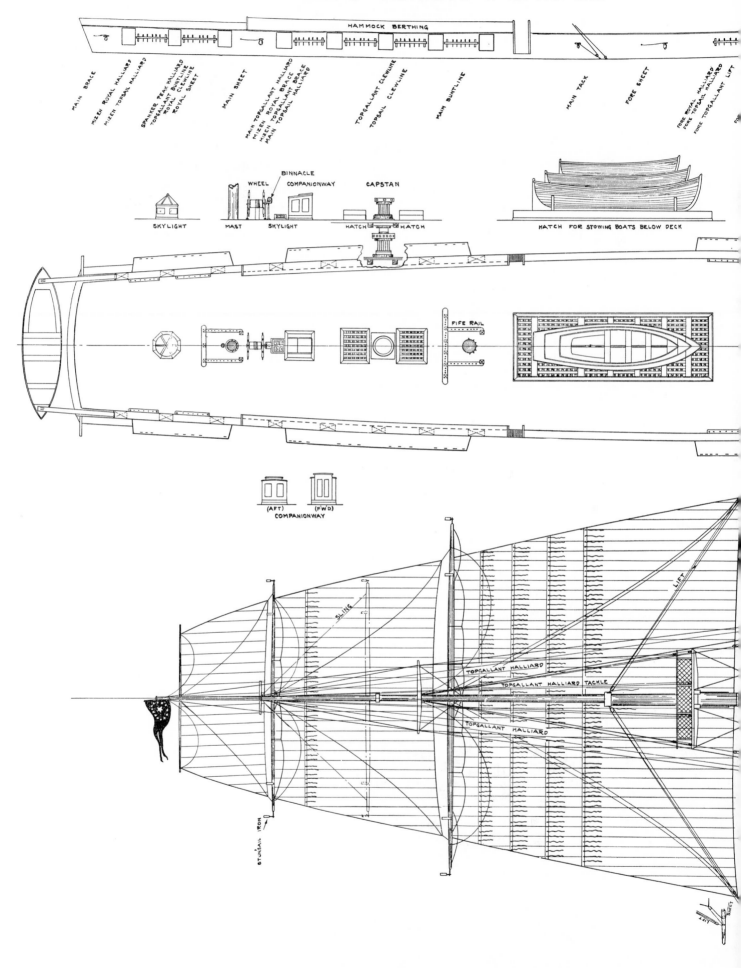

HAMMOCK BERTHING

MAIN BRACE
MIZEN ROYAL HALLIARD
MIZEN TOPSAIL HALLIARD
SPANKER PEAK HALLIARD
TOPGALLANT BUNTLINE
ROYAL CLEWLINE
ROYAL SHEET
MAIN SHEET
MAIN TOPGALLANT HALLIARD
MIZEN ROYAL BRACE
MIZEN TOPGALLANT BRACE
MAIN TOPSAIL HALLIARD
TOPGALLANT CLEWLINE
TOPSAIL CLEWLINE
MAIN BUNTLINE
MAIN TACK
FORE SHEET
FORE ROYAL HALLIARD
FORE TOPGALLANT HALLIARD
FORE TOPGALLANT LIFT

SKYLIGHT

WHEEL
BINNACLE
COMPANIONWAY
CAPSTAN

MAST   SKYLIGHT   HATCH   HATCH

HATCH FOR STOWING BOATS BELOW DECK

FIFE RAIL

(AFT)   (FW'D)
COMPANIONWAY

SLING

LIFT

TOPGALLANT HALLIARD
TOPGALLANT HALLIARD TACKLE

TOPGALLANT HALLIARD

STUNSAIL IRON

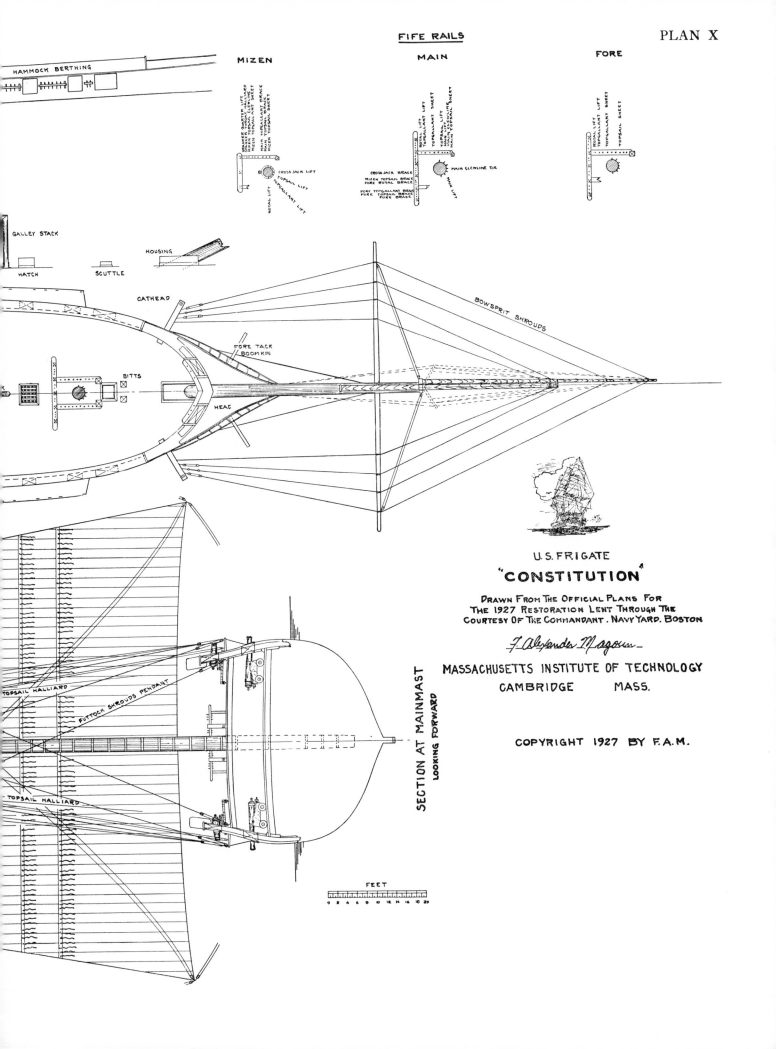

FIFE RAILS

MIZEN   MAIN   FORE

HAMMOCK BERTHING

GALLEY STACK

HATCH   SCUTTLE   HOUSING

CATHEAD

BOWSPRIT SHROUDS

FORE TACK BOOMKIN

BITTS

HEAD

SECTION AT MAINMAST
LOOKING FORWARD

TOPSAIL HALLIARD

FUTTOCK SHROUDS PENDANT

TOPSAIL HALLIARD

U.S. FRIGATE

"CONSTITUTION"

DRAWN FROM THE OFFICIAL PLANS FOR
THE 1927 RESTORATION LENT THROUGH THE
COURTESY OF THE COMMANDANT. NAVY YARD. BOSTON

F. Alexander Magoun

MASSACHUSETTS INSTITUTE OF TECHNOLOGY
CAMBRIDGE   MASS.

COPYRIGHT 1927 BY F.A.M.

FEET

jiggers, at hand, preventer-braces up and rove, men at the guns, etc., etc. A smart ship could clear for action in less than fifteen minutes.

A glimpse of service aboard the *Constitution*, under the trying and dangerous conditions of heavy weather, has been preserved for us by a member of the crew.

"A ludicrous affair occurred in the midst of the storm, which was my fortune to witness. Mr. Reed ordered one of the men who stood by to pull upon a certain rope. Just then a flash of lightning had dazzled his eyes, rendering it still more difficult to discern the nearest object. The sailor reaching for the rope, grasped the Lieutenant, through mistake, firmly by the nose! Discovering his error, he stuttered forth in confusion —

" 'I — I beg pardon, sir; it's so dark, nobody on earth can see.'

" 'Granted, my lad,' said Reed, laughing, for the accident was too ludicrous to be resented.

" 'Here's the rope,' he added, handing it himself. 'Here! here!' he shouted, as the sailor plunged at him again. 'Here it is; I've got hold of it. There, pull away.' And at it they both went.

"A hundred men or more waited the Lieutenant's bidding. The gale was at its height. All at once was head the cry — 'House top-gallant masts.'

" 'Ay, ay, sir,' echoed all around.

"Amidst the pitchy darkness, the men sprang to the shrouds. Quick as thought they were at their stations, far up in the blast. But you could not see them there. Now and then, a stream of lightning darted along the sky, bringing out all the rigging and spars in bold relief against the clouds. Then might be discerned the forms of those sea-boys, as they bent to their work, fearless and firm. Helpless indeed would men be in such a moment, without the stout heart of the sailor, to risk all for duty.

"The rigging was secured, and the masts lowered and stowed away in ten minutes or less. The ship immediately seemed relieved, and bore herself more readily through the waters."*

It was an advantage to have the wind abeam, since this tended to steady the ship and gave her a list to leeward. The leeward ship had a dual disadvantage. Her guns recoiled down hill, placing a great strain upon the breeching which sometimes parted and allowed the gun to run loose with fearful consequences. She also exposed to the enemy portions of her hull which were certain to be under water when the ship was on the other tack. The guns on the ship to windward recoiled up hill, placing less strain on the tackles. Given two vessels of equal speed, the windward ship could accept or decline battle the more easily.

Fleet actions were fought in a close-hauled line ahead; that is, the ships were arranged one behind the other, sailing as near to the direction from which the wind was blowing as possible. Hence the term "line-of-battle" ship. The Commodore who could manoeuver his fleet or the skipper who could get his ship to "cross the T," that is, in a position where his line was perpendicular to that of the enemy but in such a way that his broadside was available against the enemy's bow or stern, had a tremendous advantage. Thus all of his guns could be brought to bear from a position where practically none of the enemy's could reply. Captain Stewart's seamanship in repeatedly accomplishing this against the *Cyane* and the *Levant* will be remembered. His ship is obsolete. His tactics are still emulated.

The English people are just completing the reconstruction of the *Victory*, Lord Nelson's flagship at Trafalgar, but as Hollis has pointed out, she can never mean to

* Gunner Moses Smith: *Naval Scenes in the Last War.*

England what the *Constitution* means to us. The *Victory* was but the leader of a powerful fleet in a battle which only crowned an old kingdom's long dominion over the sea; the *Constitution*, alone, championed the cause of a newborn nation against a formidable adversary, always with honor, and always with triumph. What other ship of history has taken part in forty-two engagements, captured twenty vessels, and never suffered defeat?

V

THE CLIPPER SHIP "FLYING CLOUD"

THE construction of merchant ships is a child of the desire to trade; a desire which began to find complete expression in the United States only after the War of 1812 had come to a successful conclusion. In the years preceding that struggle both England and France, mutually at war and actuated by the dual purpose of injuring each other and of preventing our prospering merchant marine from becoming the common carrier of the world, had issued edicts forbidding any neutral nation to trade with the enemy. These decrees were vigorously enforced by the seizure and confiscation of millions of dollars worth of American shipping. The treatment had the desired effect. The adz, the hammer, and the caulking iron lay idle in our shipyards until Congress created a navy to protect our trade.

With the peace of 1814 began an era of wooden shipbuilding which was to have its climax in the white winged clippers of 1850. The perfection then attained came through an intelligent study of many poor or indifferent ships, and with the coöperation of a Congress which has since shown a conspicuous lack of ship-mindedness.

By the legislative weapon which prohibited foreign vessels from bringing to our shores cargoes from any but the country under whose flag they sailed, the exasperating obstructions presented to American enterprise by foreign laws were speedily broken down. Shipbuilding experienced a boom profoundly influenced for a time, however, by the form and rig of vessels previously built for war. The straight rise of floor from the keel toward the bilge, the small sheer, the short lower mast surmounted by an immense hoist of topsail were all typical naval practice, as were indeed the hemp rigging, the broad channels, the immense tops to the masts, and the maximum beam still only two-thirds of the length from the bow.

The immediate predecessors of the clipper ships were the famous New York-to-Liverpool packets; a fleet of dry, speedy, handsome ships which were so excellent in their appointments and so superbly handled, that their success in gaining for us a monopoly of the passenger, mail, and express traffic to Europe was as inevitable as was the envy it engendered abroad. Up to 1850 the packets were one- or two-decked vessels with a poop-deck aft and a topgallant forecastle forward. The registered tonnage of 900 to 1,000 tons afforded sufficient space for the stowage of freight in the hold, some of the lighter cargo going between decks when insufficient room below made this necessary. The steerage passengers lived in the 'tween deck space amidships, the more fortunate in the well appointed cabins aft which were lighted not only by port holes, but by deck skylights, candles, and whale-oil lamps.

In their prime, the packets offered the only regular passenger and mail service between the United States and the Continent. Rain or shine, in calm, in fog, or in a gale, one of the Black Ball liners sailed for Liverpool on the first and sixteenth of every month.

Such packets as the *James Baines* and the *Red Jacket* were able to make the run from New York in twelve or thirteen days. The secret of their great superiority in speed over the ships of other nations lay, to a large extent, in the way in which they were handled. Captains of the British East Indiamen ordered all light sails furled at sunset, no matter how fine the weather. Royals were stowed and the yards sent on deck as regularly as the sun went down. If the evening sky was lowering the top-gallant sails and the mainsail were stowed, and a single reef taken in the topsails. These precautions seemed too conservative to the Yankee skippers. From the time they cast off until the time they ran their lines ashore at their destinations the packets were driven day and night, and in all sorts of weather, to the utmost speed possible. Though decidedly the fastest ships built up to that time, much of their speed was due to the skill and energy of their commanding officers.

This was well understood at the time. Writing in 1835, De Tocqueville* said: "The European sailor navigates with prudence; he only sets sail when the weather is favorable; if an unfortunate accident befalls him, he puts into port; at night he furls a portion of his canvas; and when the whitening billows intimate the vicinity of land, he checks his way and takes an observation of the sun. But the American neglects these precautions and braves these dangers. He weighs anchor in the midst of tempestuous gales; by night and day he spreads his sheets to the winds; he repairs as he goes along such damage as his vessel may have sustained from the storm; and when he at last approaches the term of his voyage, he darts onward to the shore as if he already descried a port. The Americans are often shipwrecked, but no trader crosses the sea so rapidly. And as they perform the same distance in a shorter time, they can perform it at a cheaper rate.

" . . . I cannot better explain my meaning than by saying that the Americans affect a sort of heroism in their manner of trading. But the European merchant will always find it very difficult to imitate his American competitor, who, in adopting the system I have just described, follows not only a calculation of his gain, but an impulse of his nature."

Such were the antecedents of the clippers and their crews, ushering in the golden era which came in the early 1840's. After countless centuries upon the sea, man at last created an altogether perfect thing: magnificent, flawless, final; the ultimate development of the wooden sailing ship in construction, in speed, and in beauty. Its day was short. It was also faultless.

The evolution of the clipper ship was much accelerated by a demand for the fast transportation of teas, spices, coffee and dried fruit from the Orient, but the great stimulus came when gold was discovered in California. The resulting rush of emigration created a trade wholly unparalleled in the history of the route around Cape Horn. Provisions, furniture, clothing, tools, and hosts of enthusiastic treasure seekers clamored to be hurried to this new El Dorado.

In the year 1847-1848 only four ships cleared from Atlantic ports, bound for San Francisco. In 1849 seven hundred and seventy-five vessels made the voyage. Speed and cargo capacity were the great essentials. Each month clippers were launched which were to displace more water and to spread more canvas than ever, expressly intended to excel everything which the science of naval architecture had previously produced.

* De Tocqueville: *Democracy in America*; American translation by Reeve, page 403.

THE CLIPPER SHIP "FLYING CLOUD"

At the very climax of this development Donald McKay built the *Flying Cloud*; queen of the sea, mistress of the waves, a vessel whose excellencies have never been equalled or excelled.

McKay was *the* designer of clippers. Many other men of genius were his competitors, among them Thatcher Magoun of Mystic River fame, but no one of them approached the heights of achievement attained by the Nova Scotia boy who built his ships in East Boston.

He was born in 1810 at Shelbourne. At sixteen he began to learn his trade in the shipyards of New York. So rapid was his progress that before the age of thirty he became a master shipwright, and in 1841 was the junior partner of Currier & McKay, shipbuilders, of Newburyport, Mass. To the astonishment of everyone the vessels which this yard produced proved superior to those designed and built in New York or Baltimore. The favorable attention of shipowners followed as a corollary.

The firm of McKay & Pickett, formed in 1843 for the building of packet ships, had equal success; too much success to allow its continuance, for Enoch Train, an influential Boston merchant, soon heard of the superior mechanical ability and energetic manner of Donald McKay and persuaded him to open a yard in Boston. Newburyport is not fifty miles away, yet it was on a trip to Europe for the purpose of establishing a Liverpool office for his projected packet line, that the influential merchant first heard of the great builder of ships.

At the age of thirty-four Donald McKay opened his famous shipyard at the foot of Border Street, East Boston. Here came into being the superlative sailing ships of all time. Even their names enliven the imagination and conjure up visions which can never fail of beauty: the *Flying Cloud*, the *Lightning*, the *Stag Hound*, the *Sovereign of the Seas*, the *Westward Ho*, and the *Great Republic*.

The untiring energy of this great man produced nearly sixty ships, all of which he designed and superintended during the construction. On September 20, 1880, he set sail for that unknown port to which all flesh departs, leaving behind him achievements superior to those which have exalted many lesser men. Yet with the same colossal inability to appreciate worth which made it possible for an ignorant tenant to burn McKay's models for firewood during the recent coal strike, the City of Boston has never erected even a brass plate to his memory.

Those who know the facts visualize him not alone in terms of hollow water-lines, of towering rigging, and of rapid voyages, but also in terms of the industrial methods which he perfected. He was not only a naval architect; he was also an efficiency engineer.

Previously all frame timbers had been hewn out of the rough log with a broad axe, and timbers required to be cut lengthwise were sawed through by hand. McKay had visions of better things. He erected a steam sawmill in his yard for the performance of both these operations. The saw hung in a mechanical device by which the operator could tilt it in either direction as desired. In this way the bevel of the cut could be controlled. With the aid of this machinery three men were able to saw out the frames faster than a dozen could put them together.

Another improvement, which McKay's fertile brain introduced, seems absolutely indispensable now. A derrick made its appearance in his yard to lift the heavy timbers and beams into place; a far more rapid and less expensive method than the brute force exerted by a gang of laborers. Where men had formerly carried huge planks on their shoulders, oxen now dragged the timber to the derrick by means of which other teams exerted the force to swing the member into place.

Inevitable changes in the kind of timbers used for the building of ships took place. The accessible New England oak, which for two hundred years had supplied the ship-building industry, was running low. The demand for southern lumber increased. Where the modern shipbuilder orders steel plates and shapes of the required size, McKay made a complete set of patterns for the timber of his vessels. These were carried into the woods during the winter where a gang of men felled trees of the requisite form and number to produce every timber called for, hauled them to the rivers before the spring thaws, and loaded coasting steamers by which the trees were sent north where skillful men fashioned them into ships.

The *Flying Cloud* was originally contracted for by the merchant who persuaded McKay to come to Boston: Enoch Train. For the rest of his life he regretted that he sold her for $90,000. to Grinell, Minturn & Co. while she was still on the stocks. This New York house, after her launch on April 15, 1851, fitted her out for the California trade where flour was bringing $40.00 a barrel, sugar $4.00 a pound, boots $45.00 a pair, and laudanum $1.00 a drop. The miners could wash $100. to $1,000. worth of gold dust in a day, and what few supplies were available had to be transported from the east coast. "Easy come, easy go." Freight rates at thirty-five cents a cubic foot would have been profitable. The ship owners easily obtained a dollar a cubic foot, and even a dollar and a half. Sometimes the profit from one voyage would pay the original cost of the ship. Eleven months after she was finished the *Great Republic* had earned $200,000. Great fortunes were amassed — and lost — in the merchant ventures of those heroic days.

With high hopes of great financial return Grinell, Minturn & Co. watched the *Flying Cloud* sail out of New York harbor on her maiden voyage, June 2, 1851. Little did they realize that she was destined on this voyage to exceed by forty-two miles the fastest day's run ever made under sail or steam up to that time, and that her speed to San Francisco was to be equalled only twice; once by herself and once by the *Andrew Jackson*,* but never to be beaten by anything except a boiler and an engine.

Twenty-one days out she crossed the equator. On August 31, 1851, eighty-nine days and twenty-one hours from her New York anchorage, she was anchored in San Francisco harbor. On her fourth voyage, arriving April 20, 1854, she lowered the elapsed time by thirteen hours, a record never beaten.

The first voyage was a national triumph. It reduced by twenty-five per cent the records of two years before. For four consecutive days she had averaged 314 miles. On August 1st she logged 374 nautical miles, an average of nearly sixteen knots. In twenty-six consecutive days she sailed 5,912 miles. In order to give some conception of the heroic conduct of Capt. Josiah Perkins Creesy and his men, Arthur Clark quotes an abstract of the *Flying Cloud's* log:†

"June 6th (three days out from New York). Lost main and mizen topgallant-masts, and maintopsail yard. — June 7th. Sent up main and mizen topgallantmasts and yards. — June 8th. Sent up maintopsail yard. — June 14th. Discovered mainmast badly sprung about a foot from the hounds, and fished it. — July 11th. Very severe thunder and lightning, double reefed topsails, split fore- and maintopmast staysails. At 1 P.M. discovered mainmast had sprung, sent down royal and topgallant yards, and studding sail booms off lower and topsail yards to relieve strain. — July 13th. Let men out of irons in consequence of wanting their services, with the understanding that they would be taken care of on arriving at San Francisco. At 6 P.M.,

* 89 days, 20 hours pilot to pilot; 90 days, 12 hours anchorage to anchorage.
† Clark: *The Clipper Ship Era*, page 179.

PLATE XXVII

Photograph by Edwin Levick, New York

MODEL OF THE CLIPPER SHIP "FLYING CLOUD," BUILT BY H. E. BOUCHER MFG. CO.
FOR FREDERICK C. FLETCHER

carried away the maintopsail tye and band round mainmast. — July 31st. Fresh breezes, fine weather, all sail set. At 2 P.M. wind southeast. At 6 squally; in lower and topgallant studding sails; 7, in royals; at 2 A.M. in foretopmast studding sail. Latter part, strong gales and high sea running. Ship very wet fore and aft. Distance run this day by observation is 374 miles. During the squalls 18 knots of line was not sufficient to measure the rate of speed. Topgallantsails set. — August 3d. At 3 P.M. suspended first officer from duty, in consequence of his arrogating to himself the privilege of cutting up rigging, contrary to my orders, and long-continued neglect of duty. — August 25th. Spoke barque *Amelia Packet*, 180 days from London for San Francisco. — August 29th. Lost foretopgallant mast. — August 30th. Sent up foretopgallant mast. Night strong and squally. Six A.M. made South Farallones bearing northeast ½ east; took a pilot at 7; anchored in San Francisco harbor at 11:30 A.M. after a passage of 89 days, 21 hours."

Captain Creesy was a Marblehead boy, born in 1814. When appointed to the command of the *Flying Cloud* he had already proved his worth as a skipper in the China and the East Indies trade, exhibiting that unusual combination of qualities essential in the sea captain of that period. Beside the mastery of navigation, he possessed the physical strength to manhandle even the roughest of his rough crew. The poised, courteous manner necessary in dealing with the gentlewomen of breeding who were often on the passenger list was also expected of him. These antipodal requirements produced a remarkable type of man; robust, abrupt, dictatorial, gracious, genteel, polite.

One of the able successors of Captain Creesy was Capt. Alexander Winsor who, from the port of New York, first set sail as the commanding officer of the *Flying Cloud* on Friday, December 9, 1859. In the next three years he made two voyages in her to China, not around Cape Horn, but via London and the Cape of Good Hope. An account from his "journal," describing the near loss of the ship in a typhoon, while en route from Foochow to London, is here printed for the first time by courtesy of his grandson, Mr. Bancroft Winsor:

"Wednesday, August 8, 1860

"Begins with brisk breezes from N.E. and dark cloudy weather, standing to E.S.E. by the wind. Weather looks threatening, sent down royal yards, put double gaskets on all the furled sails and double reefs in the topsails. Barometer falling fast, typhoon coming on. At 4 P.M. passed between Pinicle and Crag Islands. Saw them both. Wind increasing and steady heavy rain. Furled the mainsail and jib at 10 P.M. close reefed the topsails, furled the foresail and mizen topsail. Now it is blowing hard and a big sea. Bar'tr 29.20 at midnight, it is blowing furiously; at daylight the wind veered E. and E.S.E. and increased, if possible. Now at 8 A.M. it is perfectly frightful. Cannot see three seas off. Wind howling in the rigging so that I cannot make a man hear me four feet off. Raining in torrents and the sea making a complete break over the ship fore and aft, deck full of water, spars and water casks adrift, lashings cannot hold them and at 8 A.M. the starboard anchor washed off of the bow. Stove out all the ring bolt and everything it was lashed to. I may safely say the ship is completely under water. I never saw anything like it before and the most lamentable part of it is that we are on a lee shore and driving almost square on about 20 or 25 miles off and utter destruction is our fate unless we can wear the ship around and that seems to me an utter impossibility, but I must make the effort. I called all hands to me and told them our situation and begged them to use their utmost strength on the braces. The ship is under two close reefed topsails and how they have stood so long is a wonder to me. We succeeded in wearing the ship safely. Now she heads up N.E. and lies four points off the land and goes ahead four knots, and makes not more than three points lee way and if our mast and sails stand we can go clear of the land. Ship makes some water but nothing alarming. Carried away main spencer gaff and lost foretopmast staysail and jibs washed off of the boom and blowed to pieces. So ends the day. Barometer 28.60

"Thursday, August 9, 1860

"The gale continues with all its force, but the barometer begins to rise a little, now 28.70. It is astonishing to me how our masts have stood as they have. At 4 P.M. it began to show signs of abating. Less rain and clouds broken. At 6 P.M. less wind but an awful sea. Decks full of water and ship laboring hard. At midnight strong breezes, high sea, but good weather. Did not make any sail till about daylight. Then wore ship and let two reefs out of the topsails and set all hands to repairing damages. At meridian made all sail. In examining the ship I find her very badly strained all over, the butts all started in the decks and waterways, plank shear, etc. and the copper a good deal broken abreast of the fore rigging. She has suffered in every part. Still I think there is but few ships that could have done so well and come out with so little damage, and not another that could have brought us off of a lee shore as she did. I feel that we all owe our lives to her superior sailing qualities and extra strength. Ninetenths of the ships in the world would be obliged to put into port for repairs after experiencing such a gale as this, but in two days our ship will be in good order again."

The crews were a motley lot. Never were they pure American stock, but invariably a queer patchwork of nationalities of whom the best were Scandinavian. Some were deep water sailors of wide experience. Some were from coasting vessels. Some were adventure seekers of no nautical experience whatsoever whose only reason for signing on was to get to California.

The officers navigated their ships by sheer force of character, often maintaining their authority over the more desperate and mutinous members of the crew with a brawny fist, a belaying pin, or even a capstan bar. The discipline of our merchantmen became, due to the self-reliance of our officers, superior to that of any other nation. Its excellence went hand in hand with the preëminent place held by that of our navy.

Good sailors received excellent treatment and were in great demand; refractory and incompetent ones were dealt with by he-man methods. There was no other way. The safety of the ship depended upon it. Under the expert, if physical tutelage of the mates, the carpenter, the cook, and the boatswain, even a green crew of rough characters soon learned to "shake a leg" when the captain issued an order. The rule, which has even in recent years been painted above the wardroom door of one of our battleships, was then very much in force: "Growl you may, but obey you must."

The crew was never quite the same on any two voyages, either in individuals or in numbers. Some general conception of its make-up may be gathered from the following table:

Captain	1
Mates	4
Boatswains	2
Carpenters	2
Sail Makers	2
Stewards	3
Cooks	2
Able Seamen	75
Boys before the mast	10
Total	101

THE CLIPPER SHIP "FLYING CLOUD"

The tedium of the rapid click, click, click of a capstan and the regular tramp around of the crew's feet as they reeled in the warp by which their ship was slowly hauled out of dock, was relieved by the rough singing of chanties, usually senseless, often obscene in their wording, but always producing in the sailor that elusive, enigmatic something which martial music creates within the soldier. Chanties were a part of the enthusiasm of the times.

> "A Yankee sloop came down the river,
> Hah, hah, rolling John,
> Oh, what do you think that sloop had in her?
> Hah, hah, rolling John,
> Monkey's hide and bullock's liver,
> Hah, hah, rolling John."

And so on in endless repetition until the line was cast off or the anchor was apeak, as the case might be. The first mate, in charge on the forecastle with the third mate and boatswain as assistants, would yell through his trumpet, "Avast heavin' there for-'ard." Or in obedience to the captain's orders issued from the quarter deck, "Lay out there some of you and loose them head sails. Aloft there my hearties and spread the royals. Hey, you in the green shirt, look alive. Ease down them clewlines handsomely or I'll have ye up before the Old Man for playing jump rope. Ease down handsomely I say. Overhaul the buntlines. Belay there. That's well. Now on the main topsail sheet, rouse her home, my bullies, rouse her home."

At sea, with all sails set, in a crisp northeasterly breeze, and the gear shipshape, the old salts undertook the education of the lubbers before the mast. "Know the longest name of any rope aboard, son? Well, I'm looking at it right now. Naw it isn't either. It's the main t'gallant st'u'n sail boom tricing line. Take a good look the next time you lay aloft and don't get caught on that question again or I'll split yer damned head open to see wher's yer brains."

The racing of rival clippers was enthusiastically watched by the inhabitants of two continents, the classic example being that of the *Ariel*, the *Taeping*, and the *Serica*. These three vessels left Foochow, China, May 30, 1866, on the same tide. So evenly were they matched that even after a race half way around the globe all three ships were docked at London on the same tide of September 6th.

Days of wooden ships and iron men; days of oak and hemp and northeast wind when sailors were hairy-chested superhumans, and ships, complex, sensitive, vagarious structures whose vanity and exasperating deviltry were sufficient grounds for their being affectionately classed as feminine gender, even without the additional impossibility of predicting, in spite of long experience, exactly what a ship would or would not do under given conditions. These were precisely the characteristics for which a true sailor loved his ship. He knew that for all her foibles she would not fail him when the waves dashed high, if only he in turn would take good care of her.

But like the beautiful coquettes of the land, the day of the clippers was short-lived. The more dependable if more homely steamships captured the affections of the merchants, although deep-water sailors had nothing but contempt for "such contraptions" and for those who stoked their furnaces.

In 1863 the *Flying Cloud* was sold to James Baines of Liverpool, England, to compete in the Australian wool trade. The combination of the Civil War and the inevitable decline which came to the California trade, did much to discourage shipping in America. But the final blow, from which the clippers could never recover, fell with the universal adoption of steam, a transition in which England took the lead and from

THE CLIPPER SHIP "FLYING CLOUD"

which she emerged once more mistress of the seas. Hampered by prejudicial laws enacted by a Congress chiefly recruited from our fertile plains, American vessels have been driven from the sea. The one exception is our coastwise trade, in which foreign-owned ships are forbidden to engage.

The *Flying Cloud*, like our merchant marine, is no more. Her last days were spent with Maskey & Co. in the unromantic business of carrying lumber from St. John to London. In 1874 she ran aground on Beacon Island bar just off the New Brunswick coast, broke in two, and was burned in June, 1875, for whatever of her metal could be salvaged.

"Sic transit gloria mundi." The *ship*, in the old sense of the term, has gone forever. In its place we have a floating power plant. The black hull of the clipper and her spread of white canvas are to be found only on the indelible pages of history. Black smoke and white steam, oil burning boilers, and the unspeakable noise of Diesel engines betoken the advance of science and the demise of romance on the seas.

How altogether human it is that the service performed by steam toward the perfection of the sailing ship is almost never alluded to. Nevertheless the appearance of steam tugs by which it was possible to get a ship in and out of her berth made it possible to design the clipper for speed and seaworthiness alone without attention to the conflicting demands of handiness in restricted waters. The result was greater size, increased lengths, and therefore more speed.

The chantey, the creak of the running rigging in the blocks, and the sing-song, colorful orders of the mate are sounds which have been replaced by the gasping noises of exhaust steam and the ringing of the engine-room telegraph. The whine of the wind in the shrouds of the clippers was the swan song of the merchant sailing ship.

HULL

In order to gain the favorable attention of merchants on the water front the clippers had to be attractive as well as swift. The *Flying Cloud* was a marvel of neatness and finish. Her lines, concave forward and aft up to a few feet above the water-plane, became gradually convex as they rose from there to the gunwale. The sharpness of the bow, however, was preserved entire, with a plain simplicity altogether beautiful.

Her stern was semi-elliptical in form and corresponded well with the after-body. Upon it appeared her name and port of hail, the name being also inscribed on each side of the bow. Even the novice cannot fail to appreciate her grace and beauty.

Plan XI was traced from what is alleged to be Donald McKay's original line drawing, now part of the Clark Collection at the Massachusetts Institute of Technology. Capt. Arthur Clark's known friendship with Mr. McKay makes this assertion entirely possible although it is the author's personal opinion that the drawing was made for the Captain from the figures given on page 77 of Henry Hall's "Report on the Shipbuilding Industry of the United States," written in 1884 for the Department of the Interior. Exactly the reverse may well be the case. In any event the lines may be taken as authentic.

The old confusion between the displacement and the tonnage rating, already discussed in connection with the *Mayflower* and the *Constitution*, is met again in the *Flying Cloud*. The method of arriving at her registered tonnage was no more sensible than any used for previous ships.

Let "L" be the distance measured on the deck from the fore part of the stem to the after part of the stern post; "B" the maximum breadth outside the planking; "D"

PLATE XXVIII

Model of the Clipper Ship "Flying Cloud," Built by H. E. Boucher Mfg. Co.
for Frederick C. Fletcher

the depth of hold from the plank of the deck to the ceiling of the hold (actually this was assumed as ½ B). The tonnage was then calculated by the formula:

$$\text{Registered tons} = \frac{(L - \tfrac{3}{5}B) \times B \times D}{95}$$

A tabulation of the hull characteristics of interest to the naval architect would include:

Length knight heads to taffrail	235' - 0"
Length on deck	225' - 0"
Length load water-line	209' - 6"
Length of keel	208' - 0"
Moulded beam	40' - 0"
Beam, extreme	40' - 8"
Depth, moulded	23' - 9"
Deadrise	30"
Tumble-home	6"
Sheer	3' - 0"
Height between decks	7' - 8"
Registered tonnage	1783
Displacement at 20' draft	2375.7
Displacement at 17'-6" draft	1951
Tons per inch immersion at 17' - 6"	13.91
Area load water-line	5660 sq. ft.
Area midship section	486.9 sq. ft.
C. of B. above base	11.23 ft.
C. of B. abaft amidships	2.15 ft.
Inertia of water-line	530467 ft⁴.
Metacentric radius	8.28 ft.
Water-line coefficient	0.682
Midship line coefficient	0.820
Block coefficient	0.515

The amount of theoretical information which the shipbuilders of 1850 had was remarkable when one considers that they had no such model tank experiments to follow as are now available. They knew that equal cargo capacity and greater speed could be obtained by increasing the beam instead of having so flat a floor. They knew that the lines of the bow could be filled in with less detriment than those of the stern. They knew that a vessel with a rising floor could go about her business when off a lee-shore, while one with a flat floor would be going bodily to leeward. They knew how to balance the conflicting claims of capacity and velocity so that the volume of cargo transported in a given year would be a maximum.

The clippers were first built with extremely sharp floors and sailed with a drag. Some of the Baltimore-built vessels drew sixteen feet aft and only eight feet forward. After 1850 the long, sharp bow was considered the best for speed, the maximum cross-section was placed half-way aft instead of two-fifths of the length from the stem, and the ships sailed on an even keel.

Nearly 1,000,000 feet of oak, and over fifty tons of copper, exclusive of sheathing, went into the hull of the *Flying Cloud*. The following excellent description of her hull was written by Duncan MacLane of the "Boston Atlas":

"Her keel is of rock maple, in three depths, sided 16 in. and moulded 44", or 37" clear of the garboards; deadrise at half-floor 30 in., rounding of sides 6 in., and sheer about 3 feet. Her bow below the planksheer is slightly concave, and at the load displacement line may be about two inches concave from a straight line. As it rises, however, the lines are gradually modified until they assume the convex, to correspond with her outline on the rail.

"At 18 feet from the apron inside, on the level of the between-decks, she is only eleven feet wide. She has the sharpest bow we ever saw on any ship. Although she is ten inches fuller on the floor than most of the other barge clippers which have been built here. She has neither head nor tail-boards, but forming the extreme, where the line of the sheer and the carved work on the naval hoods terminate, she has the full figure of an angel on the wing with a trumpet raised to her mouth. The figure is finely designed and exceedingly well executed and is a beautiful finish to the bow. It is the work of Mr. Gleason, who made the figure-head for the 'Shooting Star.'

"Her name, in gilded letters, is let into the curve of the bow, between the mouldings of the rails, and it also ornaments the quarters.

"Her great length, and boldly defined sheer, give her a splendid appearance broadside on. Her lines aft are fuller than those forward; and her stern which is elliptical, is small and neat, and is formed from the line of the planksheer. Her name and port of hail are carved and gilded upon it, surrounded by finely-designed ornamented work. In her general outline, she bears some resemblance to the 'Stag Hound,' but though her bow is somewhat sharper, she is ten inches fuller on the floor than that splendid ship.

"Her bulwarks are five feet from deck, or rather her main-rail is that height, surmounted by a monkey-rail 16 in. high. She has topgallant forecastle thirty feet long fitted for the accommodation of one watch of the crew, and carrying in after wing two W. C. Abaft the foremast is a house 41 ft. long by 18 wide by 6½ high, which contains quarters for the other watch, also the galley and other apartments. Her poop-deck is the height of the main-rail, 68 ft. long, surrounded by an open rail on turned stanchions. In the front of the poop is a small portico, which protects the entrance to the cabins, of which she has three. The first contains the pantry, and staterooms for the officers, and the second, or great cabin, is beautifully wainscoted with satinwood, mahogany, and rosewood, set off with enamelled pilasters, cornices, gilt work, etc. The panels are of satinwood, Gothic in their form, and are set in mahogany frames edged with rosewood. The after cabin is small, and is fitted in the same beautiful style. It contains two useful apartments, and is otherwise neatly arranged.

"A few particulars of the style of her construction will show that she is a very strong vessel. We have already stated that her keel is in three depths, moulded 44″, and sided 16 in.; her floor-timbers average 12″ by 17″ on the keel, and are bolted in the usual style with 1¼″ copper and iron bolts, and she has three depths of midship keelsons, which combined are moulded 45 in., and sided from 17″ to 15″, making her nearly 9 feet through her back-bone. She has also two depths of sister-keelsons, 16″ x 10″, crossbolted at right angles and diagonally through the naval timbers. Ceiling on the floor 4½″ thick, square-bolted, and on the bilge there are two keelsons, 16″ x 10″, extending the whole length of the vessel. She has also a stringer 10″ x 16″ on which the lower ends of the hanging knees rest, and all the other ceiling in the hold is 7″ thick, scarphed and square-fastened. Her lower deck beams 15″ square, and those under the upper deck amidships 9½″ x 16″. Hold stanchions are clasped with iron above and below, and are also kneed to the beams and kelson. Her ends are almost filled with long pointers and hooks, some of the pointers extending almost 40 ft. along the skin.

"Her chain lockers are in the hold abaft the foremast, and abaft the mainmast she has a large iron tank for water. The hanging and lodging knees connected with the beams of both decks are very stout and closely fastened. The between-decks waterways are 15″ square, the strake inside of them 10″ x 14″, and that over them 10″ x 16″, bolted in superior style. Under the upper deck beams she has a clamp 7″ thick; the rest of the ceiling between it and the standing strake over the waterways is 5½″

thick. She has a long and stout hook forward, and the thick work aft is carried round the stern. The stanchions are of turned oak, secured with iron rods, bolts, screws, and nuts, and the deck planking is of hard pine, 3½ in. thick. Her combings and mast-partners are well kneed off, and securely bolted.

"The upper deck waterways are 12" x 14", with two thicknesses, and the coering board is 6" x 16". Her bulwark stanchions are of oak, and between the main and rack rails there is a stout clamp, which extends both forward and aft. The main rail is 6" x 16". Her garboards are 7" thick, the next 6", the third 5", and the rest of the planking on the bottom 4½". Her wales, of which she has 18 strakes, are 5½" x 7", and she is planked up flush to the planksheer. The boarding of her bulwarks is neatly tongued and grooved, and altogether is beautifully finished. Outside she is black, — inside, pearl color.

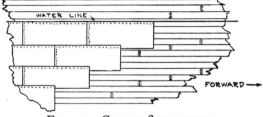

FIG. 43. COPPER SHEATHING

"Her frame is mostly superior white-oak and scantlings of southern pine; she is copper fastened. Her hood ends are bolted alternately from either side, through each other and the stem, so that the loss of her cutwater would not affect her safety or cause a leak. She is easoned with salt, has air-ports below, brass ventilators along the line of her planksheer and in the bitts, and Emerson's patent ventilators for clearing the hold. She is a full rigged ship, and her masts rake alike 1¼" to the foot.

MASTS				SPARS			
	Length	Dia.	Heads		Length	Dia.	Yd. Arms
Fore	82	35	13	Fore	70	20	4-6"
Top	46	17	9	Top	55	15	5
Topgal.	25	11		T'gal.	44	10	3
Royal	17	10		Royal	32	7	2
Skysl	13	8½	Pole 5	Skysl	22	6½	1½
Main	88	36	14	Main	82	22	6
Top	51	18	9½	Top	64	17	5
Topgal.	28	12		T'gal.	50	15	3
Royal	19	11		Royal	37	10½	2
Skysl	14½	9½	Pole 5½	Skysl	24	7	1½
Mizzen	78	26	12	Crossjack	56	16	4
Top	40	12½	8	Miztop	45	11½	4½
T'gal.	22	9		T'gal.	33	10	2¼
Royal	14	8		Royal	25	7	1½
Skysl	10	7	Pole 4	Skysl	20	6	1

Main deck to truck 200 ft. }
"   "   "   " 166 " } different authorities

"Bowsprit 26½" dia. 20 ft. outboard, jibboom 16½" dia., divided at 16 feet from the cap for inner and 13 for outer jib, with 5 ft. end; spanker boom 55 ft., gaff 40, main spencer gaff 24 ft. and other spars in proportion."

The bottom of the hull was copper sheathed to protect it from barnacles and other marine growth. In putting on sheathing the copper plates were nailed over the planking from the water-line down, beginning at the after end and working forward. Had the butt edges been forward instead of aft, the resistance to propulsion through the water would have been increased. Similarly, the longitudinal laps being up instead of down did not offer resistance to the water as it came up from under the hull.

From the sheathing to the rail-cap, the hull was painted entirely black. Some few clippers had a boot-top, as a narrow, colored stripe along the water-line is called. In tabular form the painting scheme was:

Black	*Light Blue*
Hull above sheathing	Waterways
Bowsprit	Tops of deck houses
Channels	*Natural*
White	Masts
Deck houses	Jib boom beyond bowsprit end
Rail cap and monkey rail	Yards
Inside the bulwarks	Decks
Small boats	

The usual practice was to paint the lower masts white to the tops. The *Flying Cloud* and a few other ships kept their lower masts scraped bright and varnished.*

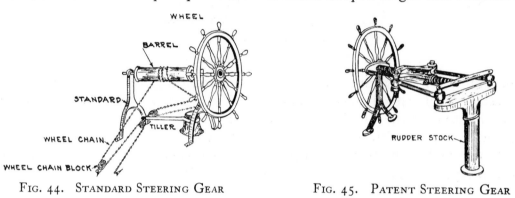

FIG. 44. STANDARD STEERING GEAR   FIG. 45. PATENT STEERING GEAR

HULL FITTINGS

Steering Gear

The standard steering gear in use at the time consisted of two tackles which were operated by a barrel attached to the wheel, and which in turn caused the tiller to be thrown from side to side. This mechanism, all except the steering wheel, was covered by a little deck house, making a very neat appearance.

But this was not the gear installed on the *Flying Cloud*. She had a patented steering gear which avoided all lost motion. The wheel turned a great screw, the two ends of which were threaded in opposite directions. Sleeves travelled on these two threads and operated a yoke on the rudder stock, one pulling, one pushing as the wheel was turned over. A ship-shape, oval cover protected the mechanism from the elements and left the deck entirely clear.

The helmsman stood on a wooden grating which offered him a surer footing besides the advantages of being dryer and warmer. Instead of the double chain which on the *Constitution* prevented the rudder from being carried away by a storm which might unship it, the *Flying Cloud* had but a single chain.

Side Lights

When Grinnell, Minturn & Co. first dispatched their famous clipper, the red light of the port side and the green to starboard had not yet come into use. It was a custom

* Fletcher Model; Henry Hall: *Report on the Shipbuilding Industry, etc.*

soon to be adopted, however. In connection with his research on this point the author was told by an old sea captain an excellent story worthy of preservation. Returning from a long voyage, a certain skipper was endeavoring to make port before complete darkness fell. He encountered an out-going vessel carrying side lights, whereupon the man on watch shouted "Tell the Captain there's a blooming drug store coming down the channel!"

The early clippers, like the packet ships, carried a white light at the bowsprit cap during the hours of darkness. An additional precaution was the flare kept in readiness in the waist for the purpose of warning passing vessels or signalling a pilot.

Hawse Pipes

One on each side led directly to the forecastle through which the anchor chain was carried to the pump-brake windlass later described under equipment. The adoption of chain anchor cables in place of hemp made little alteration in the size, location, or design of the hawse pipe itself. In spite of the many advantages of the chain, clippers occasionally were still fitted out with hemp cables.

Figurehead

Conforming with the general practice of her time, the beauty of the *Flying Cloud's* bow was increased by a figurehead. On each side of her bowsprit rose the wings of an angel, whose outstretched hands held a golden trumpet through which, if only the Creator had given life to the wood carver's image, might have sounded a reply to the wreathed horn of old Triton himself.

Bitts

In order to tie the ship up alongside a dock, a series of bitts were fitted along her deck. The heavy wooden bitts of former days were now replaced by cast-iron ones, held fast to the ship's timbers by long, wrought-iron bolts. These were much neater in appearance, less destructive to the hawsers, and easier to use than their massive predecessors.

SPARS AND RIGGING

There were many different rules laid down at various times for the proportions of the spars of merchantmen. For example — the following explicit directions are found in the "Kedge Anchor," which went through several editions in 1854:

Mainmast equal to two-and-a-half times the ship's beam.

Foremast equal to eight-ninths the mainmast.

Mizenmast equal to five-sixths of the mainmast.

Bowsprit two-thirds of the mainmast, one-third of which ought to be in-board.

Main-topmast three-fifths of the mainmast.

Main-topgallant-mast one-half of the main-topmast, exclusive of the pole, which is generally one-half the length of the topgallant-mast or a little longer.

Fore-topmast three-fifths of the foremast.

Fore-topgallant-mast one-half of the length of the fore-topmast, exclusive of the pole, which is half the length of the topgallant-mast.

Mizen-topmast three-fifths of the mizenmast.

Mizen-topgallant-mast one-half the length of the mizen-topmast, and the pole one-half the length of the topgallant-mast.

Jib-boom the length of the bowsprit, two-thirds of which length is rigged without the bowsprit-cap.

Main-yard twice the ship's extreme breadth.

Main-topsail-yard two-thirds of main-yard.

Main-topgallant-yard two-thirds of main-topsail-yard.

Fore-yard seven-eights of main-yard.

Fore-topsail-yard two-thirds of fore-yard.

Fore-topgallant-yard two-thirds of the fore-topsail-yard.

Royal-yards two-thirds the length of the respective topgallant yards.

Cross-jack-yard same length of main-topsail-yard.

Mizen-topsail-yards the same length of the main-topgallant yard.

Mizen-topgallant-yard two-thirds of mizen-topsail-yard.

Spritsail-yards five-sixths of the fore-topsail-yard. *Remarks:* Some have the spritsail-yard the length of the fore-topsail-yard, or nearly so; if it should be much shorter, the jib-sheets will chafe against the spritsail-braces.

Spanker-boom the length of the maintopsail-yard; it is however made sometimes longer, and sometimes shorter, according to fancy. Mizen-gaff two-thirds of the spanker-boom — liable to the same variation. Topsail yard-arms to be long enough to haul out close-reef-earing.

It has been customary to allow for every three feet of the mainmast's length, one inch of the diameter in the partners; nine-tenths of an inch in diameter in the middle, between the partners and the extremity of the head, and two-thirds under the hounds, and all other masts in the same proportion; and with these proportions masts have been usually made; I am, however, of opinion that one-quarter of an inch to the foot is much better.

For every four feet of their length, allow one inch of diameter in the slings, and half that diameter within the squares at the yard-arm.

Yards

The following table, a study of which will show how little Donald McKay was influenced by the rules of other men, yet how consistent in his own practice, was prepared by Mr. St. Clair Smith, Jr., and is here printed by his kind permission. Attention is called to the fact that the length of a yard-arm must be added to each end of Mr. Smith's "L" as given for the yards, in order to get the total length of the spar.

"FLYING CLOUD"

L=length in feet.   Y.A.=length of yard arms in feet.   D=diameter in inches.   M.H.=lap of the mastheads in feet.

REGISTERED TONNAGE

Flying Cloud 1782		*Flying Fish* 1505	
Staghound 1535		*Sovereign of the Seas* . 2421	

FOREMAST

	L	D	M.H.	Top	D	M.H.	T. Gal.	D	Ryl	D	Sky	D	Pole	D
Flying Cloud	82'	33"	13'	46'	16"	9'	25'	10"	17'	9"	13'	8"	7'	6"
Staghound	82'	32½"	13'	46'	16"	9'	25'	10"	17'	9"	13'	8"	7'	6"
Flying Fish	82'	33"	13'	46'	....	....	24'	.....	16'	....	12'	..	..	..
Sovereign of the Seas	89¾'	41"	16'	50'	19"	10'	27½'	14"	18'	11½"	....	..	10'	6½"

FORE YARDS

	Lower			Top			T. Gal			Royal			Skys'l		
	L	D	YA	L	D	YA	L	D	YA	L	D	YA	L	D	YA
Flying Cloud	70'	21"	4½'	55'	14"	5'	44½'	10"	3'	32'	8"	2'	22'	6"	1½'
Staghound	72'	20"	4½'	57'	15"	5'	42'	10"	3'	32'	7"	2'	24½'	6½"	1½'
Flying Fish	70'	...	....	55'	....	..	41'	....	..	32'	..	..	22'	..	..
Sovereign of the Seas	80'	22"	5'	63'	17½"	5½'	47'	14"	3½'	37'	8"	2½'	....	..	..

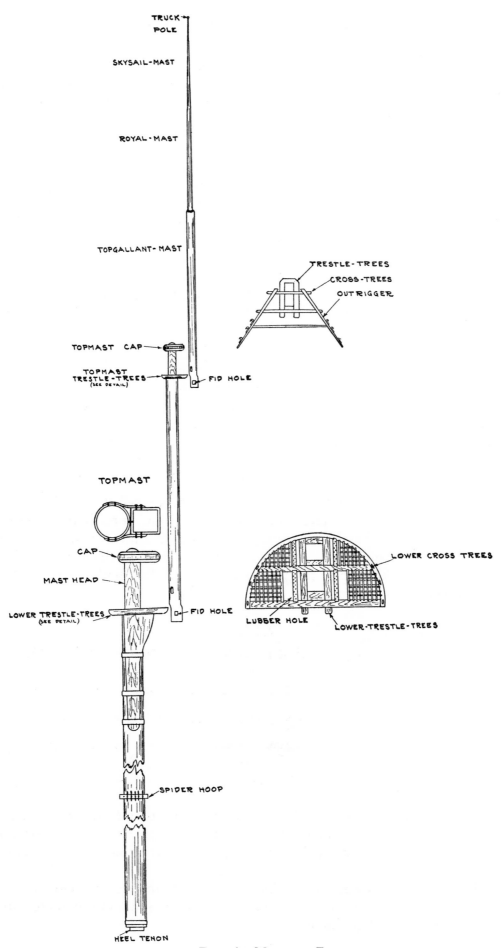

TRUCK POLE

SKYSAIL-MAST

ROYAL-MAST

TOPGALLANT-MAST

TRESTLE-TREES
CROSS-TREES
OUTRIGGER

TOPMAST CAP

TOPMAST
TRESTLE-TREES
(SEE DETAIL)

FID HOLE

TOPMAST

CAP

MAST HEAD

LOWER CROSS TREES

LOWER TRESTLE-TREES
(SEE DETAIL)

FID HOLE

LUBBER HOLE

LOWER-TRESTLE-TREES

SPIDER HOOP

HEEL TENON

FIG. 46. MAST AND FITTINGS

MAINMAST

	L	D	M.H.	Top	D	M.H.	T.Gal.	D	Ryl	D	Sky	D	Pole	D
Flying Cloud	88'	36"	14'	51'	20"	9½'	28'	12"	19'	11"	14½'	10"	10'	6"
Staghound	88'	33"	14'	51'	17½"	9½'	28'	12"	19'	11"	15'	10"	9'	6"
Flying Fish	88'	....	...	49'	....	....	27'	....	18'	....	14'	....	..	..
Sovereign of the Seas	93'	42"	17'	54'	19½"	11'	30'	15"	20'	12"	14'	10"	8'	6"

MAIN YARDS

	Lower			Top			T.Gal			Royal			Skys'l		
	L	D	YA	L	D	YA	L	D	YA	L	D	YA	L	D	YA
Flying Cloud	82'	24"	4½'	64'	16"	5'	50'	15"	3'	37'	11"	2'	24'	8"	1½'
Staghound	86'	22"	4½'	68'	17"	5'	53'	15"	3½'	42'	10½"	2½'	32'	7"	1½'
Flying Fish	80'	....	....	64'	....	..	49'	....	..	39'	....	..	31'	..	..
Sovereign of the Seas	90'	24"	5'	70'	20"	5½'	54'	15"	4'	42'	11"	3'	35'	9"	2'

MIZENMAST

	L	D	M.H.	Top	D	M.H.	T.Gal.	D	Ryl	D	Sky	D	Pole	D
Flying Cloud	78'	24"	12'	40'	12"	12'	22'	9"	14'	8"	10'	7"	6'	5"
Staghound	78'	26"	12'	40'	12½"	8'	22'	9"	16'	8"	11'	7"	6'	5"
Flying Fish	78'	....	....	38½'	....	....	21'	....	14'	....	10'	....	..	..
Sovereign of the Seas	82¾'	34"	14'	43'	16"	9'	24'	11"	17'	9½"	....	....	8'	6"

MIZEN YARDS

	Lower			Top			T.Gal			Royal			Skys'l		
	L	D	YA	L	D	YA	L	D	YA	L	D	YA	L	D	YA
Flying Cloud	56'	14"	4'	45'	11"	4½'	33'	10"	2½'	25'	7"	1½'	20'	5"	1'
Staghound	60'	16"	4'	48'	11½"	4½'	36'	10"	2½'	27'	7"	1½'	22'	6"	1'
Flying Fish	59'	....	....	44'	....	..	34'	....	..	26'	..	..	21'	..	..
Sovereign of the Seas	70'	20"	4'	56'	15"	4½'	43'	11"	3'	32'	7"	2'	....	..	..

The rake of all masts was 1¼ inch per foot. This caused the wind to lift instead of to depress the vessel. It obviated the tendency to pitch. It made the bracing of the yards more easy. The difficulty of saying with absolute authority what the spar dimensions of any of these old ships were is emphasized anew by the discrepancies found between this table and that on page 117. As a matter of fact both are possibly correct for differing periods of her career.

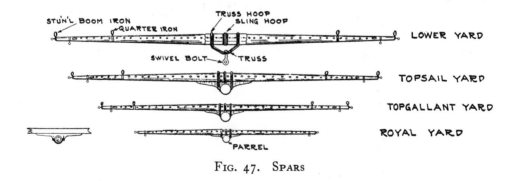

FIG. 47. SPARS

Model enthusiasts are reminded that the lower masts rest on the keelson. Their entire length is decidedly not above the deck. In the *Flying Cloud*, for example, the heights of the lower masts above deck are: foremast, sixty-four feet; mainmast, seventy-one feet, six inches; mizenmast, sixty feet.

The bowsprit, twenty-six and one-half inches in diameter, projected outboard for twenty feet; above it, the jib-boom, sixteen and one-half inches in diameter, stretched fifty-two feet forward of the stem.

The length of the spanker boom was fifty-five feet and its diameter eighteen inches. The spanker gaff measured forty feet, with a twelve-inch diameter.

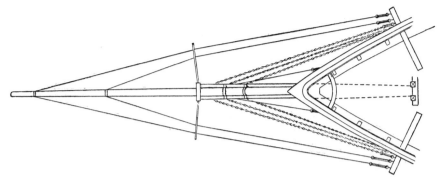

FIG. 48. BOWSPRIT

All standing rigging was tarred in order to protect it from the weather. A rule for compounding the mixture by which to do this reads like a cooking recipe:— ½ barrel of tar, 6 gallons of whiskey, 4 pounds of litharge, 4 pounds of lamp black, 2 buckets of boiling beef-pickle or hot salt water. Mix well and apply immediately.

Spare deadeyes, made in two pieces with a small bolt to hold them together, were to be found in the gear locker; a provision for temporary repairs at sea without having to remove a chain-plate to the smith shop, should the standing rigging break a deadeye.

All rigging was cable laid. Such rope consists of nine strands, each strand having an equal number of yarns. These nine strands are laid into three by twisting three of the smaller ones into one large one. The three larger ones are then laid up, or twisted together, in a left-handed direction.

Shroud-laid rope is made in the same manner except that it consists of four strands instead of three, and a small strand which runs through the middle termed the heart of the rope.

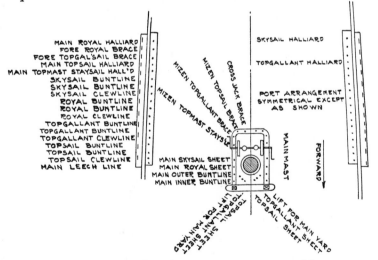

FIG. 49. BELAYING PIN ARRANGEMENT AT THE MAINMAST

The chain sheet pendants, shown on Plan XII, were probably not found on the *Flying Cloud* during her first voyages. Their accuracy was guaranteed by an old sailor who professed familiarity with the ship. Apparently, however, the hemp sheet pendant retained its simplified form for some time after 1850.

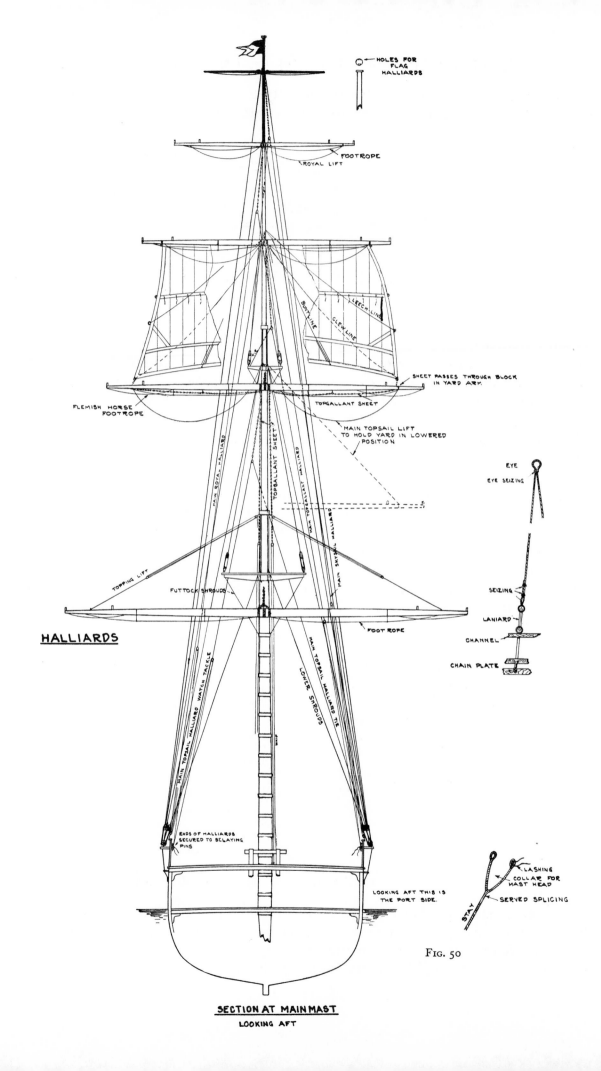

HOLES FOR
FLAG
HALLIARDS

FOOTROPE

ROYAL LIFT

LEECH LINE

BUNTLINE

CLEWLINE

SHEET PASSES THROUGH BLOCK
IN YARD ARM

FLEMISH HORSE
FOOTROPE

TOPGALLANT SHEET

MAIN TOPSAIL LIFT
TO HOLD YARD IN LOWERED
POSITION

EYE

EYE SEIZING

TOPGALLANT SHEET

MAIN ROYAL HALLIARD

MAIN SKYSAIL HALLIARD

SEIZING

LANIARD

CHANNEL

TOPPING LIFT

FUTTOCK SHROUDS

FOOT ROPE

CHAIN PLATE

HALLIARDS

MAIN TOPSAIL HALLIARD WATCH TACKLE

MAIN TOPSAIL HALLIARD TIE

LOWER SHROUDS

WHIP

ENDS OF HALLIARDS
SECURED TO BELAYING
PINS

LOOKING AFT THIS IS
THE PORT SIDE.

LASHING

COLLAR FOR
MAST HEAD

SERVED SPLICING

STAY

FIG. 50

SECTION AT MAIN MAST
LOOKING AFT

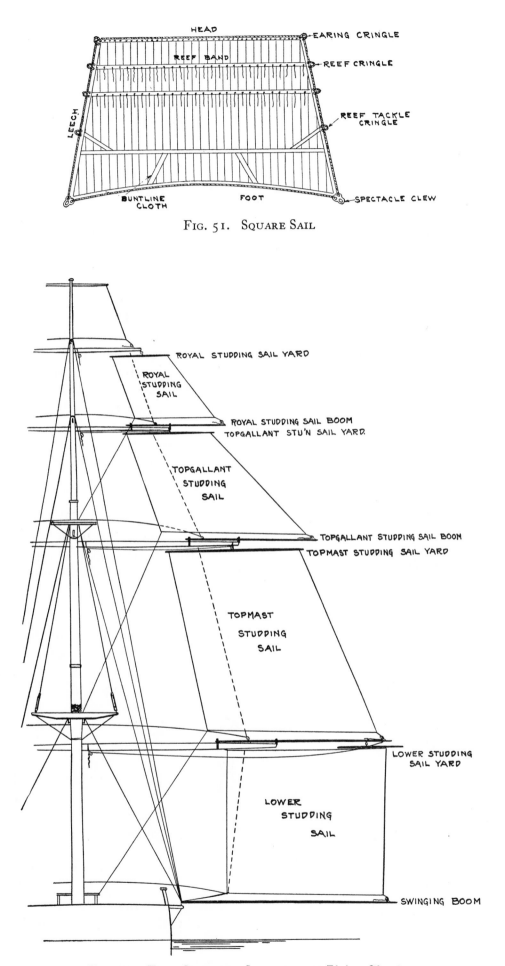

HEAD

EARING CRINGLE

REEF BAND

REEF CRINGLE

LEECH

REEF TACKLE
CRINGLE

BUNTLINE
CLOTH

FOOT

SPECTACLE CLEW

FIG. 51. SQUARE SAIL

ROYAL STUDDING SAIL YARD

ROYAL
STUDDING
SAIL

ROYAL STUDDING SAIL BOOM
TOPGALLANT STU'N SAIL YARD.

TOPGALLANT
STUDDING
SAIL

TOPGALLANT STUDDING SAIL BOOM
TOPMAST STUDDING SAIL YARD

TOPMAST
STUDDING
SAIL

LOWER STUDDING
SAIL YARD

LOWER
STUDDING
SAIL

SWINGING BOOM

FIG. 52. FORE STUDDING SAILS ON THE *Flying Cloud*

Equipment

Sails

The construction of the square sail naturally reached its highest development with the clippers. Through the eyelets in the head the sails were lashed to the iron jackstays on the spars. Tackles from the yards to the reef cringles hauled the sail up when it had to be shortened. The sheets and the clew-lines made fast to the spectacle clews at the lower corners. Extra cloths reinforced the canvas wherever necessary.

Besides the sails shown on Plate XII, the *Flying Cloud* was equipped with main topgallant, main royal, mizen topmast, and mizen topgallant staysails. She carried royal, topgallant, and topmast studding sails at the fore and main, with square lower studdingsails and swinging booms at the fore.

The "stun' s'ls," as the sailors called them, greatly increased the sail area, and were used in light weather. Because it was both difficult and dangerous to handle these sails, seamen disliked them heartily. The knowing ones began to refuse to ship on vessels on which they could see the stun' sail booms. Mates, who were clever, consequently stowed their stun' sail booms out of sight, below decks, when signing on a new crew, ordering the booms rigged only after the vessel was at sea. When the sailors had been fooled once by such a ruse, they examined the yards for stun' sail boom irons before deciding whether to join or not.

The topsails were provided with four reef bands — an unusual number. The topgallants had single reefs. Bowlines, found as far back as the *Santa Maria*, still appeared in the topsails and the topgallants of the *Flying Cloud*.

Extra Spars

As seen from the extract of her log quoted on page 110, it was no unusual thing to have to replace a mast or a spar. An extra topmast was carried over the starboard waterway, and a round half-dozen of lighter spars on the forward deck house flanking the upturned small boats.

Anchor

The evolution of the anchor has been extraordinarily slow. Previous to the stockless anchors of the present day there was very little change from even before the Middle Ages. To be sure, the anchor of 1850 had a shorter stock than that of 1492, but in general principle it remained unchanged.

The rule for the proportioning of anchors had even less scientific basis than that used today, although both rules are brave in high-sounding deductions.

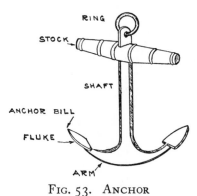

FIG. 53. ANCHOR

"For the sheet and bower anchors take two-thirds the number of feet which the ship draws with all her stores, etc., on board, and add to it the breadth of beam, allowing one hundred weight for every foot. The stream anchor is to be one-third of the sheet or bower. In stocking an anchor add together the length of the shank and half the round of the ring for the length of the stock. The stock is as many inches in thickness in the middle as the shank is long in feet, and is tapered to one-half the size at the end."*

* William Brady: *The Kedge Anchor*, 1854.

This anchor is for hemp cables. If for chain cables, the length of shank could be reduced one-quarter, but no reduction in weight was allowed.

Application of the rule would give a 6,400 pound anchor for the *Flying Cloud*. The sheet and the bower chains were of $2\frac{1}{2}$ inch wrought iron, 120 fathoms long.

Windlass

The so-called pump-brake windlass was a great improvement over its predecessors, though much inferior to those of a few years later. On each side of the central samson post an iron-toothed rim served as a ratchet. Between these a pawl operated over another iron-toothed surface and prevented the windlass from overhauling, that is, from slipping back. Links from the crosshead, which on the *Flying Cloud* appeared

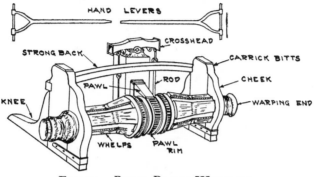

FIG. 54. PUMP-BRAKE WINDLASS

above the forecastle deck, operated on the ratchets and forced the windlass to turn as the hand levers were worked up and down. These levers fitted into sockets in the crosshead and could be removed in order to clear the forecastle.

The great difficulty of this design lay in the impossibility of letting the anchor chain run free. There were several turns around the whelps on the barrel of the windlass which had to be overhauled by hand until sufficient chain had run out to reach bottom. This process was called "ranging" the cable.

Capstans

Of these there were four in all: two single-acting capstans on the poop-deck, one double-acting capstan on the forecastle, and one just abaft the mainmast. A series of

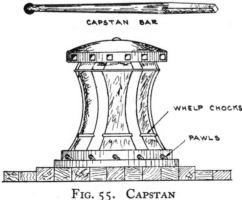

FIG. 55. CAPSTAN

little pawls at the bottom kept the capstan from overhauling and made the rapid click, click, click which accompanied the red-shirted sailors as they pushed the bars around. Without these pawls a sudden force on the hawser would have felled the sailors as the drum spun around and catapaulted the bars out of their holes with fearful and destructive effect. Capstan bars were removable; those belonging to the poop-deck stowed on the after side of the deck house beneath the fire buckets; those for the forecastle and waist, on a rack along the bulwarks.

Pump

The fire and bilge pump was no longer below, but now occupied a strategic position between the fife-rails of the mainmast. The old hand levers had been replaced by rotating fly wheels. Removable handles belonged on each end of the shaft, either handle being sufficiently long for two men to operate it at a time.

"Man the pumps" is an order that has in it a hint of romance and catastrophe. Actually it was back-breaking labor which had to be periodically performed as a matter of routine because even the tightest ship leaks a bit.

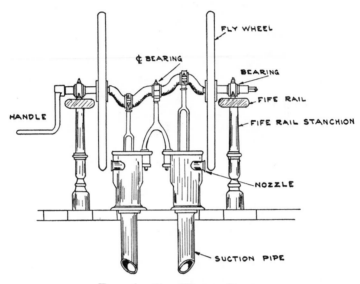

FIG. 56. FLY-WHEEL PUMP

Sometimes it was deadly serious business. On one of her voyages, a few days out of Whampoa, the *Flying Cloud* ran on a coral reef. The crew succeeded in getting her off but not, however, until she was so badly strained that the water leaked into her hold at the rate of eleven inches every hour. Over a hundred days later she arrived in New York with a cargo valued at a million dollars — safe, because the crew had continuously manned the pump in shifts from the time she ran aground.

Flags

From the mainmast every clipper flew the house flag of the firm to which she belonged. That of Grinnell, Minturn & Co. was a white, red, and blue swallowtail.*

From the mizen was flown her private signal — a red pennant.

At the peak the national ensign fluttered in the breeze, proclaiming to all that the ship was American. The British were our only rivals. The flags of these two nations, and these two only, flew from the peak halliards of clipper ships.

* Clark: *Clipper Ship Era*, page 303, gives it as red, white and blue. A lithograph published in 1852 by N. Currier, New York, gives it as white, blue and red. As this book goes to press, a letter from Grinnell Martin of New York, a grandson of one of the owners of the *Flying Cloud*, brings the information that from the fly to the pole the flag was white, red and blue. Thus there is authority for various arrangements, though material left by Capt. Alexander Winsor, commanding officer of the *Flying Cloud*, 1859-1862, more than substantiates the correctness of Mr. Martin's statement. There was no star, as is sometimes erroneously supposed.

PLATE XXIX

DECK VIEW OF THE MODEL OF THE CLIPPER SHIP "FLYING CLOUD," BUILT BY F. VAN L. RYDER

The top of the deck house is here removed, showing the cabin forward with its mahogany staircase leading below. In the center is the galley with its ranges. The after end is divided into two staterooms, with bunks, wash bowls, etc.

MODEL OF THE CLIPPER SHIP "FLYING CLOUD," BUILT IN 1927 BY F. VAN L. RYDER

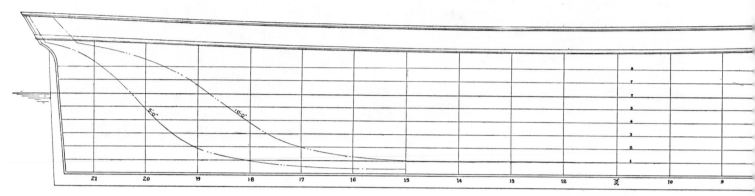

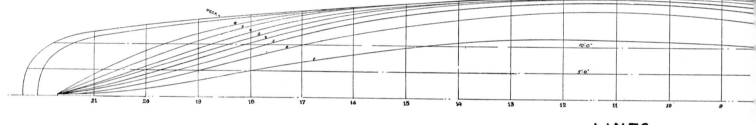

LINES

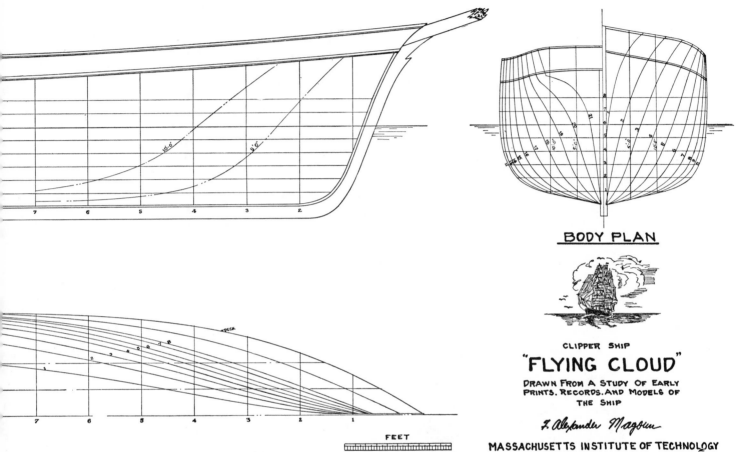

BODY PLAN

CLIPPER SHIP
"FLYING CLOUD"
DRAWN FROM A STUDY OF EARLY
PRINTS, RECORDS, AND MODELS OF
THE SHIP

F. Alexander Magoun

MASSACHUSETTS INSTITUTE OF TECHNOLOGY
CAMBRIDGE   MASS.

COPYRIGHT, 1926, F. ALEXANDER MAGOUN

FEET

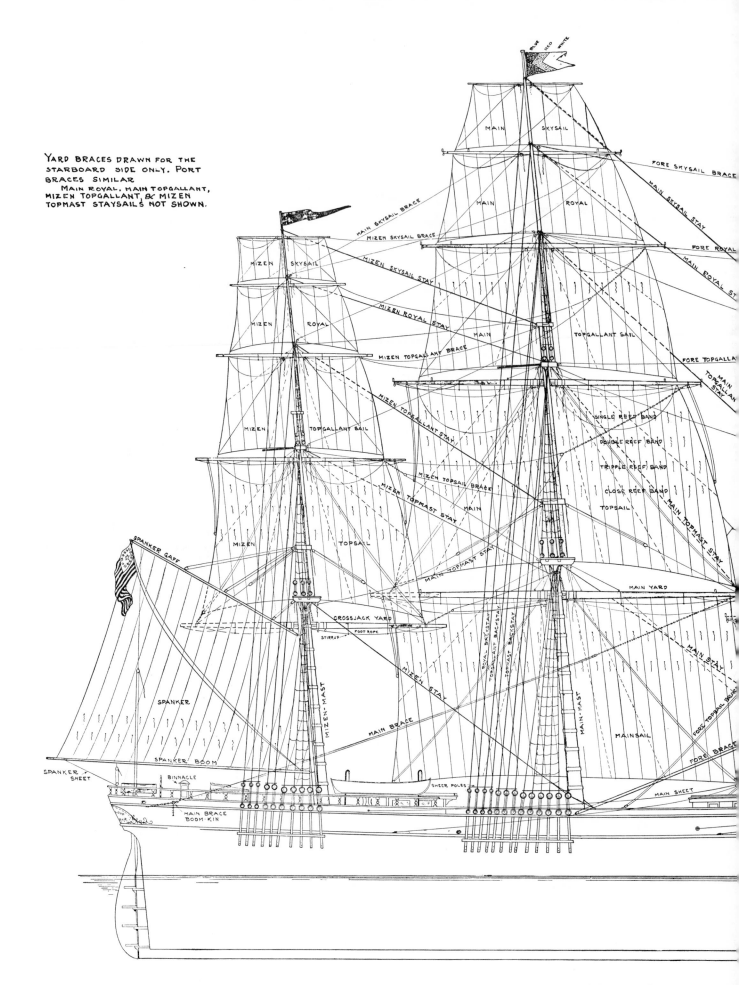

YARD BRACES DRAWN FOR THE
STARBOARD SIDE ONLY. PORT
BRACES SIMILAR
MAIN ROYAL, MAIN TOPGALLANT,
MIZEN TOPGALLANT & MIZEN
TOPMAST STAYSAILS NOT SHOWN.

MAIN SKYSAIL

FORE SKYSAIL BRACE

MAIN SKYSAIL STAY

MAIN SKYSAIL BRACE

MAIN

ROYAL

FORE ROYAL

MIZEN SKYSAIL BRACE

MIZEN SKYSAIL STAY

MAIN ROYAL ST

MIZEN SKYSAIL

MIZEN ROYAL STAY

MIZEN

SKYSAIL

MIZEN

ROYAL

MAIN

TOPGALLANT SAIL

FORE TOPGALLA

MIZEN TOPGALLANT BRACE

MAIN TOPGALLAN STAY

MIZEN TOPGALLANT STAY

MIZEN

TOPGALLANT SAIL

SINGLE REEF BAND

DOUBLE REEF BAND

TRIPPLE REEF BAND

MIZEN TOPSAIL BRACE

CLOSE REEF BAND

MIZEN TOPMAST STAY

MAIN

TOPSAIL

MAIN TOPMAST STAY

MIZEN

TOPSAIL

MIZEN TOPMAST STAY

SPANKER GAFF

MAIN TOPMAST STAY

MAIN YARD

CROSSJACK YARD

FOOT ROPE

STIRRUP

ROYAL BACKSTAY

TOPGALLANT BACKSTAY

TOPMAST BACKSTAY

MAIN STAY

SPANKER

MIZEN STAY

MIZEN-MAST

MAIN-MAST

MAIN BRACE

MAINSAIL

FORE TOPGALLANT BRACE

SPANKER BOOM

FORE BRACE

SPANKER
SHEET

BINNACLE

SHEER POLES

MAIN SHEET

MAIN BRACE
BOOM-KIN

SAIL PLAN

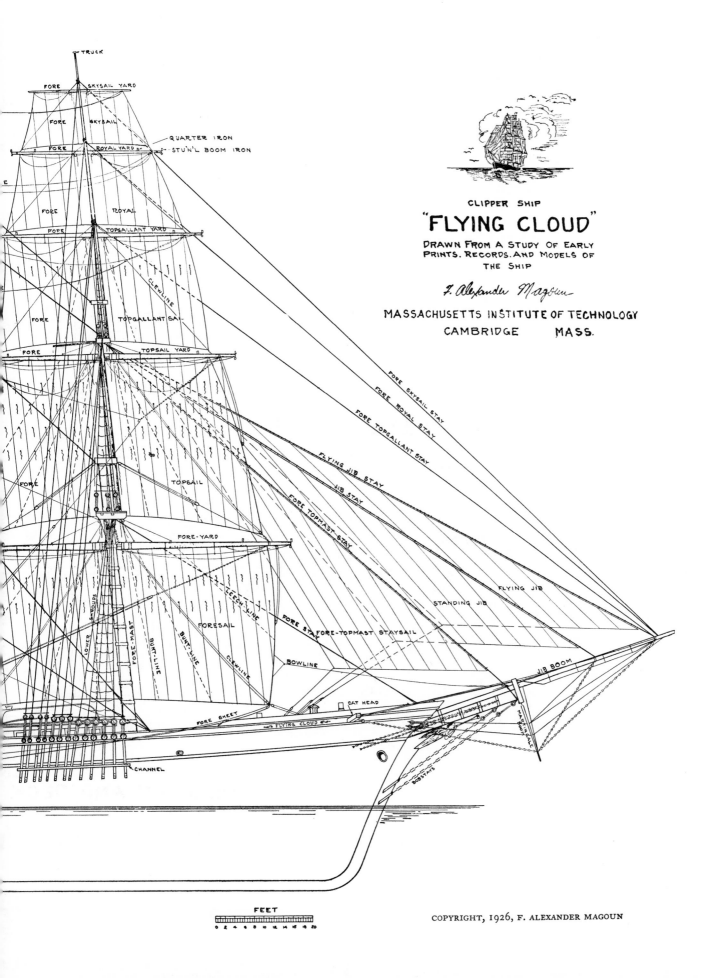

CLIPPER SHIP
"FLYING CLOUD"
DRAWN FROM A STUDY OF EARLY
PRINTS, RECORDS, AND MODELS OF
THE SHIP

F. Alexander Magoun

MASSACHUSETTS INSTITUTE OF TECHNOLOGY
CAMBRIDGE   MASS.

FEET

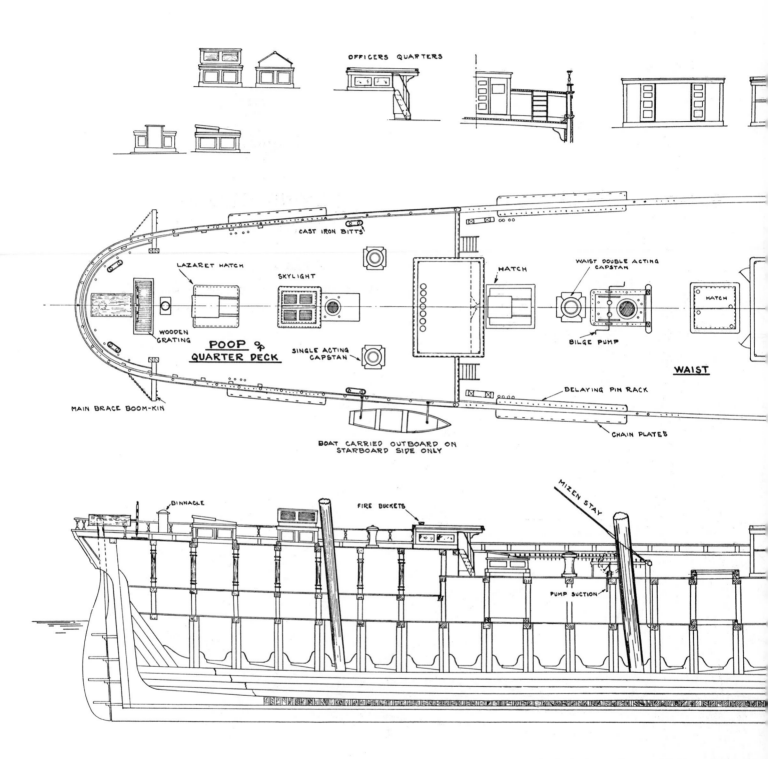

OFFICERS QUARTERS

CAST IRON BITTS

LAZARET HATCH

SKYLIGHT

HATCH

WAIST DOUBLE ACTING CAPSTAN

WOODEN GRATING

POOP ⚓ QUARTER DECK

SINGLE ACTING CAPSTAN

BILGE PUMP

HATCH

MAIN BRACE BOOM-KIN

WAIST

BELAYING PIN RACK

BOAT CARRIED OUTBOARD ON STARBOARD SIDE ONLY

CHAIN PLATES

MIZEN STAY

BINNACLE

FIRE BUCKETS

PUMP SUCTION

PROFILE AND DECK

PLAN XIII

CLIPPER SHIP
"FLYING CLOUD"

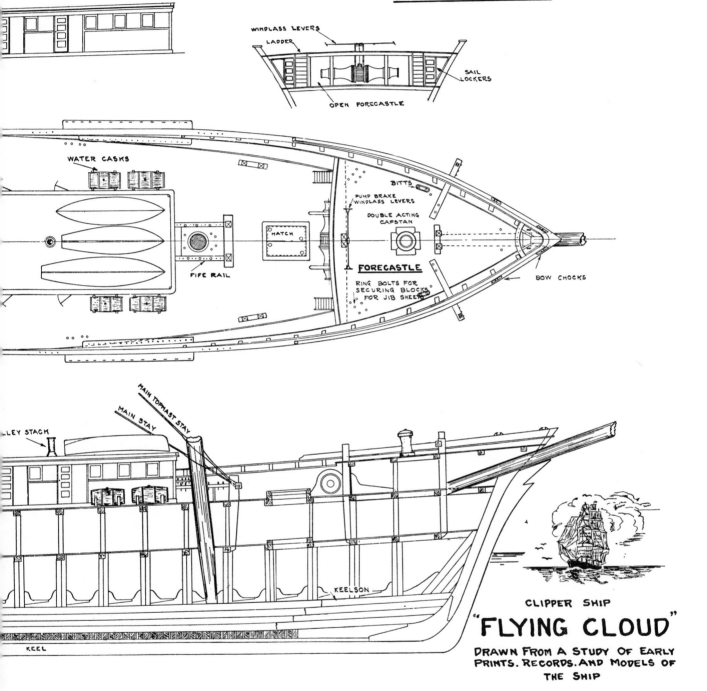

WINDLASS LEVERS
LADDER
SAIL LOCKERS
OPEN FORECASTLE

WATER CASKS

BITTS
PUMP BRAKE WINDLASS LEVERS
DOUBLE ACTING CAPSTAN

FORECASTLE
RING BOLTS FOR SECURING BLOCKS FOR JIB SHEETS
BOW CHOCKS

HATCH

FIFE RAIL

MAIN TOPMAST STAY
MAIN STAY
GALLEY STACK

KEELSON

KEEL

CLIPPER SHIP
"FLYING CLOUD"
DRAWN FROM A STUDY OF EARLY PRINTS. RECORDS. AND MODELS OF THE SHIP

F. Alexander Magoun

MASSACHUSETTS INSTITUTE OF TECHNOLOGY
CAMBRIDGE   MASS.

FEET
0 2 4 6 8 10 12 14 16 18 20

COPYRIGHT, 1926, F. ALEXANDER MAGOUN

THE CLIPPER SHIP "FLYING CLOUD"

Small Boats

Lest they be carried away by the sea, the small boats were not stowed outboard on davits, the one exception being a cutter swung just forward of the starboard mizen shrouds for immediate use in case of a man overboard. The other three boats were turned upside down and lashed on top of the forward deck house where they offered shelter to the poultry during a voyage.

The wisdom of carrying one boat on davits was proven on April 2, 1856, when the *Flying Cloud* was making twelve knots in the vicinity of Madagascar. From her cabin window the captain's wife, Mrs. Creesy, saw a sailor go overboard. She rushed on deck to throw over a life buoy and give the alarm. Immediately the ship was hove to and the boat launched. A long search followed. When the boat came back without the sailor, Creesy ordered a second boat put over and the hunt was vigorously pursued as long as daylight lasted. Four hours later, almost dead, the man was picked up two miles from the ship. Under Mrs. Creesy's motherly nursing he soon regained his strength.

Quarters

A description of the provisions for both crew and passengers has already been given. See page 116.

Food

As a rule the food was excellent and there was plenty of it. British crews were allowed so much a day. American crews could help themselves to beef, pork and bread as long as it lasted.

Water was a different matter. Its consumption had to be carefully regulated, the carpenter usually being charged with the responsibility of pumping a gallon for each person on board, from the great iron tank in the hold, and pouring it into a scuttle-butt on deck. Each day the amount remaining in the tank was meticulously entered in the log-book. From the scuttle-butt, the cook, the stewards and the sailors obtained their water, and woe indeed to the man who wasted it.

Grog formed a part of the rations on the British ships. Not so aboard the American clippers. It is true that the crew often spent their wages for drink when ashore, but no alcohol was allowed at sea. Total abstinence was much encouraged by our ship-owners, both because the ships were then better managed, and because this superiority reaped its monetary reward in lower insurance rates.

A captain would sooner have thought of putting to sea without his medicine chest than without a cow or a nanny goat. The latter possesses excellent sea legs, a bequest from rock-jumping ancestors. She is also blessed with a stomach of such courage that nothing in the shape of vegetable fiber dares to disagree with it. Nevertheless, Captain Cressy preferred a gentle bovine, who chewed her cud within the narrow confines of a pen erected on the forward hatch.

Hogs thrived well at sea, enjoying the scraps from the mess table until one day they appeared upon the menu. Ducks, geese and hens were always found in the forward end of the deck, persisting sometimes unto the third and fourth generation of sea-going poultry. They furnished fresh eggs for the captain's omelette, and like their dryland cousins, they had a noisy way of their own when there was excitement near them. Sometimes, no doubt, even the cow bemoaned her lot.

The solution of the problem of taking care of all these animals has already been hinted at. Beneath the upturned boats the poultry found security and shelter. Across the forward hatch was lashed the cowhouse within whose narrow confines the Jersey might dream of shade trees and friendly hills, but from which she could see only the rolling endless ocean.

A negro cook of enviable genius always presided over the galley, which, on the *Flying Cloud*, was in the center instead of at the after end of the forward deck house (See Plate XXIX).

Cargo

During the California gold rush the cargo consisted of sundry items on the outward voyage, principally furniture, tools, and food supplies. From San Francisco, ships crossed to China in order to return to New York with tea. Under the British flag the *Flying Cloud* carried wool from Australia and later, lumber from New Brunswick.

Operation

The clippers were much easier in a seaway than the older types of vessel; they rolled and heaved less, and consequently offered greater comfort to the passengers besides delivering their cargoes in better condition. The long, narrow bow would cut through a heavy sea which the tremendous buoyancy of a *Mayflower's* bow would rise upon. This drenched a clipper's deck in a swirl of foaming spray, but what cared the crew for wind or weather?

Their ships could sail to windward under conditions impossible for the navigation of any previous type. They could be operated to advantage by a breath of air, or by a gale. But compared to the simplicity with which the throttle of a turbine may be closed in answer to a ring of the engine-room telegraph, the procedure following the order "All hands shorten and furl sails," was extremely complex. Following this first order the crew would man the clew-ropes, buntlines, leech-lines, down-hauls, and brails, having the bunt ropes and jiggers overhauled, and ready for hooking to the gluts, and hands by the halliards, out-hauls and bowlines, to let them go.

"Aloft, topmen!" was the second command after which time was allowed to reach the futtock-rigging.

"Aloft, lower-yardmen!"

"Haul taut, clew up, haul down, lie out and furl."

Gather up the slack of the sails smartly, and pass the leeches, points, and bowlines, bridles in taut along the yard towards the bunt, slack down the buntlines, hook the bunt-jiggers, toss up, and skin the sail taut and smoothly in the headband, keeping the bunt square in the slings, and heaving the clews forward in the wake of the quarter-blocks, slew the head-earing cringles up fair, and pass the gaskets at right-angles with the yard, parallel with each other, and without turns.

"Lie in, down booms, and down from aloft" — square the heel of the booms, keeping them at equal distances apart on each side of the bunt, and parallel with the yard, secure the glut to the tye by a temporary racking, unhook the bunt-jiggers, stop the bowlines to the jackstays, on each side of the bunt, and haul them taut, together with the jig and staysail halliards, and see that the clew-lines are close up. Then square yards: after which, haul taut reef-tackles, sheets and all slack ropes.

In trimming the sails the yards on a given mast were not all at the same angle. Instead the sails were "checked in" as it was called, the light upper sails being closer to the wind than the larger lower courses. By this system, the helmsman could keep half an eye on the royals, which warned him when he steered too close to the wind by backing before the lower sails came aback.

Incomplete charts and the necessity for navigating in strange waters made the sounding lead even more indispensable than it is today.

Heaving the lead was generally performed by a man who stood in the main chains to windward. Having the line all ready to run out, without interruption, he held it at a distance of nearly a fathom from the lead, and having swung it backwards and forward three or four times, in order to acquire a greater velocity with the swing, he then swung it over his head, and thence as far forward as was necessary; so that by the lead sinking whilst the ship advanced, the line might be almost perpendicular when it reached the bottom. The person sounding then proclaimed the depth of water in a kind of singing manner. Thus: if the mark of five fathoms was close to the surface of the water, he sang out, "By the mark five!" and as there were no marks at 4, 6, 8, etc., he estimated those numbers and sang, "By the deep four!" etc. If he considered it to be a quarter, or a half, more than any particular number, he sang out, "And a quarter five!" "And a half four!" etc. If he conceived the depth to be three-quarters more than a particular number, he called it a quarter less than the next; thus, at four fathoms and three-quarters, he called, "A quarter less five!" and so on, according to the depth of the water.

FIG. 57. HEAVING THE LEAD

The *Flying Cloud* is considered by most naval architects to have been the finest of the clippers notwithstanding the fact that to the *Lightning*, another product of Donald McKay's intellect, goes the honor of the longest twenty-four hour run. On her maiden trip from Boston to London she logged 436 miles in a day, part of which was at the rate of 18½ knots. This is the record for any type of sailing vessel on any sea and is equalled after nearly a century of improvements by very few steamships now crossing the Atlantic.

The longest distance covered by the *Flying Cloud* in any one day measured 427½ miles, accomplished without the assisting current of the Gulf Stream which gave to the *Lightning* an additional knot or two. In a neck and neck race the *Flying Cloud* would have been faster than any other wind-driven vessel ever made by the hand of man.

VI

THE FISHING SCHOONER "BLUENOSE"

FISHING has occupied the attention of men, both as a sport and as a livelihood, since first they went down to the sea in ships. As long ago as 1500 B.C. fishing villages were scattered along the coast of Phœnicia, where the land was unfitted for agriculture. This was the beginning of a commerce which was to expand until it reached from England, on the north, to the southern extremity of the Cape of Good Hope.

From such small beginnings have sprung the great fleets of many nations: Phœnicia, Carthage, Spain, England, and the United States. Realizing the importance of the fishing industry, it has always been given every encouragement by far-seeing statesmen. During the sixteenth century, when England had practically no merchant marine of her own, the people were forbidden by law to eat meat on two days a week in order that a profitable market for fish might be guaranteed, and the creation of a larger shipping fostered. In this way the enormous ship-building industry of the British Isles received its start and derived a great deal of its early vigor.

The opportunities offered by the Grand Banks as a fishing ground were appreciated and exploited long before the successful colonization of America. John Cabot proclaimed the size and abundance of North Atlantic fish to European dealers as early as 1497, making special mention of the "baccalos" or codfish. Cargoes of these were caught for European consumption in 1504. By 1517 there were fifty vessels at the Banks. By 1540 an establishment had been created on the shores of Newfoundland for salting and curing the catches. Ever since that time the Grand Banks have been a prolific source of sea food.

Those of us who are prone to think of things North American in terms of the last century, will be astonished to learn that before 1600 there were over four hundred vessels engaged in Grand Banks fishing, half of them British. In the next ten years more adventuresome fishermen, who possessed an investigating turn of mind, discovered that cod could be taken close inshore to what is now Maine and Massachusetts, in six or seven fathoms of water. These fish were even larger and better than those which could be caught in the forty-five fathoms off Newfoundland. Fishermen had been earning £6 or £7 apiece. The New England fisheries offered as much as £14.

The inevitable result was a desire to colonize this region with fishing villages since in this way merchants could lower their costs very considerably. The student of history is continually impressed by the recurring proof that the ultimate urge has always been an economic one.

James I made a grant in 1606 to the Plymouth Company which was formed for the purpose of establishing such colonies along the coast. A succession of little villages of differing nationalities were planted, most of them unsuccessful at first. The very beginning of shipbuilding within the present limits of the United States resulted from one of these attempts. During the summer of 1607 two ships, the *Gift of God* and the *Mary and John*, left forty-five persons at Stage Island near the mouth of the Kennebec River. Disheartened by the severity of the winter which followed, they built the *Virginia*, which not only carried them home in safety but subsequently made several voyages across the Atlantic.

These early failures were followed by settlements that thrived altogether too well to please the English capitalists. People in the New World, stimulated by the excellent timber available and the rewards of independence, began the construction of boats and the catching of fish on their own account. Fourteen years after the *Mayflower* sailed up Massachusetts Bay a certain citizen of Marblehead owned eight fishing vessels.

The original fishing craft built in North America were birch bark canoes with ribs of ash to which the bark was sewed. In ten days an experienced Indian could make one having more speed, if paddled by three men, than an eight-oared shallop. The first settlers of Plymouth, Salem, Ipswich and Portsmouth purchased canoes in large numbers for fishing in smooth waters. Calm weather fishing could be carried on in a canoe as far as two or three miles off shore.

A larger type of boat was necessary for the catching of cod in the open sea. That the Pilgrim Fathers had intended to use their shallop for this purpose has been mentioned in an earlier chapter. Experienced ship-carpenters came to Plymouth as early as 1642, and boat building began in earnest.

The probate records of Suffolk County, Mass., record only ketches and shallops among the fishing fleet until the beginning of the eighteenth century. The ketches had a nine or ten foot depth of hold, drew some seven feet of water, had a complete deck with cabins aft, and were built almost entirely of white oak. The masts were usually spruce; the registered tonnage about thirty.

The shallops were open boats of approximately the same size. Some had but one sail, some two, both sails being square. The present manifestation of the shallop is found in the lugger.

Marblehead and Gloucester rapidly became the centers of the fishing industry which expanded with a steady and permanent growth. From the times of the old pinkey, that peculiar craft without bowsprit or shrouds, with its two masts, hemp sails and crew of three men, most of the Gloucester boats have been built at Essex. This quaint old town, lying a few miles inland on a little crooked river, was once called Chebacco, a name from which the famous Chebacco boats received their name.

The same rapid evolution which manifested itself in the merchantmen of the early nineteenth century had its counterpart among the fishing fleets. During the very days when the packet was becoming the clipper, the pinkey became the schooner. Some more venturesome Essex ship-builder departed from the established precedents of his colleagues, sharpening the bow of his vessel and hollowing her run. The fishermen were candidly distrustful. What an idiotic rake! What a sheer! But in spite of sailormen's misgivings she was manned, became successful, and almost immediately proved the prototype of a new class of fishing schooners.

In those days the larger craft registered from twenty to forty tons, a figure which with growing accumulations of capital and improved shipyard facilities has grown to over one hundred and fifty tons. And with the coming of better ships came the introduction of more productive methods. No longer did the fishermen rely upon hand lines over the side of the vessel. Each schooner carried a number of small boats of the dory type in which the crew could scatter around "on their own hook" as soon as the fishing grounds had been reached.

In 1820 John Rowe of Gloucester made and successfully operated the first trawl. To a long line, which he afterward stretched across Brace's Cove, he attached many short lines, each with a baited hook. Quantity production had invaded another industry.

The lines of a trawl are made of tarred cotton, fifty fathoms long and about the size of a lead pencil. Lest it become hopelessly tangled, to the vexation of the fisherman and the immunity of the fish, the line is coiled round and round in a tub, often but the slimy remains of a one-time flour barrel from which the upper portion has been removed. When the schooner "brings to" at the fishing grounds, furls her canvas, and bends the riding-sail, dories are put over the side by means of a block and tackle from each mast. Two fishermen leap into each boat as it goes over, receiving the tubs of trawls that make up their quota, the buoys, the buoy-lines, and the anchors. Rowing in a direction previously determined by lot, they drop an anchor with its buoy, and begin the laying of a long line of trawls which is to form one of the radii diverging from the schooner. The anchor buoy at the outer end, perhaps a mile or a mile and a half from the ship itself, carries a flag to mark its location and identity. The dory then rows aboard, to wait until afternoon or perhaps the following morning.

Leaving only the captain, the cook, and perhaps a boy on board, the dories are once more hoisted out to pull the trawls. In foggy weather, not an infrequent variety, the finding of the outer buoy is no easy task. By beginning there, instead of at the schooner, the long pull can be made with no load, the alternative being to row the entire catch all the way in from the flag.

Seemingly endless fathoms of line (about forty in all) are hauled up before the anchor appears. With it comes the head of the trawl and perhaps the first fish. Haddock drop into the bottom of the dory as a lamb in the shambles of the slaughter house. They scarcely stir after being slatted off the hook. Big fifty-pound codfish are equally complacent with a sort of adult fatalism quite different from the determined struggles of their younger progeny.

Sometimes a hook comes up with only the skeleton of a fish on it. Little insects called sand fleas have eaten the cod completely; an exasperating feat which they can accomplish in two or three hours.

As the trawl is pulled and the fish are taken off, it is coiled in the tubs again from which it will be recoiled into other tubs as the hooks are baited. When all the gear has been recovered, the dory is rowed back to the schooner and the fish are pitched on to the deck with a two-tine fork. If the catch is not large, the captain shifts a few miles away where he will "bring to" again, bait up, and try once more.

On foggy days a horn is blown at frequent intervals while the dories are hauling trawls. But even so, fishermen are often lost, rowing about for days without food, sometimes to be picked up by another schooner, sometimes never to be heard from again.

Mackerel swim near the surface in schools and are caught with a seine, one edge of which is provided with sinkers, the other with floats, so that it will hang vertically in the water. Experienced fishermen can actually "smell" a school in the vicinity. From the after hatch, where it lies coiled up and wet with brine to prevent rotting, the purse-seine, 1,500 or 2,000 feet in length, is thrown into a boat. Under the direction of the seine boss it is rowed out, cast into a circle and pursed. While the fishermen in the dories estimate the size of their catch (which is not yet caught, however) the captain and the cook manoeuver the schooner until a portion of the cork-line can be gotten on board. The fish are then between the vessel's side and the seine boat. A large dip-net, operated by a tackle and a long handle, scoops the live mackerel onto the deck by the half-barrelful. This causes great alarm among the fish in the seine, who rush from one side to the other, often bursting the net in their frantic efforts to escape. Once a hole has been made, its size increases with the same rapidity which marks the escape of the fish.

Sometimes, after the net has been cast completely round the school and hopes for a catch of perhaps 500 barrels are high, the mackerel will suddenly sink to the bottom and not one of them is captured. They vanish for some unknown reason, to emerge again farther away. In order to entice the fish a form of bait called "chum," used to be thrown upon the surface of the water, which, like the trout fisherman's fly, might work and might not.

Fishing schooners on the Banks are divided into two classes: those that go out to be gone for two or three weeks, or less, if luck is with them, with ice in their bins unless the ship is sufficiently up to date to have an ice machine for keeping the fish fresh; and the salt bankers, which stay until their hold is full, making only two or three trips in the run of a season. In winter the salt bankers are laid up or used for the transportation of freight.

To the latter class belongs the *Bluenose*, twice crowned queen of the Lunenburg fleet. The preservative in her bins is salt instead of ice, one barrel of salt being required for every four barrels of fish. The fresh fish come to market much as they were taken from the water. Aboard the salt bankers the catch is thrown into a trough with small dip nets, from which it is cut open, gutted, and washed, to be sorted according to size, sprinkled with salt, and stowed below through the hatchway.

After the cargo has been discharged at the dock it is transferred to the flakes and dried. In the skinning lofts, nimble fingers then remove the skin and bones, leaving only solid pieces of fish to be packed in boxes labeled "Boneless Codfish," later to reappear when some housewife wishes to serve it boiled — with drawn butter and egg sauce, or with pork scraps, beets, and potatoes.

"Fisherman's luck" is an expression not without secure foundation. Those sturdy disciples of self-projection who declare that there is no such thing as luck should go angling. In 1873 a Nantucket fisherman launched his dory, pulled two miles off shore, caught 2,114 pounds of codfish, and was back in three hours. In February, 1880, two brothers, of Folly Cove, hauled nine tubs of trawls — some 4,500 hooks — and got five pounds of fish! Schooners have come back from the Banks with half a million pounds. They have come back with almost nothing.

As for the size of individual fish, the following may not comprise the largest specimens ever caught, but they most certainly rank high.

Halibut — 637 pounds — found dead in Damask Cove, Boothbay, Maine. One is reminded of the bride, who, wishing to conceal her ignorance, told the fishman, when asked how much halibut she wanted, that two would be enough! She may have had in mind the smallest specimen on record, a twenty-ounce fish brought into Gloucester in 1880, and sent to New York by mail.

Codfish — 110 pounds, five feet long.

Horse mackerel — 545 pounds.

Lobster — 15 pounds, 38 inches long.

Sea Bass — 79 pounds. The game fight which even a small bass makes will ac-

THE FISHING SCHOONER "BLUENOSE"

count for the two hours which elapsed from the time he was hooked until he could be gotten into the boat.

The dark moments, the dangers, and distresses of fishermen are widely known and little appreciated. Even the amount of moral courage required for a land lubber to get out of an uncomfortable, rolling bunk, struggle up on to a cold, wet, cheerless deck and handle cold, wet, slimy lines with colder, wetter, slimier fish — all for the experience — can never be understood except by those who have allowed themselves to be deluded into trying it.

In fifty years, four hundred vessels and 2,000 fishermen went out of Gloucester, never to return. A single incident, positively authenticated, which did not end in tragedy, will convey a bare hint of the dreadful apprehensions in the minds of those women who wait along the beach and upon the headlands when the seas run high.

Two fishermen* in a dory had safely hauled the larger part of their trawl, when a huge wave struck the boat, throwing the men overboard and filling the dory with water. One of the fishermen was fortunately not thrown far. He grasped the gunwale and pulled himself aboard, where frightened for his own safety, he fastened the trawl to anchor the bow, and made desperate efforts to bail out the boat. His less fortunate comrade came to the surface some ten or fifteen feet away, only to go down again, encumbered with heavy clothing and with awkward sea boots. As he sank for the second, and as he thought, the last time, his hand struck the trawl some fifteen feet under water. Instinctively he grasped it and began to overhaul the line. A big fish hook immediately caught in his forefinger, passing completely through it near the end. Still full of courage, the man reached his other hand as far up the trawl as he could, and tore the hook bodily out of the finger. As he reached the surface, seemingly at the very limit of human endurance, another hook caught in the leg of his trousers. Gasping for breath, he shouted to his companion, but no assistance came. With one mighty, final effort he pulled himself over the side of the boat and fell senseless to the bottom. When his consciousness was restored the fisherman insisted on hauling the rest of the trawl before returning to the vessel with his torn and bleeding finger.

Unknown danger is the father of superstitions. The fishermen have many. Both certain boats and certain men, though of apparently excellent qualities, are known as Jonahs. Sometimes things may be Jonahs: a suitcase carried on board, a violin, a bucket setting on deck partly full of water, or the driving of nails on Sunday. But the fisherman who refuses to begin a voyage on Friday is no more silly than the high society girl who is afraid to be married on that day, or the farmer who nails a horseshoe over his door. As Shakespeare says, "The earth has bubbles, as the water has; and these are of them."

A custom which has in it all the appeal of children counting "eni, meni, miny, mo," in order to discover who will be "it," is that of thumbing the hat to determine the order of the watches. All hands are called aft where they form a circle around an inverted hat, thumbs on top of the rim. The skipper then turns his head away, reaches over, touches one of the thumbs, and counts around from left to right any number previously determined. The first one which this count reaches takes the first watch, the rest follow in the order of rotation.

In order to stimulate the development of faster fishing schooners, and to preserve the type, Mr. H. W. Dennis of the *Halifax Herald* and the *Halifax Evening Mail*,

* William T. Lee and Jack Devine of the *Grace L. Fears*, in November, 1880.

offered a prize which amounted to $4,000. and a $50. cup for the fisherman which should win the Atlantic seaboard championship in a series of forty-mile races. This prize was first won by the American schooner *Esperanto*, of Gloucester, Mass.

In 1921 the *Bluenose*, a Lunenburg salt banker, designed by W. J. Roué, of Halifax, succeeded in lifting the trophy in a race against the schooner *Elsie* from Gloucester. In 1922 she retained the supremacy against the fisherman *Ford*. In 1923 her contest with the *Columbia*, greatly marred by protests and enmity on both sides, finally broke up when Capt. Angus Walters disgustedly set sail for Halifax and the committee declared "no race." As a prelude to such an unhappy ending, the American-designed *Mayflower*, although engaged in fishing on the Banks, had sometime previously been declared a yacht and therefore not eligible.

It is a great misfortune that these races which might have become a friendly classic should so soon have terminated in quarreling. Professional yachtsmen who witnessed the races were not surprised at the outcome. Fishermen contend with the vacillating ocean and with conditions laid down by God Almighty. They do not care for the seeming inconsistencies of committees and the unfamiliar stipulations of racing rules. These men are at their best in the fog, the dashing spray, and the drifting snow off Newfoundland. Their genius lies in catching the denizens of the deep — anything from a shrimp to a whale — and in facing, unafraid, hardship, torture, or sudden death.

HULL

All fishermen sail with a drag. This particular form of hull can be most easily kept up to the wind when "laying to," a very desirable characteristic since meeting the waves bow on reduces the liability of water breaking over the deck.

Another distinguishing feature is the very low freeboard, necessary to facilitate getting the dories over the side, and to make possible the pitching of the new-caught fish on to the deck.

In order to make the after part of the vessel, where the helmsman must stand, somewhat dryer than it would otherwise be, the deck breaks forward of the mainmast, the quarter deck rising in a little step which stops the flow of moderate quantities of water coming over the bows, and causes it to spill out through the scuppers.

The construction of the hull is largely of white oak. Frames are built up of "floor timbers," "futtocks," and "top timbers," tapering gradually from the keel to the plank-sheer. The frame spacing is about two feet. On the outside is the planking; on the inside is the ceiling, which contributes to strength but not to water-tightness.

Length over all	142' - 0"
Length load water-line	110' - 0"
Draft	15' - 8"
Beam	27' - 0"
Displacement	270 tons
Sail area	9770 sq. ft.
Ballast (stowed inside for races)	110 tons

The hull is painted black above the narrow white boot top, with a copper brown under water body which is not sheathed. A white moulding stripe at the lower edge of the rail gives her a snappy appearance, which is well carried out by the white deck erections and inner bulwarks. Inboard, the bowsprit is painted white. Outboard it is scraped bright. Below decks the masts are varnished; from the upper deck to the booms they are painted white; from there to the trucks they are scraped bright.

HULL FITTINGS

Steering Gear

As on the clipper ships, the wheel is directly above the rudder. Instead of being vertical, however, it is slanted in order that it may still fulfill the requirement of perpendicularity to the rudder stock. A little house covers the mechanism; a worm wheel affair, which requires the wheel to be on the port side of the center line.

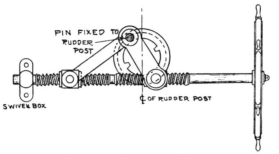

FIG. 58. STEERING GEAR

Side Lights

These are now required by law, and the boards upon which the lights are fixed may be found in the standing rigging of the foremast. The port light is of course red, easily remembered by associating it with the color of port wine; the starboard light is green.

Hawse Pipes

A hawse pipe on each side of the bow offers opportunity for the anchor cables to pass from the deck through the bulwark and into the water. A short length of chain cable is carried, usually stowed below, for use in the more shallow water of a harbor. On the banks the anchor is held by a long wire rope, a much lighter fastening than chain would be. Halibut fishermen still use the old hemp hawser for anchoring, 400 fathoms being the requirement for such deep sea anchorages.

SPARS AND RIGGING

A table of dimensions of the masts and spars of the *Bluenose* is extremely simple compared to that of the *Flying Cloud*.

Spar	Length	Maximum Diameter
Foremast	83' - 0"	19"
Foretopmast	46' - 0"	11"
Boom	33' - 9"	10"
Gaff	33' - 6"	10"
Mainmast	96' - 0"	20"
Main topmast	51' - 0"	11"
Boom	80' - 0"	14"
Gaff	47' - 0"	11"
Bowsprit	17' - 6"	16"
Fore staysail boom	27' - 6"	8"

Eighty-three feet of the mainmast are above deck; seventy-five feet of the foremast. The foremast rakes 5" in 64 feet; the mainmast rakes 2'-4" in 70 feet.

All standing rigging is made of wire cable which possesses the great advantages of strength and of immunity from stretching perceptibly with changes in the weather.

The topmast shroud cuts through the edge of the side-light board which is fastened to the lower shrouds.

In the square-riggers the crew were constantly under the necessity of going aloft. The absence of this requirement in the handling of the fore and aft rig makes it unnecessary for the ratlines to span more than two shrouds. One man in the rigging can usually perform any service necessitated by occasional mishaps.

The lack of backstays and channels will be observed. Although popular with yacht designers, the backstay has never appealed to the fisherman, nor does he see the necessity for channels when he can satisfactorily attach his chain plates directly to the hull.

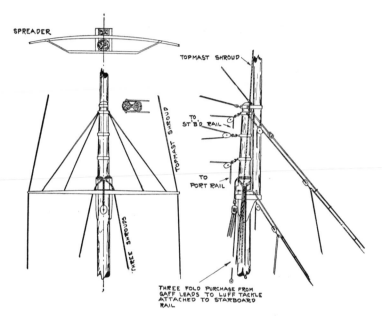

FIG. 59. MAST HEAD ARRANGEMENT

One result of the low bulwark is its loss as a convenient location for a belaying pin rack. A substitute at a more workable height above the deck is provided by lashing a stout bar across the shrouds. To the pins which it carries and to those in the spider hoops around the masts are made fast the lines of the running rigging. In order that several of the crew may heave in together on a halliard, a snatch block on the deck makes it possible for them to "walk away" with the rope.

Although essentially much simpler than the square rig, the fore-and-aft rig has its complications. The main peak halliard has a jig end made fast to a starboard belaying pin; the port end has a luff tackle by which it can be hauled up. The lead of the fore peak halliard is to the opposite hand. An enlarged detail of the mast-head arrangement should help to clear up any difficulty experienced with Plan XV.

From the lower end of the gaff the throat halliard passes through a triple block and functions parallel to the mast. The staysail halliard belongs to port, the jib halliard to starboard, and the jib topsail halliard to port.

The difficulties and disagreements encountered in endeavoring to redraw old ships find excellent illustration in this, a very recent vessel. The plan calls for both the fisherman's topping lift attaching to the extreme end of the main boom, and the yachtsman's quarter lift made fast at the main sheet. Only one is necessary, and Plate XXX shows that the yachtsman's practice was actually followed. Plan XV corresponds with the original plan. The quarter lift, consisting of two pieces, one on each side of the sail, is much the more sensible arrangement since it offers support to the boom at exactly the place necessary, namely, where the sheet tends to bend it.

On most yachts the fore-staysail sheet is on a traveler. Fishermen use a double sheet with a set of blocks to each side of the deck for this, as well as for the fore sheet and the main sheet.

For the reefing of sails, the jibs are provided with down hauls and the mainsail has a tackle made fast to a cringle at the after extremity of the reef band. The topsails may be furled either at the masthead, or just below the truck on the topmast. If the

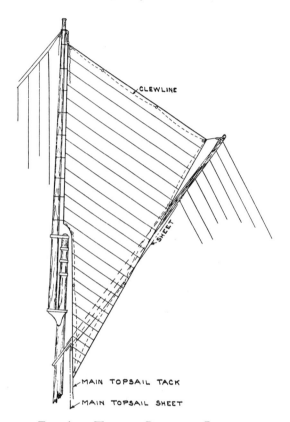

FIG. 60. TOPSAIL RUNNING RIGGING

halliard and sheet are let go and the clewline hove in, the sail comes into a nice ball at the masthead. On the other hand, if the tack and sheet are let go, the sail will be clewed up below the truck.

In order to get the fore-topsail about it must first be clewed up; double sheets and double tacks being required for the operation of this sail.

EQUIPMENT

Sails

There are eight in all: jib topsail, jib, fore staysail, fore sail, fore topsail, fisherman's staysail, main topsail, mainsail. Of these the only ones now in common use are the jib, the fore staysail, the fore sail, and the mainsail. Many years ago the fore topsail began to be omitted. Now the auxiliary gasoline engine is responsible for the almost universal disappearance of all top hamper.

The life of a suit of sails is from two and a half to three years, but repairs have to be made on them continually.

Anchor

The fisherman's anchor is entirely of wrought iron and has what is called a housing stock, that is, one which can be slipped through the hole in the shank of the anchor and brought around from the perpendicular parallel to it. Besides the two large anchors carried for the schooner herself, each dory has small anchors for use with the trawls.

Windlass

Just abaft the bitts at the bowsprit end is a pump-brake windlass much like, in style and quite so in operation, that of the *Flying Cloud*. The handles are similarly removed and stowed along the rail when not in use, the ratchet and the pawls are the same, even the construction of the drum is almost an exact counterpart.

FIG. 61. FISHERMAN'S ANCHOR   FIG. 62. BILGE PUMP

Pumps

Each dory is provided with a little scoop like those used by grocers for filling sugar bags. These scoops lie in the bottom of the boats and are flat enough to fit between the boats when they are nested. This makes it unnecessary to remove them, with the consequent guarantee that the fisherman will always have something with which to bale.

The bilge pumps of the schooner herself are similar in design to those used by contractors for the draining of cellar holes under construction. On each side of the mainmast is such a pump which, when the handles have been stowed, offers practically no obstruction to the deck.

Small Boats

In order to tend the trawls it is necessary to have a large number of small boats which must satisfy the triple demands of stability at sea, large carrying capacity, and ease of stowage on the deck of the schooner. For this work no improvement has ever been made on the Yankee invention of the dory. It is swift, easily handled, roomy, and if properly managed, difficult to capsize.

Dories are built in sizes from twelve to sixteen feet, the smaller ones being used for hand-line fishing, the others for haddock trawling, and the very large ones for halibut.

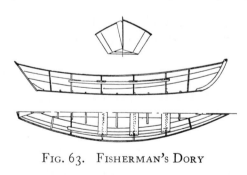

FIG. 63. FISHERMAN'S DORY

Contrary to the general impression, practically all the boats carried by any one schooner are usually of the same size. When the thwarts are removed the slanting sides make it possible to stow one dory within another in a "nest" which thus occupies no more deck space than a single boat. Five or six boats to a nest are common. In summer as many as ten or twelve boats have been stacked together in this way, making twenty-four boats in the two nests.

The frames of the dories are spaced from 27″ to 30″ apart, are of white oak and

PLATE XXX

Photograph by Edwin Levick, New York

THE FISHING SCHOONER "BLUENOSE" UNDER FULL SAIL

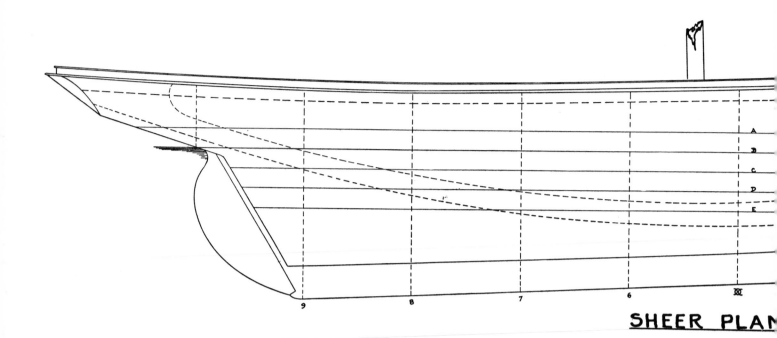

A
B
C
D
E

9   8   7   6   ⅩⅠ

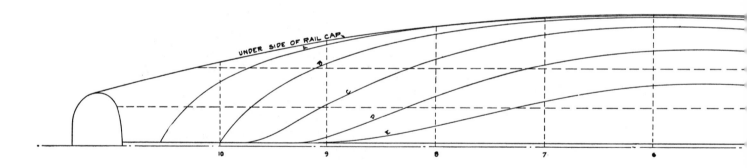

UNDER SIDE OF RAIL CAP.

10   9   8   7   6

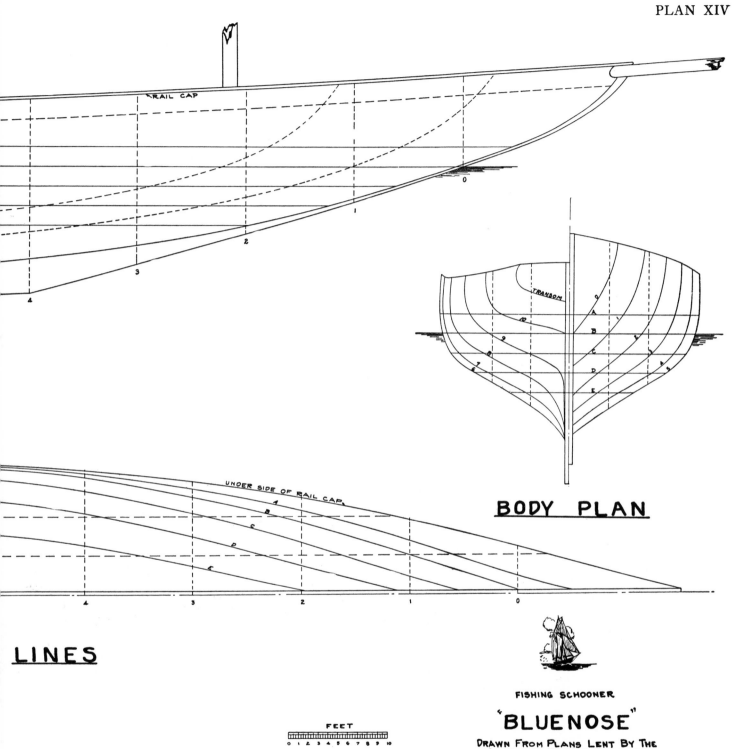

RAIL CAP

TRANSOM

BODY PLAN

UNDER SIDE OF RAIL CAP

LINES

FEET
0 1 2 3 4 5 6 7 8 9 10

FISHING SCHOONER

"BLUENOSE"

DRAWN FROM PLANS LENT BY THE
COURTESY OF HER DESIGNER,
MR. W. J. ROUE.

F. Alexander Magoun

MASSACHUSETTS INSTITUTE OF TECHNOLOGY

CAMBRIDGE   MASS.

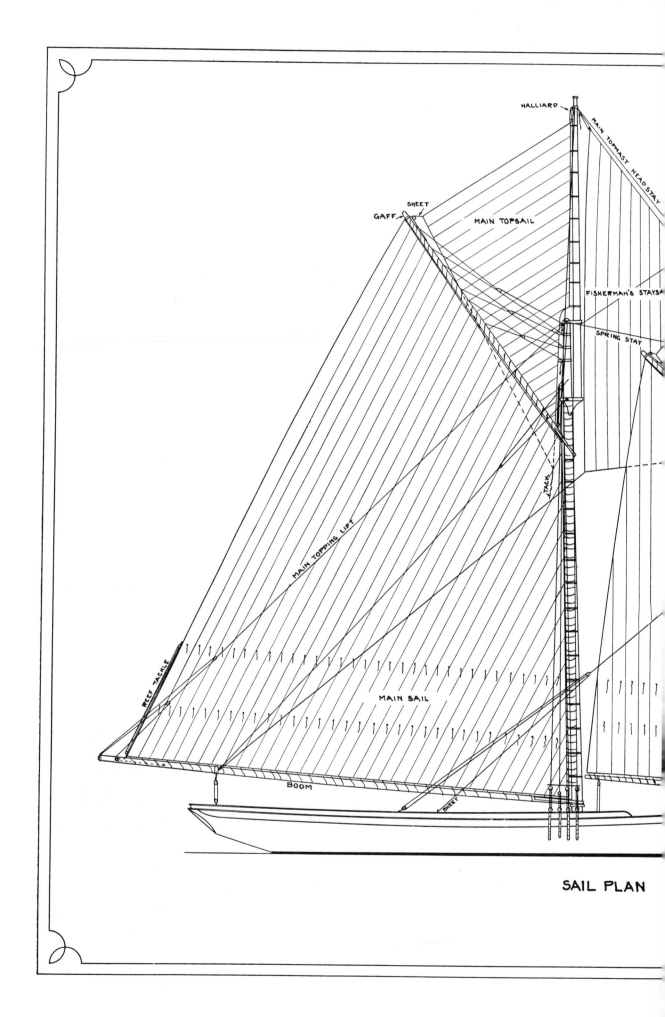

SAIL PLAN

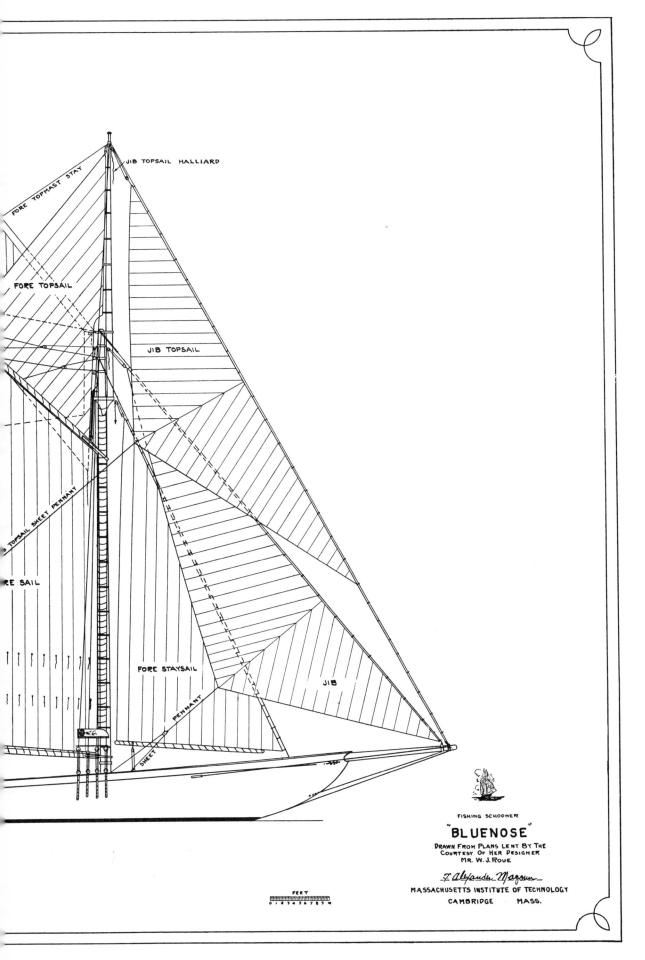

FISHING SCHOONER
"BLUENOSE"
DRAWN FROM PLANS LENT BY THE
COURTESY OF HER DESIGNER
MR. W. J. ROUE

F. Alexander Magoun

MASSACHUSETTS INSTITUTE OF TECHNOLOGY

CAMBRIDGE   MASS.

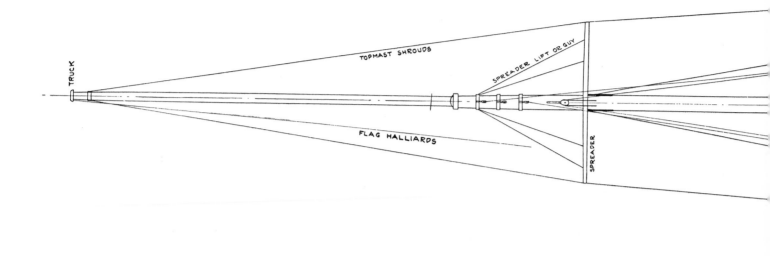

TRUCK

TOPMAST SHROUDS

SPREADER LIFT OR GUY

FLAG HALLIARDS

SPREADER

STEERING GEAR   DECK HOUSE   HATCH

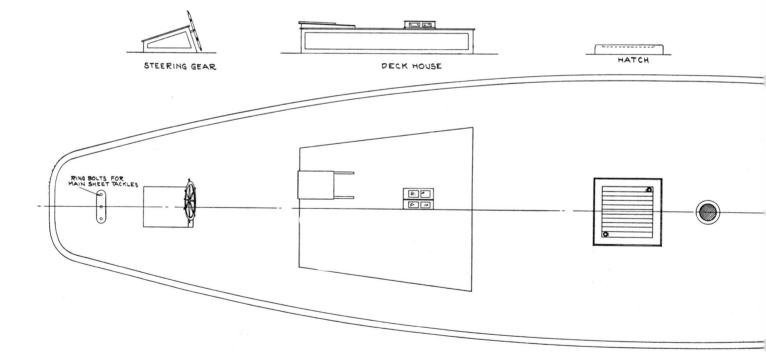

RING BOLTS FOR
MAIN SHEET TACKLES

DECK PLAN

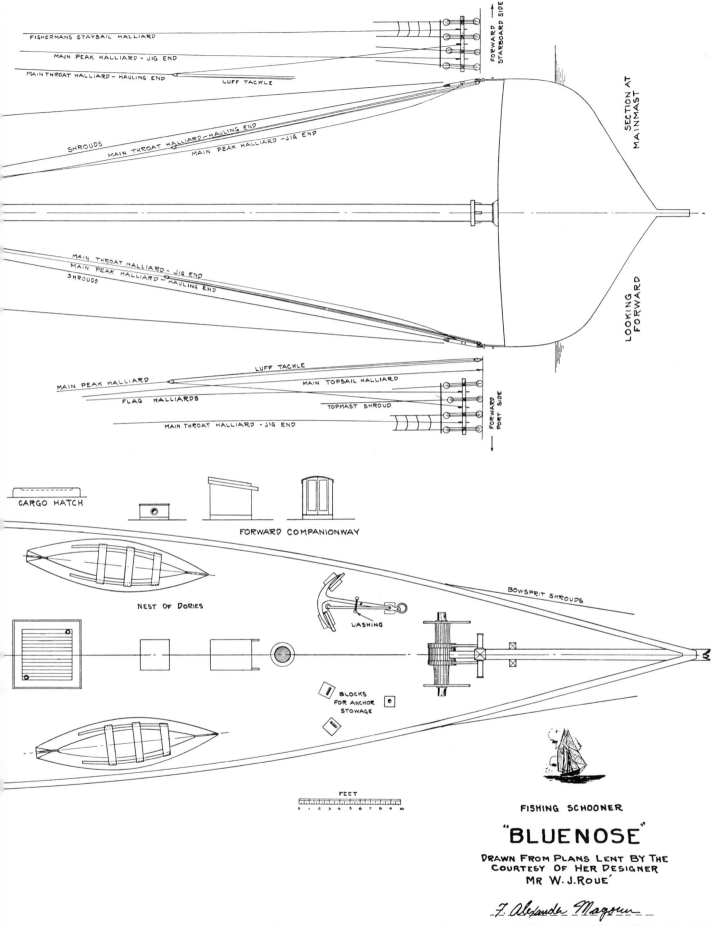

FISHERMANS STAYSAIL HALLIARD

MAIN PEAK HALLIARD - JIG END

MAIN THROAT HALLIARD - HAULING END   LUFF TACKLE

FORWARD STARBOARD SIDE

SECTION AT MAINMAST

SHROUDS   MAIN THROAT HALLIARD - HAULING END

MAIN PEAK HALLIARD - JIG END

LOOKING FORWARD

MAIN THROAT HALLIARD - JIG END

MAIN PEAK HALLIARD - HAULING END

SHROUDS

LUFF TACKLE

MAIN PEAK HALLIARD   MAIN TOPSAIL HALLIARD

FLAG HALLIARDS   TOPMAST SHROUD

FORWARD PORT SIDE

MAIN THROAT HALLIARD - JIG END

CARGO HATCH

FORWARD COMPANIONWAY

NEST OF DORIES

LASHING

BOWSPRIT SHROUDS

BLOCKS FOR ANCHOR STOWAGE

FEET
0 1 2 3 4 5 6 7 8 9 10

FISHING SCHOONER

"BLUENOSE"

DRAWN FROM PLANS LENT BY THE
COURTESY OF HER DESIGNER
MR W. J. ROUÉ

F. Alexander Magoun

MASSACHUSETTS INSTITUTE OF TECHNOLOGY

CAMBRIDGE   MASS.

are cut from a branch which grew in the crooked shape desired, or are made by fastening two pieces together into an elbow; usually the latter.

The construction of these efficient boats is extremely simple. The floor is sawed to the proper shape from ⅞″ white pine boards that have been tongued and grooved. These boards are fastened by strips of oak which are placed between the positions later to be occupied by the frames. The curvature of three or four inches given to the bottom of the dory is easily accomplished by placing blocks of the desired size under the forward and after ends, the middle being held down by a pole braced to the ceiling of the shop.

In this position the frames, the stem post and the V-board of the stern are secured to the bottom in anticipation of the planking. Three white pine planks ⅝″ thick go into the making of each side. They are cut to a pattern in order to match the curvature of the bottom, and to give the desired sheer which may be as much as fourteen inches. By beveling the upper edge of each plank, as a clapboard is beveled, the strakes overlap in the old, old clinker-built style.

A narrow batten or rising is fastened to the frames for the thwarts to rest upon. Thus these are held in place only by virtue of their tight fit, and can be easily removed when it is desired to stow the boats.

Thirteen-foot dories have two thwarts, with parting boards or bulkheads beneath them to keep the fish from shifting about. One pair of oars is sufficient. Fifteen-foot, or trawl dories have three thwarts, three parting boards, and two pairs of oars which are worked between thole pins — not in oar locks.

Dimensions of a 15-foot fishing dory

Length over all	19′ - 4″
Depth	22″
Width at floor	2′ - 7″
Flare amidships (each side)	14″
Width across gunwales	5′ - 3″
Weight	250 pounds
Draft (light)	3½″
Load at 13″ draft	2000 pounds

Several trans-Atlantic voyages have been successfully made in these little boats. The first man to cross, absolutely alone, was Alfred Johnsen, a Gloucester fisherman of Danish birth. In a sixteen-foot dory he sailed June 15, 1876, arriving at Liverpool on August 21st, sixty-seven days from Gloucester. On August 2d, his boat, which he called the *Centennial*, capsized, but he managed to right her and complete the voyage.

Johnsen's feat was preceded by the 1786 voyage of Capt. Josiah Shackford of Portsmouth, New Hampshire, who crossed the Atlantic in a fifteen-ton sloop accompanied only by a dog. The two men who were to have been his shipmates lost courage at the last possible moment and jumped aboard the pilot boat.

Quarters

The forecastle is reached through a companionway abaft the foremast. Here are two tiers of bunks on each side of the ship, offering accommodations for some twenty men. Along the centerline runs a collapsible table on which the meals are served. The galley itself occupies the after part of the forecastle, its stove being under the ladder coming down the companionway, A skylight hatch offers illumination for the cooking operations, and in good weather an escape for the inviting odors which they produce.

The after cabin is less crowded. Double bunks at the sides provide sleeping quarters for eight or ten more men, and the stove bolted to the deck supplies a warm refuge for the swapping of yarns and the defense or disparagement of the sailing qualities of various schooners. A barometer, a looking glass, and a chronometer are prominent furnishings, the second being indispensable even to the unshaven toilers of the sea.

Food

The "ding, dong" of the cook's dinner bell always proclaims a hearty meal of boiled salf beef, potatoes, pork, white biscuit, pilot-bread, butter, rice, pie, strong tea, or, at the first of a voyage, beefsteak. Later the finest fish are served up in a manner rarely equalled elsewhere. Sometimes there are vegetables or eggs. Apparently no alcoholic drinks of any kind have been permitted on our fishing schooners for nearly a hundred years.

Operation

Fishing schooners can log thirteen knots under the best conditions, and will stand up in a gale which no yacht could weather. More than this, their fore and aft rig enables them to work to windward of any clipper that ever swung a skysail yard. Owing to their small freeboard, the deck is often completely under water, only the after deck house and the strength of his hands keeping the helmsman from being swept overboard.

Sometimes a gust will send the rail under so far that as the ship straightens up it brings gallons of water on to her deck. Several buckets full may go down the companionway, wetting the bedclothes of the lee bunks. Whether this be tragedy or comedy depends upon which side of the ship one's bunk is on.

Many able men, among them Capt. J. W. Collins, have tried to improve the seaworthiness of the fishing schooner by various alterations. Considering the conditions under which they are operated, the rig leaves something to be desired.

All hands except the captain and the cook are usually at the trawls. The schooner will be tacking in the vicinity when suddenly a squall strikes, making it imperative to shorten sail. That this may be accomplished with all speed the big mainsail is lowered first, but unfortunately its removal destroys the equilibrium between the center of effort of the sails and the center of lateral resistance of the hull. The latter remains unchanged; the former has been moved forward by a considerable distance, making it almost impossible to get the schooner about.

By adopting the ketch rig, in which the large sail is on the foremast and the smaller one on the main, the bigger sail could be lowered without affecting the balance at all. The area of canvas might be much reduced, yet the center of effort of the remaining sails coincide exactly with that of the whole.

At the present time the fishing schooner, as here described, is fast passing. One sees great oil trucks backed up on the fish piers, a hose leading to the tank below from which flows the sure propulsive energy once provided (if there was any wind) by the topsails and the staysail. Only the stub lower masts remain to compete with the "put, put, put" of 300 horse power machinery.

A variety of nationalities compose the crews which once were mostly native-born. From their humble cottages back of the waterfront, waiting wives scan the harbor for each returning sail, often to see the flag at half-mast — for whom?

VII

CHRONOLOGICAL TABLE

A complete chronological table showing the development of improvements from the savage on a log to the modern "Leviathan" would be a monumental work. For the convenience of those who wish a ready reference by which to place the more important details in their proper period a partial table has been prepared.

Because we have little accurate knowledge of ships in the Middle Ages, the years preceding 1300 may be dismissed with the observations that:

Egyptian oared boats developed into ships with square sails which had backstays.

The Romans introduced shrouds and brailed up their sails to the yards.

The Norsement lowered the yard, but developed the reef and bowlines.

All vessels were clinker built.

Fourteenth Century

Jacob's ladder up after side of mast to top.

No ratlines.

Shrouds set up by blocks.

Yards made from two pieces.

Ties led through a calcet.

Parrels in use.

Equal shear fore and aft.

Bonnets.

"Castles" at both ends of ship.

Bowsprit used for attachment of bowlines.

In Northern Europe:

Rudder still on starboard side.

Shrouds set up to hearts or thimbles inboard.

Reef points being developed.

Ratlines.

Fifteenth Century

More than one mast now.

Fuller bow giving greater stability.

Carvel planking.

Wales for protection in rubbing against wharves.

Channels beginning to take the place of hearts set up inboard.

Southern European ships still without shrouds.

Jacob's ladder on the mainmast only.

On largest ships:

    Foremast — square sail.

    Mainmast — square sail.

    Mizenmast — lateen.

Sometimes a tiny topsail, sheeted to the rim of the top, *not* to the yard.

Mizen yard originally handled by a mouton, or rope, which attached to the lower end of the yard, and by which it was drawn back and swung around the forward side of the mast. Columbus had a ship-style lift at the upper end of the yard which was consequently swung abaft the mast.

Carracks usually had no mizen top to interfere with lateen yard.

Braces had pendant blocks.

Sheets still single ropes.

Bonnet and drabler laced to bottom of main course by eyelet holes and loops called latchets.

Near end of century, spritsail added and an "outrigger" for mizen sheet.

Sixteenth Century

Chains over outside edge of channels instead of through holes near edge.

Shrouds.

Ratlines.

Mizen lift superseded mouton.

Combination of topmasts and topsails of appreciable size.

Gun ports cut in hull.

Round stern superseded by square tuck.

Beginnings of studding sails.

Bowsprit still to starboard.

Fore tack boomkin developed.

Whip staff introduced.

Seventeenth Century

Futtock shrouds set up to main rigging.

Crowfoot attachment of rigging characteristic, the object being the distribution of stress.

Braces, bowlines, and even the standing parts of the halliards attached to stays.

No staysails yet.

Spritsail topsail and mizen topsail distinguishing features.

Quarter galleries, open at first, but later closed on account of the ease of setting fire to a ship by tossing a torch on to the gallery.

Profuse ornamentation.

Paintings and bas-reliefs on sterns.

Topsail yards still short.

Topgallant sails beginning with a consequent reduction in the size of the courses.

After the middle of the century:

Introduction of reef bands.

Beginning of staysails. Had been used on small craft as an emergency rig for at least two centuries.

Stays no longer used as attachments for halliards.

End of century:

Spritsail yard fixed instead of sliding.

Ties replaced by jeers.

Bowsprit on center line, always gammoned to stem.

Bobstay on bowsprit.

No bowsprit shrouds yet.

Iron bands on anchor stock.

CHRONOLOGICAL TABLE

Eighteenth Century

Steering wheel replaces whipstaff.
Addition of reef to courses and topsails.
Tops no longer round, the square sides giving a better spread to the topmast shrouds.
Jib added.
Jib-boom introduced, carried on port side of bowsprit.
Bowsprit shrouds appear.
Spritsail topsail disappearing.
Dolphin striker added below bowsprit end.
Main brace boomkins.
Bonnets gone.
Studding sails and royals became common.
Mizen still carried a lateen until the middle of the century when the forward part of the lateen was omitted, becoming the spanker. The long lateen yard continued, even after the sail was reduced, until some genius discovered that this piece could be omitted and so arrived at the modern gaff.
Futtock shrouds on a pendant carried down to deck.
Skysails appear.
Circular stem replaces square beakhead-bulkhead.

Nineteenth Century

Ornamental additions fast disappearing.
Spritsail discontinued, though yard used as an outrigger for bowsprit shrouds.
Tremendous expansion of sail area.
Chain anchor cables replace hemp.
Wales going.
Bowlines disappearing.
Futtock shrouds brought to truss hoop on lower mast.
Double topsails.
Sails give way to steam.

INDEX

INDEX

INDEX

INDEX

INDEX

INDEX